D0160937

Chicano Drama
Performance, Society and Myth

This is the first book since Jorge Huerta's ground-breaking earlier study, *Chicano Theater: Themes and Forms* (1982), to explore the diversity and energy of Chicano theatre. Huerta takes as his starting point 1979, the year Luis Valdez's play, *Zoot Suit*, was produced on Broadway. Huerta looks at plays by and about Chicanas and Chicanos, as they explore, through performance, the community and its identity caught between the United States and Mexico. Through informative biographies of each playwright and analyses of their plays, Huerta offers an accessible introduction to this important aspect of American theatre and culture.

Overall, Huerta establishes a pattern of theatrical activity that is closely linked with both Western European traditions of realism and an indigenous philosophy seen in contemporary Chicano culture. Further, Huerta examines how the playwrights challenge the Roman Catholic Church and its priests, while demonstrating an abiding faith. The final chapter explores plays that challenge the tradition of the patriarchy by openly discussing the issues of homosexuality. The book contains photographs from key productions and will be invaluable to students, scholars and general theatregoers.

JORGE HUERTA is a leading authority on contemporary Chicano and Latino theatre, a professional director, and Chancellor's Associates Professor of Theatre at the University of California, San Diego. Huerta founded El Teatro de la Esperanza in Santa Barbara, in 1971, and was also co-founder of Teatro Máscara Mágica, in San Diego, in 1989. He has published numerous articles and reviews, three anthologies of plays, and a major study, *Chicano Theater: Themes and Forms* (1982).

The American theatre and its literature are attracting, after long neglect, the crucial attention of historians, theoreticians and critics of the arts. Long a field for isolated research yet too frequently marginalized in the academy, the American theatre has always been a sensitive gauge of social pressures and public issues. Investigations into its myriad of shapes and manifestations are relevant to students of drama, theatre, literature, cultural experience and political development.

The primary intent of this series is to set up a forum of important and original scholarship in and criticism of American theatre and drama in a cultural and social context. Inclusive by design, the series accommodates leading work in areas ranging from the study of drama as literature to theatre histories, theoretical explorations, production histories and readings of more popular or para-theatrical forms. While maintaining a specific emphasis on theatre in the United States, the series welcomes work grounded broadly in cultural studies and narratives with interdisciplinary reach. Cambridge Studies in American Theatre and Drama thus provides a crossroads where historical, theoretical, literary and biographical approaches meet and combine, promoting imaginative research in theatre and drama from a variety of new perspectives.

Chicano Drama

Performance, Society and Myth

JORGE HUERTA

University of California, San Diego

CAMBRIDGE
UNIVERSITY PRESS

PUBLISHED BY THE PRESS SYNDICATE OF THE UNIVERSITY OF CAMBRIDGE
The Pitt Building, Trumpington Street, Cambridge, United Kingdom

CAMBRIDGE UNIVERSITY PRESS
The Edinburgh Building, Cambridge CB2 2RU, UK   www.cup.cam.ac.uk
40 West 20th Street, New York, NY 10011–4211, USA   www.cup.org
10 Stamford Road, Oakleigh, Melbourne 3166, Australia
Ruiz de Alarcón 13, 28014 Madrid, Spain

© Jorge Huerta 2000

First published 2000

Printed in the United Kingdom at the University Press, Cambridge

Typeface Adobe Caslon 10.5/13pt   *System* QuarkXPress™   [SE]

A catalogue record for this book is available from the British Library

Library of Congress Cataloguing in Publication data

Huerta, Jorge A.
Chicano drama : performance, society, and myth / Jorge Huerta.
p.   cm. – (Cambridge studies in American theatre and drama : 12)
Includes bibliographical references and index.
ISBN 0 521 77119 6 (hardback) – ISBN 0 521 77817 4 (paperback)
1. American drama – Mexican American authors – History and criticism.   2. Literature
and society – United States – History.   3. Mexican Americans in literature.   4. Myth in
literature.   I. Title.   II. Series.

PS153.M4 H84 2001   812.009′86872–DC21   00-036300

ISBN 0 521 77119 6 hardback
ISBN 0 521 77817 4 paperback

To the memory of my dear friends, colleagues and collaborators
Miguel Delgado
Estela Portillo-Trambley
José Guadalupe Saucedo
Ruben Sierra
Que en paz descansen siempre

Contents

Illustrations

Acknowledgements

I want to thank all of the theatre artists who have been my collaborators and my inspiration. Also, thanks to my student research assistants: Kat Avila, Ken Cerniglia, Ricardo Chavira, Laura Esparza, Gregg Huerta, Ron Huerta, David Lugo-Beauchamp, Juan Pazos, Tatiana Piccone, Analola Santana, Liberty Smith and Michael Stegen. A very special thanks to Maria Figueroa, Michal Kobialka, Adam Versenyi and John Clum for their invaluable feedback. Without the support, guidance and patience of Victoria Cooper and Don Wilmeth, I could not have completed this book. Thanks also to the staff of the Department of Theatre and Dance at UCSD: Sondra Buffett, Robin Doane, Paulette Gregg, Linn Fridy, Hedayat Jafari and Barbara Vilbrandt. To the University of California, UC-Mexus, Program and the staff at UCSD-TV: Vice Chancellor Mary L. Walshok, Lynn Burnstan, John Menier, Matt Alioto, Marci Bretts, Suzanne Cedevic, David Cain and Patricia Taylor, thanks for making our video series, "Necessary Theatre," a reality. I could not have completed this book without the financial support of my Chancellor's Associates Endowed Chair III. Finally, a great big *gracias* to my wife, Ginger, whose love, wisdom, encouragement and support make it all possible.

Introduction

Brief overview of Chicano theatre prior to *Zoot Suit*

This is a book about Chicana/o drama from 1979 to 1999, the last two decades of the twentieth century. My point of departure is 1979 because that was the year Luís Valdez's play with music, *Zoot Suit*, was produced on Broadway, marking a turning point not only for Mr. Valdez, but for an entire generation of Latina and Latino theatre artists.[1] Also, I wrote my first book about Chicano theatre in 1980, in the wake of the *Zoot Suit* phenomenon in New York and Los Angeles. In the twenty years that have passed since that first book, much has changed in Chicana/o theatre and some of those developments are the substance of this book. I write this book as a scholar but also as someone who has been intimately involved in many of the plays I discuss, as an audience member, as director of a reading or a fully staged production. I know all of the directors and playwrights, some as ex-students, others as collaborators and fellow travelers in the peripatetic world of the theatre.

In reality I could not have written this book in 1980 because the majority of plays I am writing about had not yet been scripted. Yet, although I focus on the plays and playwrights that have emerged since 1979, these playwrights all call themselves Chicana or Chicano, recognizing the political ramifications and history of such a conviction. By continuing to call themselves Chicana/os they are claiming an identity that is neither Mexican nor Anglo-American, but a synthesis of both. As self-proclaimed Chicanos they recognize a history of struggle in the barrios that continues to this day.

---

[1] I use the term, Latina/o when the reference can be applied to all people of Latin American descent, whether Cuban, Puerto Rican, Chicano, etc. When a reference applies to only one of the many Latina/o populations, I will be specific. Although this introduction is about Chicana/o theatre, often what I say can apply across Latina/o cultures.

Finally, these playwrights acknowledge that they did not spring out of a void, writing plays in isolation. Several of the playwrights I discuss were directly influenced by individuals such as Luís Valdez, Estela Portillo-Trambley or Carlos Morton, or they were inspired to act or write because of a Chicano teatro they had seen. Therefore I would like to give the reader a brief overview of the events that preceded *Zoot Suit*, the evolution of a Chicano Theatre Movement.

As I will discuss in Chapter 1, Luís Valdez founded the Teatro Campesino in 1965 as the cultural and performing arm of the farm workers' union being formed by Cesar Chávez, Dolores Huerta and others. The Teatro Campesino immediately became synonymous with the farm workers' struggle and later, with the Chicano Movement. By 1968 the Teatro Campesino had gained national and international recognition and had also spawned many other teatros, seemingly wherever they had performed. Noting the growing number of teatros, Valdez and his Teatro members decided to host a Chicano Theatre Festival in 1970 in Fresno, California, the company's home base. Several Chicano teatros attended, as well as a Puerto Rican group from New York City, The Third World Revelationists, and Los Mascarones, of Mexico City, establishing a sense of international struggle and inter-American cooperation. The first festival led to another the following year.

During the Spring break of 1971 the second Chicano theatre festival was sponsored by the Teatro Campesino on the campus of the University of California, Santa Cruz. Soon after the 1971 festival a group of representatives from various teatros met at the Teatro Campesino headquarters and founded TENAZ, *El Teatro Nacional de Aztlán* (the National Theatre of Aztlán). "Aztlán" is the Nahuatl (Aztec) word for "all the lands to the north, the land from whence we came." The Chicanos interpreted Aztlán as the Southwestern United States, home of the largest concentration of Mexicans and Chicanos in the country. By adopting a Nahuatl term as part of their name, the members of TENAZ were proclaiming their Native American roots, celebrating their indigenous heritage as encompassing all of North (and South) America. The word, "Tenaz" means "tenacious" in Spanish and the acronym was intended to honor the tenacity of all Native peoples, despite centuries of European colonization.

TENAZ became a national coalition of teatros, Chicano theatre groups that were initially composed mainly of individuals more motivated by politics than by "art." TENAZ was an important part of a Chicano Theatre Movement, indeed a driving force, sponsoring annual festivals, workshops, symposia and publications in efforts to assist groups with their aesthetic and political growth. Because the Teatro Campesino was the only full-time teatro in the early days, with an office and a (modestly) paid staff, that organization took on much of the administrative duties of TENAZ. Luís Valdez was the undisputed leader of the Chicano Theatre Movement and he and his fellow Teatro Campesino members were looked up to as role models by the younger, emerging *teatristas* (theatre workers). Although the Teatro Campesino was very well known in theatre circles, few people outside of the Chicano Movement knew that there were many other teatros, from Chicago to San Diego, San Antonio to Seattle, in operation during the 1970s.

Many of the early teatros emerged from community organizations as well as from college and university Chicano student groups. With names like Teatro M.E.Ch.A. (Chicano slang for match)[2] and Teatro Justicia (Justice), it was clear that these theatre groups were more intent on bringing about social justice than following any traditional rules of aesthetic theory. Metaphorically, at least, they wanted to light fires of social justice wherever there were Mexicans and Chicana/os being oppressed. In other words, the message was much more important than the medium. The Teatro Campesino's *actos* became the standard model for these young troupes because the *acto* form is easily emulated and adaptable to any sociopolitical motive or situation. Anyone with a cause can collectively create an *acto*, but the cause is essential.

The *acto* was the perfect form for those teatro members who were not experienced in performance techniques. The *actos* can be characterized as brief, collectively created sketches based on a commedia dell'arte model of slapstick, exaggeration, stereotypes and allegories poking satiric jabs at any given enemy or issue(s). The targets of the *actos* ranged from institutions to individuals, elected officials or organizations such as a Police Department; targets that were easily recognizable to the delighted audience members. Unlike Valdez, who had studied theatre in college, most of the other people involved in the early teatros had little or no experience in theatrical techniques. What the incipient *teatristas* lacked in formal training, however, they compensated for in sheer vitality and commitment. And their audiences, like the first striking farm workers, were totally in tune with what they were seeing on stage. One of the most important premises of the theatre, that critical connection between performer and audience, was unwavering in the initial stages of teatro Chicano.

---

[2] "M.E.Ch.A." is also the acronym for Movimiento Estudiantil de Aztlán (Chicano Student Movement of Aztlán) a student movement which continues to this day on high school, college and university campuses all across the country.

Even from the beginning of what we can call contemporary Chicano theatre, this was a theatre movement based on the need to make a difference in the community, not through Art but through Action. Social action, political action – any kind of action and activism that could educate and motivate first the community members themselves, and then, if possible, members of the broader society. However, this was a developing movement and the membership of the teatros was in constant flux, gaining and losing members constantly. Despite the transient nature of the field, some individuals persevered, intent on making teatro their way of life, regardless of the sacrifices. By the mid-1970s some teatros had offices and some even had performance spaces, but the members of these teatros were still often students or community workers who had to study as well as work to get by financially. Professional theatre training was a luxury to which few, if any, early teatro members could aspire, even if they wanted such training.

Early *teatristas*, including Valdez, were unabashed in their disdain for traditional theatrical practice and purposes. At a time when the regional theatre movement was being infused with foundation monies and the National Endowment for the Arts was beginning to recognize a growing professionally oriented regional theatre movement in the Anglo communities, most *teatristas* purposely avoided any connections to these funding agencies. If they did not take monies from the establishment they felt they would be free of any controls those agencies might impose upon them. Representing a community that had been ignored by the government and most of its agencies anyway, these *teatristas* were virtually snubbing their noses at the System as they openly criticized it.

This was a period of intense volunteerism in the theatre when few, if any, people were paid for their cultural work. Instead, these dedicated individuals, who called themselves "cultural workers," were eager to challenge the status quo any way they could. They were not interested in a "A Life in the Theatre," as much as they were intent on using theatre to change people's lives. For them, the theatre was an obvious and accessible platform for sharing ideas with their communities. Their stages were not civic auditoriums or fully equipped theatres, but rather, community-based spaces such as schools, churches, parks and community centers. "If the Raza [the people] will not come to the theatre," Valdez wrote in 1971, "then the theatre must go to the Raza."[3] And the teatros did, indeed, go to the people.

TENAZ continued to give the Movement continuity and a sense of

---

[3] Luís Valdez, *Actos* (San Juan Bautista: Cucaracha Press, 1971), p. 4; and in Luís Valdez, *Early Works: Actos, Bernabe and Pensamiento Serpentino* (Houston: Arte Publico Press, 1990), p. 10.

something much larger than the individuals and the teatros in which they participated. By 1976 the Teatro Campesino stepped out of TENAZ, and Teatro de la Esperanza assumed many of the administrative responsibilities, along with other teatros that were still operating. TENAZ continued to be a national coalition and teatros from all over the nation were involved in the yearly festivals, workshops and meetings.[4] With time, many teatros dissolved or transformed into new teatros with former members of other groups. Most people found full-time employment in other fields, some continued to work with their community-based teatros. Then "*Zoot Suit* fever" hit Los Angeles.

Why would a Chicano take a play to Broadway?

I can still picture the moment. The year was 1977 when Luís Valdez told me he was going to write and direct a play about the infamous Sleepy Lagoon Murder Trial, produce it in Los Angeles and then move it to New York's Broadway. "Why do you want to do that?" I asked incredulously, knowing that there were two reasons they called Broadway the "Great White Way." One reason has to do with the brightness of the (white) lights. But to theatre artists of color, there is another, more subtle reason for that description. Although serious African-American plays had been produced on Broadway, their numbers were (and still are) few. And a play written, directed and performed by Chicana/os or Latina/os had never been produced on Broadway. Never. But Luís Valdez decided that he was going to be the first Chicano writer/director on the Great White Way.

What could the Chicano Theatre Movement possibly gain by a Chicano play on Broadway, I thought. In response to my original question ("Why?"), Luís said simply: "They won't take us seriously until we succeed on their turf, on their terms." "They" were the New York Establishment. "They" were the regional theatre producers who only seemed to value plays that had come from Broadway or at least New York. "They" were the New York theatre critics who still looked down their noses at most plays that had come from west of the Hudson River. And, of course, "they" were not Latino or even Chicano. But they did, in fact decide what was "Great" or even "Good Theatre."

I didn't know what to say to Luís. But I knew that this man was a

---

[4] I was one of the founding directors of TENAZ, but stepped out of the organization in the mid 1980s due to other commitments. In 1992 I attended the Chicano Theatre Festival in San Antonio and was drawn back into the organization as President of the Board of Directors.

visionary and that if he said he was going to do something, he did. This was
the charismatic leader who had gathered together a group of striking farm
workers and created the ever-evolving Teatro Campesino. And this was the
man who, along with his Teatro Campesino members, had inspired an
entire movement of Chicano theatre groups all across the country. The
"Father of Chicano Theatre" was going to Broadway.

Zoot Suit opens doors

Valdez did write that play, titled it *Zoot Suit*, and it was co-produced by the
Teatro Campesino and the Center Theatre Group of Los Angeles at the
Mark Taper Forum in the heart of the city. *Zoot Suit* opened in Los Angeles
in 1978, breaking all previous box office records for any theatrical production in that city. When the producers understood that audiences could not
get enough of *Zoot Suit*, they moved the production to the larger Aquarius
Theatre in Hollywood and the people kept coming. Another production
went to Broadway in 1979, both productions directed by the playwright. As
we will see later in this book, *Zoot Suit* closed in New York after four weeks
of attempting to overcome negative reviews. Still, a Chicano and many
other Chicanas, Chicanos, Latinas and Latinos, had taken a play to
Broadway and although they had been "rejected" by the East Coast
Establishment, they had made their mark. Like the play's central figure, the
ubiquitous Pachuco, the production team walked proudly out of what had
been for those months of rehearsal and production, *their* theatre, on their
terms. The play was still selling out in Los Angeles and it would soon be
made into a motion picture, directed by the playwright.

The success of *Zoot Suit* in Los Angeles became a watershed moment in
the history of Latino theatre and of all theatre in the United States. With
his very conscious move into the so-called mainstream, Valdez opened the
doors to other professional venues, for himself and for other Latina/o
theatre artists as well. Producers and artistic directors across the country saw
the huge profits generated by the production of *Zoot Suit* in Los Angeles
and began to seek ways to tap into the Latino market. They also wanted to
expand their audience base beyond their traditionally white, upper-income
patrons. *Zoot Suit* proved popular across ethnic, class and cultural lines in
Los Angeles but most importantly, while that play was being performed in
the theatre, while El Pachuco strutted nightly across that stage, that space
belonged to La Raza. Luís Valdez had ushered-in the era of professional
Chicana/o theatre and the theatre would never be the same.

Zoot Suit had set a new, professional standard for Chicano theatre artists, moving some to study theatre practice, formally and informally. While few *teatristas* were able to see *Zoot Suit* in New York, during the eleven months the play was in Los Angeles, Chicanas and Chicanos from all parts of the country made their way to the Mark Taper Forum or to the Aquarius Theatre to witness this singular event. While some of the more established Chicano theatre companies had begun to develop plays written by individuals before the advent of *Zoot Suit*, more teatros began to develop plays and playwrights in the 1980s. Just as the Teatro Campesino's early *actos* had inspired people to create their own statements in that genre, now the people involved in the teatros had a totally different kind of professional production to invigorate and stimulate them.

Zoot Suit was unlike anything a Chicana/o theatre troupe had ever achieved, awesome in its theatrical force and humbling in its high professional standards. Never before had so many Latinas and Latinos been brought together to make theatre in a professional venue. Some of the cast members, like Cuban-born, Tony Plana, had been trained at the Royal Academy of Dramatic Art, and others, like Evelina Fernández, had gotten her basic training in community-based Chicano teatros in East Los Angeles. Other actors, like Charles Aidman, had been on stage and screen for years, while Edward James Olmos had been a lounge singer. *Zoot Suit* changed the lives of many people both on and off the stage.

After *Zoot Suit*

After *Zoot Suit* closed in Los Angeles, most of the Latina and Latino actors in the cast were confronted with the sad reality that there would be few opportunities to act professionally on the stage or screen. Mr. Olmos' very successful career had been launched and other actors could be seen in (usually stereotypical) Latina/o roles as victims or victimizers, on film and television. But their real satisfaction came from acting in live theatre. Some actors who had come from the Teatro Movement continued to work with teatro groups whenever possible. These actors often brought their expertise to the TENAZ festivals and workshops during the 1980s in that organization's continuing efforts to promote and facilitate a higher performance standard. Although the film of *Zoot Suit* had not played long in the movie theatres, the actors who had been in that film were seen as role models by many of the younger teatro members. Those actors who had come from the barrios and "made it" in *Zoot Suit* knew that they still had a responsibility to their communities and would play-out that responsibility, literally, by acting in teatro performances whenever they could.

As the 1990s approached, the annual TENAZ festivals became semi-annual events and they were now attended by a growing number of companies that had been together for fifteen or more years. Individual directors and actors began to emerge from teatros as well as from professional training programs, all eager to work with the best scripts possible. Theatre companies such as El Teatro de la Esperanza (Santa Barbara and San Francisco, California), the Bilingual Foundation for the Arts (Los Angeles, California), La Compañía de Teatro de Alburquerque (Albuquerque, New Mexico), Su Teatro (Denver, Colorado), the Guadalupe Cultural Arts Center (San Antonio, Texas), and the Chicago Latino Theatre Company (Chicago, Illinois) each had play development programs. Many of the plays these companies were producing were evidence of their efforts to reach higher levels of professionalism, even if they were not yet able to pay living wages to their artists.

Whereas the 1960s and 1970s were a period of "*rasquachismo*," of unsophisticated performance aesthetics within the Chicano Theatre Movement, in the 1980s the teatros and individual *teatristas* became increasingly aware that there could be more to their repertoire than *acto*s. TENAZ festivals had always included representative groups and individuals from Latin America who offered symposia and workshops as well as performances which visibly demonstrated their troupes' work. People such as Emilio Carballido, one of Mexico's leading playwrights, Argentinean director/playwright/theorist in exile Augusto Boal, and director/playwright, Enrique Buenaventura, of Colombia, brought their visions to TENAZ festivals, expanding the theatrical possibilities.[5] And, by the 1980s there were a growing number of individuals studying in both undergraduate and graduate programs in theatre across the country. Some of those people have contributed to the core of this book through their works.

The projects

While the community-based teatros were developing plays by playwrights both within and outside of their own organizations, mainstream theatre companies also began to offer programs in script development. Due, in large

---

[5] The cross-pollination of ideas was more a south-to-north pattern than the reverse, because few Chicana/o teatristas or teatros could afford to travel south of Mexico. Indeed, few teatros have toured beyond Mexico City to date.

part to generous grants from the Ford Foundation and, later, the Lila Wallace Reader's Digest Fund, several mainstream (and a few, select Latino) theatres were able to launch projects to develop Latina/o audiences and plays. Two of the most important projects, both for their longevity and national outreach, were the South Coast Repertory Theatre's "Hispanic Playwright's Project" and the INTAR (International Arts Relations, Inc.) "Hispanic Playwright's-in-Residence Laboratory." The "HPP," headed by director/playwright, José Cruz González from 1986 to 1997, was responsible for the development of many Latina and Latino plays from across the country. INTAR's Laboratory was taught by director/playwright, Maria Irene Fornes in New York City from 1981 to 1992. Not coincidentally, Fornes was also invited to participate in the HPP on a few occasions. Many of the playwrights I will be discussing studied and/or collaborated with Fornes and several have had their plays read or workshopped by the South Coast Repertory Theatre.[6]

Sometimes, readings and workshops of Chicana/o Latina/o plays in the regional theatre "projects" led to fully staged productions, which then meant that the theatre companies would (usually) have to hire Latina/o production staffs. As the need for trained actors grew, the pool of actors seemed to expand as well, particularly in New York City and the Los Angeles metropolitan area. The outcome of all of this activity, in the teatros and in the mainstream theatres, was that a substantial number of plays got produced and publications of those plays often followed. All of the plays which will be discussed in this book are the products of development projects in teatros, mainstream theatres, or both.

I have focused my project on the plays and playwrights, as opposed to theatre companies or directors, because I believe that the writers are at the core of the new Chicana/o drama. With one exception, the plays that I discuss are the products of individual visions, tempered by readings, workshops and various production teams that have also contributed to each play's particular identity. I have chosen the plays in this book because I believe they tell us what it means to be a Chicana/o in the United States at the close of the twentieth century. I do not intend to essentialize a Chicana or Chicano "experience" through these plays but I do find a common thread that links them to one another; themes, ideas, even musical undertones that often invoke Indo-Hispano, Mexican sources. These plays thus form, for

[6] See Jorge Huerta, "Looking for the Magic: Chicanos in the Mainstream," in Diana Taylor and Juan Villegas (eds.), *Negotiating Performance: Gender, Sexuality and Theatricality in Latin/o America* (Durham: Duke, 1994), pp. 37–48.

me, a Chicana/o mythos, the locus of the first chapter that keeps reappearing throughout this study. Some of the playwrights I write about are familiar; pioneers, such as Carlos Morton, Estela Portillo Trambley or Luís Valdez. But other individuals were not yet writing plays in 1980 and their voices are the voices I wish to focus on in this study.

Happy families don't make good drama

All of the plays discussed in this volume are about families, the vast majority of which would be termed dysfunctional. This is not because all Mechicano families are as dysfunctional as the characters and situations in these plays, but because they make much better drama or comedy. I say this because I want the reader to understand that although the people in these plays range from martyrs to murderers, saints to sinners, as in all drama, they are extensions of reality. Each playwright expresses her/himself differently, of course, but these writers are all conscious of the fact that happy families do not make good drama. It is the dysfunctional family that fascinates us and the most evil characters that draw our attention and our ire. Perhaps it is human nature to be more interested in the villain than the heroine, even if that villain is a product of your own community.

Community is very important to each of the playwrights and because they are interested in the betterment of their communities, they expose the sores, explore the weaknesses. The playwrights do not write these plays for sensationalistic purposes, but because they see something in their plays, the characters, the plots, that are important to them. Most importantly, perhaps, is the fact that the playwrights are writing about their people, their circumstances. These are not Hollywood's distorted pictures of the Mechicano but, rather, the Chicanos' pictures of sometimes distorted Chicanos. Therefore, as you read about these plays and the characters that inhabit their worlds, remember that they are sometimes ordinary people in extraordinary circumstances or extraordinary people in ordinary circumstances. In the best of theatrical worlds, they are extraordinary people in extraordinary circumstances.

On the use of the term, Mechicana/o

I will distinguish between the Chicana/o and the Mexican when the differences are important and refer to a conflation of the two as Mechicana/o, when the conditions pertain to both groups equally or similarly. In other words, there are plays in which the characters who are United States-born confront situations that someone raised in Mexico might not have to deal with, and vice versa. The Chicana that does not speak Spanish, for example, may not suffer the same alienation a non-English-speaker might. Conversely, that same Chicana might suffer alienation in an all Spanish-speaking situation. However, language is only one of the factors that distinguish the native-born from the immigrant, as the plays in this book will attest. All of the plays are ostensibly about Chicana/os living in the United States but by their very definition, Chicana/os recognize and celebrate their Mexican cultural roots. Although these plays take place in the United States, Mexico is always in the background, contributing to the characters' fractured identities.

Why another book about Chicano theatre?

When I wrote my first book in 1980 I could not write about several of the issues, themes and circumstances that I discuss in this project. I could not have written about Chicana (read: female) plays and playwrights because there was only one Chicana playwright in print, and, unfortunately, the Chicano Theatre Movement was male-dominated. In fact, it was a *Chicano* Theatre Movement, as noted by Chicana critics, scholars and *teatristas*. Certainly, not all of the women in Teatro Chicano were standing idly by, allowing the men to dominate, but although women were active participants in decision-making processes, both politically, organizationally and artistically, most teatros were headed by men. Therefore women's issues were not as prominent as they are today. As my discussions of each of the Chicana playwrights in this book reveals, most of them began to write plays because there were so few substantial roles for women. It took the women to write about the women. Indeed the main list of playwrights discussed in this book reveals an equal number of men and women, not because I looked for this fifty-fifty split but because that is how it happened. A closer look reveals the fact that of the several playwrights that emerged after 1980, there are more women than men.

With the advent of a professionally oriented Chicana/o dramaturgy, playwrights began to write plays that require theatres, technical facilities, designers, technicians – in short all of the benefits of a well-run theatre organization. While the *acto* and docu-drama could be performed almost anywhere, most of the plays in this book need some sort of theatrical space. Many of the plays are domestic dramas but the action does not necessarily take place solely in the safety of the characters' homes. Sometimes settings shift with cinematic frequency and those changes are much more effective with lighting, sound and the other technical advantages of a well-equipped theatre space. Some of the plays retain the theatricality of the early Chicano theatre, with fluid, non-specific locales designed to be produced in almost any circumstance. But all of the plays revolve, in one way or another, around the family.

Certainly, the family has always been at the core of Chicana/o dramaturgy but in the early period that family was more symbolic or representative of all Mechicana/o families, as opposed to a particular family in crisis. Characters and situations were almost archetypal in the early *actos* and even in the rudimentary plays that were evolving. The docu-dramas, too, were designed to represent all families or individuals in crisis. Always, these families were fighting a monolithic system that could be blamed for most of their problems. In today's dramas Mechicana/o families represent only themselves and often, their problems are theirs alone. Certainly, the characters that inhabit these plays exist in the broader society as Mechicana/os, which presupposes that they are being oppressed in one way or another. But as the playwrights begin to portray the Chicana/o as her/his own worst enemy, sometimes the broader society becomes less responsible for the family's problems.

Along with women's issues and domestic dramas as areas I could not have addressed in 1980, is the representation of homosexualit(ies) in Chicana/o drama. There was only one play about a lesbian central character in print – the same singular play written by a Chicana, *Day of the Swallows*. And there were no plays that revolved around a gay male character in print. Secondary gay and lesbian characters appeared on stage sporadically, but those plays were seldom published. Today, I can write about several plays and a few playwrights who are addressing issues of homosexuality in the Mechicano communities. Further, I can discuss several plays in print, which is key to the dissemination of the ideas those plays express. Although there are a growing number of theatres, both Chicano/Latino and non-Latino, that are producing gay or lesbian-themed plays, these plays are more accessible on the page than on the stage.

Finally, with the exception of *Zoot Suit*, I could not have written about professionally produced Chicana/o plays in 1980. I have always sought professionalism in Chicana/o theatre, as the initial director of El Teatro de la Esperanza and one of the founders of TENAZ, as a professional director and as a professor in a major theatre department. By the 1980s, as I began to direct in cities across the country, I could see that Chicana/o and Latina/o audiences were also expecting a higher level of performance standard. Often, the more educated audiences seemed tired of the same ideas and the same styles of early Chicano theatre. There was a growing middle-class in the Mechicana/o communities and that sector was going to be the life-blood of any effort to professionalize Chicano theatre. With the move away from collectives and collectively created pieces, the playwrights became the hope for a new era in Chicana/o theatre.

A note on the structure of this book

I have divided this book into four chapters, each with a different focus or theme of representation. In chapter 1, "Myth or mitos," I trace the roots of an indo-Christian Chicano mythos through the plays of Estela Portillo Trambley, Luís Valdez, the Teatro Campesino and Alurista. In chapter 2, "Mystery or miracle," I continue my search for a Chicano mythos through an analysis of how Chicana/o playwrights dramatize "*El Misterio*," the mysteries of distortion and death in the contemporary Mechicana/o reality. In chapter 3, "Redemption," I turn to the influences of the Roman Catholic Church and the playwrights' responses to that institution, its priests and nuns. Chapter 4, "Damnation," addresses how homosexuality has been dramatized, from the earliest examples to the most recent plays. In each chapter the focus is on the plays as representatives of a particular outlook, either positive or negative, or both, in which the playwrights expose beliefs and attitudes about the Chicano condition.

Initially, I was only going to discuss the plays, but as I began to write I realized that I could not simply list the playwrights' names, without any biographical information. These are the individuals who are forging new ground in the field and they should not remain anonymous. Although a few scholars are writing about Chicana/o drama and dramatists, there is no single source for this information. Therefore I give biographical information about each of the playwrights in order for the reader to get as broad a picture of their trajectories as possible. With those playwrights whom I discuss more than once, the first time I write about her/him, I will give an overview of that person's educational and professional background including brief descriptions of their most important plays. Any subsequent references to a playwright will not include biographical information.

In general, I write about a play and/or playwright only once. However, there are some playwrights whose works I discuss in more than one chapter.

For example, Cherríe Moraga's *Heroes and Saints* addresses elements of *El Misterio*, Redemption and Damnation, therefore I consider this play in those three chapters. The first time I write about Moraga is when I explore the theme of *El Misterio* as it is reflected in *Heroes and Saints*. Thus, I first give a brief biography of Moraga, followed by a brief synopsis of the plot and how this play explores *El Misterio*. In subsequent references to Moraga and *Heroes and Saints* I will not reiterate the information I initially gave unless that information is crucial to the subject at hand. Hopefully, this approach will not appear redundant. In fact, this is a kind of post-modern fracturing that I sometimes attempt. Rather than discuss one play at a time, in its totality, if that play addresses more than one of the areas I am exploring, I attempt to "deconstruct" it accordingly. If some of their plays fall into different areas of my investigation, this is an indication of the playwrights' own, fractured visions of the Chicana/o. Hopefully these plays and my discussions of them will lead to a better understanding of what it means to be a Chicana or Chicano at the close of the twentieth century.

I

Mythos or mitos:

the roots of a Chicano mythology

"El indio baila
He DANCES his way to truth
In a way INTELLECTUALS will
Never understand."
Luis Valdez, 1971[1]

"It is indeed impossible to understand many Chicano literary works without
a knowledge of Nahuatl [Aztec] and Mayan mythology."
Herminio Rios-C, 1974[2]

"The linkage of indigenous thought to contemporary reality gave the
Chicano Movement mythic and psychic energies that could be directed
towards its political and economic goals."
Tomás Ybarra-Frausto, 1979[3]

"I hope they still relate to seasons and to plants and to colors and to the wind,
and to the Indian in them, or the element that is closest to the earth."
Estela Portillo-Trambley, 1981[4]

Introduction: looking for a Chicana/Chicano mythos

A mythos, by definition, means that a group of people, a culture, depends
on myths which help them to explain the inexplicable, what some would

---

[1] Luis Valdez, *Early Works: Actos, Bernabe Pensamiento Serpentino* (Houston: Arte Publico, 1990),
p. 177.
[2] Herminio Rios-C (ed.) "Introduction," *El Grito* 7 (Berkeley, CA) (June–August 1974), 4.
[3] Tomás Ybarra-Frausto, "Alurista's Poetics: The Oral, the Bilingual, the Pre-Columbian," in
Joseph Sommers and Tomás Ybarra-Frausto (eds.) *Modern Chicano Writers: A Collection of
Critical Essays* (Prentice-Hall, 1979), p. 119.
[4] Richard A. Abrams, "Chicana Playwright Struggles with 2 Cultures," *Austin-American
Statesman*, December 6, 1981, A24.

call the supernatural. A mythos also gives a people a place in the cosmos, describing and recalling their ancestors, giving them a "from the beginning," as it were. For the believers these myths are no longer myths but doctrine. To the outsider, however, that doctrine is just another myth. When students in the United States are asked to identify mythical heroes and their narratives, they usually refer to the Greeks and the Romans, for these are their legacy through any number of Western European representations in art, philosophy, literature and theatre. Indeed, to understand many of the Renaissance, neo-classical and even twentieth-century artists and writers we must know their referents in the Euro-classical world or we are not fully educated, we are told. But when do we learn about the Aztec God of the Sun, Huitzilopochtli or the Mother Goddess Tonantzin?

Cultural anthropologists have expanded our knowledge of myths beyond Mount Olympus, exploring other cultures, current and past. Extinct cultures are investigated through hieroglyphs, artwork or other visual artifacts, while contemporary cultures are also revealed by their arts as well as through careful interpretation of the peoples' stories. But always, these other cultures' tales remain in the realm of the mythical as opposed to the actual; legend rather than historical fact. We know that the feats of Hercules or Theseus are exaggerations, but somehow, those heroes and their super-human exploits remain accessible to descendants of a Western European tradition. But where do the accomplishments of the Aztec prince Cuahtemoc come into play? What of his acts of bravery in the face of Spanish brutality? And reaching even farther back in pre-Columbian time, who knows about the gifts of Quetzalcóatl?

Carl Jung claimed that we all have a collective unconscious that unites us through universal archetypes, just as Joseph Campbell demonstrated that all cultures have a hero-quest-myth. The plots remain the same while the names and places change. But one culture's mythical hero is another culture's nemesis. Thus, like all colonizers, the Spaniards had to eradicate the spiritual beliefs of the indigenous peoples in order to truly conquer them. Early missionaries fought valiantly and indiscriminately in their attempt to replace indigenous gods and origin "myths" with one Almighty God and *Old Testament* accounts of The Creation and Fall from Eden.

Noting that the natives relied heavily on theatrical spectacle in their daily rituals, the Church fathers employed theatre to proselytize the natives a few years after the Conquest. The *auto* titled "*Adan y Eva,*" was the first Spanish religious drama to be produced in Mexico when the natives mounted it in

Mexico City in 1532, just eleven years after the collapse of the Aztec empire.[5]

The 1532 version of Adam and Eve's Fall was produced with such sincerity and reverence by the neophytes that "all who saw it broke into tears," according to the chroniclers (Campa, "Spanish Religious Folk," p. 10). Thus biblical accounts became the legacy of the indigenous peoples and their mestizo descendants to this day – one myth replaced by another. The Mesoamerican redeemer figure, Quetzalcóatl, was conflated with the Christ figure and, of course, the Aztec mother goddess, Tonantzin, was supplanted by the Virgin Mary/Guadalupe. But to the Christian believer, the Virgin Mary is Truth while Tonantzin is a myth. Yet, how true are the indigenous myths for Chicana and Chicano audiences? What do they know about indigenous history, factual or mythical?

To be a Chicana or a Chicano in the United States – which is to say to have been educated in this country – means that your indigenous history and myths have basically been ignored, suppressed or denied altogether. Mechicana/o school children are given few indicators that the United States is really *their* country; leaving them feeling marginalized, invisible and, in some states, entirely unwanted. And as these brown-skinned children search for historical or mythical role models from their community, there are few people prepared or even disposed to teach them about the early Californian or Texan heroes such as Tiburcio Vazquez or Gregorio Cortez. Or what of New Mexican folk heroes and the centuries of Spanish-language traditions in that unique state?[6]

To be a Chicana/o, it must be understood, is not to be a Mexican, either. The history of Chicano/Mexicano relations has been full of contradictions since the Southwest became a part of the United States. Many of the Mexicans who fled to the north during the Revolution of 1910 undoubtedly had plans to return, and some did. But many more stayed, married and had children: the first Chicanos. When these newly hybridized Mexicans born in the United States traveled to their parents' homeland, they were not necessarily embraced by the Mexicans. For one, there was the issue of class: many of these Chicanos were from the working class and were thus perceived

---

[5] Arthur L. Campa, "Spanish Religious Folk Theatre in the Spanish Southwest," *The University of New Mexico Bulletin (First Cycle)* (1934), 8.

[6] It is another sad reality that as I enumerate historical figures that might be recognizable to readers, not one *Mexicana* or Chicana (read: woman) comes to mind. Certainly, women have always been active in the Mechicana/o communities of the United States but historical figures remain virtually unknown.

as inferior. They were often called "pochos" – a derogatory term for those Mexicans who had "deserted the homeland" and moved to the north.

Many United States-born Mexicans did not speak Spanish properly since that language was taken from them in the schools or because some parents chose not to teach their children Spanish for fear of the discrimination this would generate. Also, since little or nothing about Mexico was taught in the schools, the Chicanos did not really know Mexico. In the words of noted Chicano historian, Juan Gomez-Quiñones, ". . . ironically, they [Chicanos] were also penalized in the homeland for being Mexican . . . [Anglo] domination had deprived them of solidarity with their trans-border kin."[7] Chicanos knew about the Great Pyramid at Giza, but who was teaching them about the glories of Teotihuacan?

Thus when our playwrights began to resuscitate Mexican legendary figures along with Aztec and Mayan gods and concepts, they challenged both the Mexican and North American hegemonies. Ironically, students in Mexico are taught very little about their indigenous roots aside from the historically negative (Church and state) narratives, a continuation of the dominant discourse demonizing the colonized peoples. And if Mexicans know very little about their indigenous heritage, Chicana/os have little hope of learning anything in early childhood education in the United States. Chicanos who travel to ceremonial sites in Mexico hear what tour guides tell all of the tourists: riveting accounts of virgins being thrown into deep wells or people having their hearts torn from their bodies in savage rituals of human sacrifice. But who tells them to read the poetry of King Nezahualcoyotl or the book of origins called the *Popol Vuh*? Who teaches them about the accomplishments of those people who are also a part of their mythico-cultural history?

The problem, when inventing a mythos, is that you are compressing time. Myths are created through generations of story-telling and cultural logic which gives those stories mythic significance, not through plays or murals on barrio walls. And yet, that is what the Chicana and Chicano writers and artists, composers and poets began to do in the 1960s: create or re-create a Chicano mythos based on Mexican and pre-Columbian heroes and myths. But, apparently lacking historical knowledge of the narratives, some of these artists would conflate images from distinct cultures and time periods. Thus you see a sixteenth-century Aztec god atop a Classic Mayan pyramid (*c.* AD 500) painted without apologies or explanation. The

---

[7] Juan Gomez-Quiñones, *Chicano Politics: Reality and Promise, 1940–1990* (New Mexico, 1990), p. 203.

important thing was to get the images onto those walls, transforming drab buildings into billboards of an emerging Chicano mythos. Cesar Chávez and the United Farm Workers' Union flag, Pancho Villa, Emiliano Zapata and the Virgin of Guadalupe were the most recognizable icons. It was up to the viewers to find out who the indigenous figures were and what they represented.

A mural or painting can only tell the viewer so much about its message(s). And even though "a picture is worth a thousand words," those words may be lost if the person viewing the image has no references, no connections to that image. Study a painting of Quetzalcóatl, and you may only see what appears to be a snake with feathers. The snake as symbol has many meanings, of course, but what of the feathers? Where are the wings? What does it all mean to a contemporary Chicana/o who has probably been taught through Church narratives that indigenous religions are pagan and that the snake is a symbol of evil?

Given the various re-creations of indigenous symbols I have seen on many murals in barrios throughout the United States, it becomes clear that if the visual artists do not provide a narrative (should they?), it is up to the writers, poets and playwrights to give those images and concepts a place in the Chicano imaginary. In his introduction to a special issue of *El Grito* dedicated to Chicano drama in 1974, Herminio Rios-C wrote: "It is indeed impossible to understand many Chicano literary works without a knowledge of Nahuatl [Aztec] and Mayan mythology. Many Chicano writers are exploring this part of our history and are actualizing it in terms of contemporary realities."[8]

Something strange happens when the Mechicana/o playwright has to educate her or his audiences about their Mexican history and mythologies, substituting Aztec, Maya or Hopi beliefs for the more familiar western European myths. As Herminio Rios-C stated a generation ago, Mechicano audiences did not and still do not automatically recognize or identify with Aztec and Maya gods and goddesses. Indeed, most people cannot pronounce names like Quetzalcóatl, Itzamná or Coyolxhaqui, much less identify with them. But that was the challenge to those playwrights who wanted to bring the gods back to their contemporary Mechicano audiences: to transform Zeus into Itzamná, substitute Guadalupe with Tonantzin and replace Mount Olympus with Teotihuacan. That is what the two pioneers of Chicana/o dramaturgy, the late Estela Portillo-Trambley and Luís

---

[8] Hermino Rios-C, "Introduction," *El Grito* (Berkeley, CA) (June–August 1974), 6.

Valdez, chose to do, setting a mythico/historical quest for themselves and their communities.

Unseen spirits of the Southwest

Estela Portillo-Trambley's magicians

Estela Portillo-Trambley is regarded by most Chicana/o critics and scholars as the woman who inspired and opened the doors for all the Chicana writers that followed her. Yet, despite college, university and community-based productions of most of her plays, there have not been any fully mounted professional productions to date. This does not diminish Portillo-Trambley's importance, however, for she has left us some very important statements about who the Chicano and especially, the Chicana, really is. Portillo-Trambley passed away in late 1998, a loss to the literary and theatre communities that will be felt for a long time.

Portillo-Trambley's writings reflect her bicultural upbringing in the desert city of El Paso, Texas, where she was born in 1936. She spent most of her life in El Paso, a city in which the majority population is Mexican and Chicano; a city in which working people have to be bilingual to survive, yet a city which is still a part of the United States. In 1953 Portillo-Trambley married Robert Trambley, with whom she had five daughters.[9] Always a pioneer, Portillo-Trambley received her B.A. in English in 1956 from the University of Texas at El Paso at a time when few Chicanos and even fewer Chicanas were graduating from high school in California. From 1957 to 1964 she taught high school English and was Chair of the English Department of El Paso Technical Institute.[10]

Portillo-Trambley had a varied professional career in El Paso, from hosting a radio talk show from 1969 to 1970, to writing and hosting a television program, "Cumbres," from 1971 to 1972. This led to a full-time writing career and the position of resident dramatist at El Paso Community College from 1970 to 1975 where she also taught classes and produced and directed school productions. In 1971, Portillo-Trambley published a collection of haiku poetry, *Impressions*, and the following year she became the first Chicana to publish a play when *Day of the Swallows* was first published in

---

[9] The Trambley's also had a son, who died at an early age – one of the catalysts for Portillo-Trambley's creative writings.

[10] Suzanne Bennett and Jane T. Peterson (eds.), *Women Playwrights of Diversity* (Westport: Greenwood, 1997), p. 276.

1972. In 1973, she edited *Chicanas en literatura y arte* for *El Grito*, the first all-women's issue of a major Chicano journal.

Also in 1973, Portillo-Trambley attended a summer workshop in the University of Mexico's Escuela de Arte Dramático, studying modern Mexican playwrights such as Octavio Paz, Hector Azar and Vicente Leñero – all well-known playwrights in their own country and abroad. This experience was significant in the formation of Portillo-Trambley's understanding of theatre within a Mexican context. In a letter to me dated February 5, 1982, she described her experiences there:

> It included a symposium with Emilio Carballido. *Tales dramturgos y compania me dieron vista para comprender el tejido de artista, actor, y audiencia. El cuerpo total de teatro como taller humano . . .* It was an experience of inspiration. [Such playwrights and company gave me the insight to understand the interweaving of artist, actor and audience. The total body of teatro as a human workshop.]

In 1975 she published *Rain of Scorpions and Other Writings*, which was the first collection of short stories to be published by a Chicana.[11] Her novel, *Trini*, was published in 1986.[12] But she was always working on a play as well as her fiction. In the period between 1974 and 1977 Portillo-Trambley had four of her plays produced at the Chamizal National Theatre, on the border between El Paso and Juarez: *Morality Play* (unpublished) in 1974, *Blacklight* in 1975, *Sun Images* in 1976 and *Isabel and the Dancing Bear* in 1977 (unpublished).[13] The years between 1974 and 1977 were a time of intense writing for the playwright, who was certainly encouraged by the productions at the Chamizal, but who also knew that each of these plays still needed to be developed. Always interested in education, Portillo-Trambley received her M.A. in English from the University of Texas at El Paso in 1978. In 1983, the playwright published *Sor Juana and Other Plays*, which included the title play and three others: *Autumn Gold*, *Puente Negro* and *Blacklight*.[14]

---

[11] Estela Portillo-Trambley, *Rain of Scorpions* (Berkeley, CA: Tonatiuh International, 1975).
[12] Estela Portillo-Trambley, *Trini* (Binghampton: Bilingual Press, 1986).
[13] *Sun Images* is published in Jorge Huerta and Nicolas Kanellos (eds.), *Nuevos Pasos*, a special issue of *Revista Chicano-Riquena* 7 (invierno 1979), 18–42.
[14] Estella Portillo-Trambley, *Sor Juana and Other Plays* (Tempe: Bilingual Press, 1983). *Sor Juana* is discussed very briefly in chapter 3.

Desert magic as mythos: Day of the Swallows

Of the several plays that Portillo-Trambley published, the two that attempt
to create a Chicano mythos by incorporating indigenous icons and concepts
are *Day of the Swallows* and *Blacklight*. As mentioned above, *Day of the
Swallows*, was Portillo-Trambley's first published play and it is written in a
traditional realistic form – a style of realism that the playwright never abandoned.[15] I would describe this play as poetic realism due to the often heightened language and the romantic setting.[16] The playwright follows an
Aristotelian model in which all of the action takes place in one setting, in
the course of a day. However, although the play is true to a realistic mode
of representation, it is grounded in the playwright's belief in nature gods.
Although the people in this play are Roman Catholics, the playwright combines Christian ritual with indigenous myth; the power of unseen spirits
permeates the central character, Doña Josefa's, world.

The playwright describes Doña Josefa as: "a tall, regal woman about
thirty-five. Her bones are Indian's; her coloring is Aryan" (Garza, *Contemporary Chicano Theatre*, 210). Thus Doña Josefa is a Mestiza, a woman in
touch with both her indigenous and her Spanish cultural and spiritual roots.
Although everyone perceives her as devoutly Roman Catholic, Doña Josefa
has other forces that speak to her, her "magicians," magical powers that we
do not see. The tension between her Christian devotion and her magicians
symbolizes a Life Force that only Josefa can reconcile. In the metaphorical
struggle between the old gods and the newer, Christian faith, the indigenous gods win, immortalizing Josefa in an animistic belief in life after death.

Day of the Swallows takes place in Doña Josefa's nineteenth-century
parlor, a refuge from the harsh world of men. The action of the play begins
the morning before the Day of San Lorenzo, when the virgins of the town
wash their hair in the lake "and bathe in promise of a future husband," a
ritual tradition that will honor Josefa this year (Garza, *Contemporary
Chicano Theater*, 207). But Josefa will never participate in the ritual, for her
destiny has been sealed long before this day. From the moment the play
begins we know that something is terribly wrong in Josefa's household.
Alysea, a young woman who lives with Josefa since she rescued her from a

---

[15] *Day of the Swallows* is also discussed in chapter 4.

[16] Portillo-Trambley's *Day of the Swallows* is published in the following: Herminio Rios and
Octavio Romano-V. (eds.), *El Espejo* (Berkeley: Quinto Sol, 1972), pp. 149–93; Philip D. Ortego
(ed.), *We Are Chicanos* (New York: Washington Square, 1973), pp. 224–71; and Roberto J. Garza
(ed.), *Contemporary Chicano Theatre* (Notre Dame, 1976), pp. 206–45. All references to this play
will be to the version published in Garza, 1976.

bordello, is obviously very upset and nervous as she begins her daily chores. But Josefa maintains her composure as other characters come into their refuge. This seemingly moral woman is hiding some dark secret, and as the action unfolds we discover that the previous night she had cut out the tongue of the boy who lived with them because he witnessed Josefa and Alysea in an act of passion. The boy represents the outside world of "*¿qué dirá la gente?* – what will people say?" – and Josefa's immediate response to the horror on the boy's face is to cut out his tongue while the horrified and confused Alysea holds him down.

Nobody knows about Josefa and Alysea's relationship but Josefa's alcoholic uncle, who suspects something and threatens to blackmail her. After Josefa confesses to her only male friend, the parish priest, Father Prado, she feels that she has no other recourse but to commit suicide. The final scene of the play, the climactic moment, is when Josefa, defeated in this world but not in the realm of her magicians, the light and the lake, dons her white gown and becomes one with these powers by drowning herself in the lake. The image of Josefa's body floating in the lake is a literary one, narrated by one of the village women who is staring out of the window towards the lake since the image is virtually impossible to depict on the stage. Nonetheless, the mental picture is powerful and enhances the playwright's notions of indigenous thought when she describes the return of Josefa's spirit following her suicide: "the almost unearthly light streaming through the windows gives the essence of a presence in the room" (Garza, *Contemporary Chicano Theatre*, p. 245). In the words of Louise Detwiler, at this moment, "Josefa has returned," as she had predicted she would.[17]

Although Detwiler's project is to demonstrate how Portillo-Trambley has created characters and situations in which cultural differences (indigenous vs Spanish) exacerbate gender oppression, she carefully articulates the mythic base upon which Portillo-Trambley constructs her vision. Detwiler believes that by "tapping into the collective consciousness of her indigenous heritage in the midst of the prevailing patriarchal consciousness of the Roman Catholic legacy within her community," Josefa represents "a nexus between animism and Roman Catholicism" (Detwiler, "Cultural Difference," 147). Further, Detwiler feels that "Josefa identifies with an animistic symbol system while she rejects the patriarchal symbols of Roman Catholicism" (147). In other words, the playwright has created a world in

---

[17] Louise Detwiler, "The Question of Cultural Difference and Gender Oppression in Estela Portillo-Trambley's *The Day of the Swallows*," *The Bilingual Review/Revista Bilingue* (1996), 151.

which indigenous, female powers prevail. Detwiler sees Josefa's belief in "Earth as Mother" as a direct contrast to the Judeo-Christian concept of God the Father: "Through the worship of fertility goddesses, i.e. life-giving symbols, Josefa creates a universe that offers her those things that the life-taking patriarchal cosmology surrounding her within the community lacks: sexual passion, life, freedom, sisterhood and rebirth" (151).

Detwiler's argument is important here for her interpretation of the transcendence of indigenous thought over Roman Catholic doctrine in this play. Although the playwright admitted to an interviewer that she wrote the play "to make money" (she assumed that a play about a closeted lesbian suicide would generate popular interest), her desert upbringing and her fascination with indigenous concepts prevailed.[18] But she was also restricted by her lack of playwriting experience. As a writer of fiction, the playwright was better at describing Josefa's world in her stage directions rather than in the dialogue itself. The first words the playwright gives us are for the reader and production staff only: "The tierra [land] of Lago de San Lorenzo is within memory of mountain sweet pine. The maguey thickens with the ferocity of chaotic existence. Here the desert yawns. Here it drinks the sun in madness" (Garza, *Contemporary Chicano Theatre*, 207).

After a full page of describing the natural surroundings and giving a history of San Lorenzo, Portillo-Trambley begins Act 1, scene i with more stage directions: "Josefa's sitting room; it is an unusually beautiful room, thoroughly feminine and in good taste; the profusion of lace everywhere gives the room a safe, homey look . . . it is flooded with light, the lace, the open window all add to the beauty of the room, a storybook beauty of serenity" (208).

This play is a series of scenes between Josefa and other characters in her life, each character bringing her/his own tone to the rising tension. With the exception of the priest, the male characters represent confrontations, with dialogue that reflects the anxiety they create: from the threatening uncle to the powerful Don Esquinas, whose family virtually owns the village. But Josefa's real nemesis is the only full-blooded Native American in the play, Eduardo, who tells Alysea he is taking her away to ". . . a wilderness . . . mountain, pines. My Squaw . . . living and loving in the open" (216). Eduardo does not know about the women's relationship or the truth

---

18 In the late 1970s, Portillo-Trambley said that *Day of the Swallows* was "a play I wrote in a very short time and for a terrible reason. I was just being mercenary." Juan Bruce-Novoa, *Chicano Authors: Inquiry by Interview* (Austin: Texas, 1980), p. 170.

about David's misfortune but he is in love with Alysea and knows that he has to live on the land to be truly happy.

Eduardo becomes a link between Josefa, the indigenous man and *La Tierra*, inspiring the most poetic dialogue in the play. In the conversation between Eduardo and Josefa the playwright equates the native people with the land and the poetry that Mother Nature can inspire. But Eduardo is also a man and Josefa flatly declares that she is not interested in the love of a man: "I did not want the callous Indian youth . . . with hot breath and awkward hands . . . a taking without feeling . . . no, not that! I wanted so much more . . ."(222). Yet, there is also a mystical/sexual tension and connection between Josefa and Eduardo. It is in her first and only meeting with Eduardo that Josefa describes her magicians:

> There by the lake, I felt the light finding its way among the pines . . . to me . . . It took me . . . then . . . perhaps it was my imagination . . . it said to me: 'We are one . . . make your beauty . . . make your truth.' Deep, I felt a burning spiral . . . it roared in my ears . . . my heart . . . [Pause] It was too much to bear . . . so I ran and ran until I fell, opened my eyes, and found myself calmly looking up at the stars . . . sisters of my love! The moon had followed me; it lay a lake around me, on the grass . . . (222)
> [ellipses are the playwright's]

Thus, although the Indian male may have been a threat to Josefa's sense of sexual beauty, he also represents her indigenous roots, her love of the land, *La Tierra, Nuestra Madre* (Mother Earth). Eduardo represents the best and the worst of humanity in Josefa's world, for he is Nature personified as Man. Eduardo had previously been Clara's lover, but he abandoned her (she is, after all the wife of Don Esquinas) and Josefa sees this betrayal as unforgivable. And yet, Josefa tells Eduardo "You are easy to fall in love with," for he is the rebel Indian she would like to be (200). Eduardo has had his way with the wife of the hacienda owner and will now take Alysea away from the barrio and into a natural surrounding, ostensibly free of the Spaniards' control. Eduardo's "temple" is the forest, an allusion and illusion that complements Josefa's belief in nature gods. Both Josefa and Eduardo worship in the same temple, although their gods may be distinct.

Day of the Swallows remains the only play of its kind in the annals of Chicano drama, a visionary, troublesome play that tackles issues and themes that remain as "forbidden" as they were when the author first wrote it. Although this play has not been produced widely, it retains its importance as Estela Portillo-Trambley's attempt to challenge the hegemony of the

Mechicano belief system, both in terms of Christian thought and Mexican/Spanish patriarchal practices. It is a paean to the peoples who were in "America," long before the Europeans came and laid claim to it all. Josefa may be dead in the "reality" of western thought, but in her indigenous vision, she lives on. In Detwiler's words, "Josefa's suicide results in the creation of a more perfect union with what she believes to be divine" (Detwiler, "Cultural Difference," p. 152).

Re-claiming Aztec and Maya mythology

Luis Valdez

Luis Valdez is indisputably the leading Chicano director and playwright who, as the founder of the Teatro Campesino (Farm Workers' Theatre), inspired a national movement of theatre troupes dedicated to the exposure of socio-political problems within the Chicano communities of the United States. More than a generation later, no other Chicana or Chicano playwright or director has generated the amount of critical interest, both positive and negative, as Valdez. His eclectic work includes plays, poems, books, essays, films and videos, all of which deal with the Chicano and Mexican experience in the United States. Further, Valdez's work has inspired many articles, theses, and dissertations, as well as a major critique and analysis of his early work with the Teatro Campesino by Professor Yolanda Broyles-González, published in 1994.[19] The following brief overview of Valdez's career cannot do justice to all that he has attempted or accomplished, but will hopefully serve to introduce Mr. Valdez before I discuss his contributions to a Chicano mythos through indigenous myths, concepts and philosophies.

Valdez was born to migrant farm worker parents in Delano, California, in 1940, the second in a family of ten children. Although his early schooling was constantly interrupted as his family followed the crops, Valdez managed to do well in school. By the age of twelve he had developed an interest in puppet shows, which he would stage for neighbors and friends. While still in high school he hosted his own program on a local television station, foreshadowing his work in film and video which would later introduce him to his widest audience. After high school, Valdez entered San José State College where his interest in theatre fully developed.

---

[19] Yolanda Broyles-González, *El Teatro Campesino: Theater in the Chicano Movement* (Austin: Texas, 1994).

Valdez's first full-length play, *The Shrunken Head of Pancho Villa* (to be discussed more fully in chapter 2), was produced by San José State College in January of 1964, setting the young student's feet firmly in the theatre. After graduation, Valdez worked with the San Francisco Mime Troupe for a year before founding the Teatro Campesino in the fall of 1965. He became the Artistic Director as well as resident playwright for this raggle-taggle troupe of striking farm workers, guiding them in the collective creation and performances of brief commedia-like sketches called "*actos*" which dramatized the need for a farm workers' union.

Within a matter of months, the Teatro Campesino was performing away from the fields educating the general public about the farm workers' struggle and earning revenue for the Union. By 1967 Valdez decided that he and the Teatro had to leave the ranks of the Union in order to focus on his theatre rather than on the demands of a struggling labor organization. As a playwright, Valdez could now begin to explore issues relevant to the Chicano beyond the fields: the experiences of the urban Mechicanos. As a director, he could begin to develop a core of actors no longer committed to one cause and one style alone. He needed the full attention of his company if the Teatro was to evolve both artistically and politically.

The separation from the Union proved auspicious. In 1968 the Teatro was awarded an Obie[20] and the following year Valdez and his troupe gained international exposure at the *Théâtre des Nations* theatre festival in Nancy, France. In only four years, the Teatro Campesino had become an international symbol of the Mechicanos' rural and urban struggles. In 1971 the troupe moved to its permanent home base in the rural village of San Juan Bautista, California, where the Teatro established itself as a resident company, producing plays as well as films and publishing some of Valdez's writings about his vision of theatre. In 1973 Valdez scripted and directed *La gran carpa de los Rasquachis* (*The Great Tent of the Underdogs*) in collaboration with his Teatro. This is an epic "*mito*" which follows a Cantinflas-like (read: "Mexico's Charlie Chaplin") Mexican character from his crossing the border into the United States and the subsequent indignities to which he is exposed until his death.[21]

---

[20] The "Obie," the off-Broadway equivalent of the Broadway Tony (Antoinette Perry) Awards, is sponsored by *The Village Voice*.

[21] See Broyles-González, *El Teatro Campesino*, Ch. 1, for a very detailed analysis of the Mexican carpa and popular performance tradition as source and inspiration for the early Teatro Campesino aesthetic. See also Nicolas Kanellos, *A History of Hispanic Theatre in the United States: Origins to 1940* (Texas, 1990), pp. 95–103.

For the next few years, Valdez continued to write and direct plays, leading to his most commercially successful play to date, *Zoot Suit*,[22] which opened in Los Angeles in 1978 and in New York, on Broadway, in 1979.[23] The play was subsequently adapted into a motion picture written and directed by Valdez and released in 1981. In *Zoot Suit* Valdez combined elements of the earliest Teatro Campesino street theatre aesthetic with *Living Newspaper* techniques, professional choreography, and Brechtian narrative that kept the action moving forward. Although the play did not win sufficient critical acclaim in New York to survive there,[24] it continued to run in Los Angeles and the film became an art film to the cognoscenti.[25] *Zoot Suit* made a major impact on the professional Latina/o talent pool, launching the careers of a number of professional theatrical and film artists, most notably, Edward James Olmos. Other actors who participated in either the Los Angeles or New York versions of *Zoot Suit* and who continue to work professionally include: Evelina Fernández, Alma Martinez, Angela Moya, Lupe Ontiveros, Tony Plana, Rose Portillo, Diane Rodríguez and Marcos Rodríguez, to name a few.[26]

Re-writing a historical California myth: Bandido!

Never one to work on a single project at a time, in 1981 Valdez also directed a workshop of his next play, *Bandido!* in the Teatro Campesino's theatre in San Juan Bautista.[27] In this play Valdez attempts to revisit and revise a historical and mythical figure by dramatizing the life and death of Tiburcio

[22] *Zoot Suit* has generated more critical discourse than any other Chicano play. For an overview of the critics' responses to *Zoot Suit* in New York, see: Broyles-González, *Teatro Campesino*, pp. 189–205; Carlos Morton, "Critical Response to 'Zoot Suit and 'Corridos'," (El Paso: University of Texas, El Paso, Occasional Paper Series, No. 2, 1984); Yvonne Yarbro-Bejarano and Tomás Ybarra-Frausto, "Zoot Suit y el movimiento Chicano," *Plural* (April 1980), 49–56.

[23] See Broyles-González, *Teatro Campesino*, for the most thorough analysis of five versions of this controversial play. See also, Huerta, *Chicano Theater*, pp. 174–84.

[24] Broyles-González *Teatro Campesino*, p. 195, points out that the following publications published positive reviews of *Zoot Suit* on Broadway: ". . . *Wall Street Journal, Variety*, the *Washington Post, Daily News, Newsweek*, to name a few." On page 204, Broyles-González states: "But the [New York] critics are not omnipotent and many plays are successful in spite of negative critical opinion." History has proven otherwise in most cases, especially when the play is a costly Broadway musical. The power of the *New York Times* theatre critics over the years is legendary and frightening.

[25] For years after its initial release of the film, since it did not generate impressive box office numbers, MCA, parent company of Universal Studios, refused to release the film on video. It is now available on video.

[26] *Zoot Suit* is in Luis Valdez, *Zoot Suit and Other Plays* (Houston: Arte Publico, 1992), pp. 23–94.

[27] The revised version of this play is in Luis Valdez, *Zoot Suit*, pp. 95–153.

Vazquez, the last man to be legally, publicly executed in California when he was hanged in 1875. Thus this play is another Valdezian attempt to create a Chicano mythos by reviving a historical figure who is a part of the Mechicanos' early presence in California. Although this play focuses on a member of the Californio ruling class, by virtue of his resistance to Anglo encroachment, Vazquez is a mythical, larger than life figure to Valdez.[28] And, like the mythical indigenous figures that Valdez investigates and brings to life in his mitos, Tiburcio Vazquez is not a well-known figure in California or other states. Therefore *Bandido!* also serves as a history lesson, bringing to life an unknown but important man in order to give his Mechicano audiences their own heroes.

Known in his time as a "bandit" to the Anglos, Vazquez was a hero to many Californios who followed his exploits with great interest between 1853 and 1875. In the playwright's words:

> Although hailed as *resistance fighters* by their own people, both men [Murrietta and Vazquez] are unquestionably part of the American mythology of the Old West, for they share the distinction of having had their lives staged professionally on the melodrama stages of Los Angeles and San Francisco. Yet their claim to fame rests on their notoriety, and their enduring memory owes much to their incorporation into Western conquest fiction as *stereotypes*.
> ... The contrast between photographic portrait and melodramatic stereotype is all that survives of Vazquez in history books.
>
> (Valdez, *Zoot Suit*, p. 97)

Taking his cue from his own metaphor of realistic photograph vs. melodramatic stereotype, Valdez states in his introduction to the published version that this is a "play within a play", an "anti-melodrama" now titled *Bandido! The American Melodrama of Tiburcio Vazquez, Notorious California Bandit*. However, I would argue that this play is a "melodrama-within-a-realistic play," because the playwright contrasts differing realities of theatrical representation in this piece. Whatever the construct, Valdez attempts to revise our perceptions of Tiburcio Vazquez (if we have any) and contrast the "real" man with the Anglo historians' (and Hollywood's) misperceptions. Valdez sees Vazquez as emblematic of all early Californios who have been

---

[28] The upper-class Spanish-speaking people who lived in the territory of Alta California called themselves "Californios." For an informative discussion of the distinct types of Spanish-speaking peoples and communities in the Southwestern United States, see Carey McWilliams, *North From Mexico* (New York: Greenwood, 1968), pp. 81–97.

relegated to stereotypical "greaser" roles and thus tries to rescue him (and all Chicanos, ultimately) from that onerous fate.

The construct of *Bandido!* is that we are watching two versions of Vazquez's exploits: an Impresario's distorted, romanticized version and Vazquez's own re-creation of who he thinks he really was and is – Valdez's "photographic portrait." The "real" Vazquez is Valdez's (re)vision; the "murderous *bandido*" is the Impresario's depiction. Thus, the play starts on a melodrama stage, and then shifts to Vazquez's (realistic) jail cell, in which he awaits his trial and eventual execution with the calm assurance of an archetypal hero. The scenes then shift from one reality to another as we witness two versions of Vasquez's story. When we are with Vazquez in the jail cell, we are observing the real man; when the action shifts to the melodrama stage we are sometimes watching the Impresario's visions and sometimes we are actually watching Vazquez's interpretation. It is a construct that can be confusing on the stage, especially if the acting style is not clearly distinct from one reality to the other. As even the elongated title indicates, the melodramatic acting is exaggerated, while Vazquez's "reality" should be as real as possible.

By shifting the action between Vazquez's reality and the Impresario's objectification of the man, Valdez plays on our own perceptions. The playwright is striving to show us how much we, as audiences, are influenced by the media's representations of who Chicana/os are. As W. B. Worthen states, "In *Bandido* (and to a lesser extent in *I Don't Have to Show You No Stinking Badges!*), Valdez examines the function of popular performance genres – melodrama and television situation comedy – in the construction of identity politics and the history they present onstage."[29] Most importantly, the playwright also gives the Chicana/o a history, a presence in the state of California in this play just as he did with *Zoot Suit*. In the case of *Bandido!*, however, Valdez has taken the Chicanos further back in time to the previous century, placing them firmly in a position to proclaim: "We didn't cross the border; the border crossed us!"

Vazquez is a man on the run from the law and Pico tells him: ". . . I admit you've given all of us Californios twenty years of secret, vicarious revenge." Moments later, Vazquez urges Pico to join him in a revolution against the Gringos: "With a hundred well-armed men I can start a rebellion that will crack the state of California in two, like an earthquake, leaving the Bear Republic in the north, and Spanish California Republic in the south!"

---

[29] W. B. Worthen, "Staging *America*: The Subject of History in Chicano/a Theatre," *Theatre Journal* 49 (1997), 115.

(Valdez, *Zoot Suit*, p. 137). These are heroic ideals that place Vazquez above the common thief many historians have described. I see his character and his situation as symbolic of all Chicanos in struggle against oppressive forces. The villains in Valdez's play are both Anglo and Latino but the hero is a mythico-historical precursor of today's Chicanas and Chicanos.[30]

Invisible Mexicans: I Don't Have to Show You No Stinking Badges!

Valdez's next major play, *I Don't Have to Show You No Stinking Badges!* was co-produced by the Teatro Campesino and the Los Angeles Theatre Center in 1986 under his direction. After so many years of battling the insensitivity of Hollywood it was inevitable that Valdez's next major stage play would expose the problems of stereotyping in tinseltown.[31] While he had tackled melodramatic portrayals of Chicanos in *Bandido!* and stereotypical representations throughout his playwriting career, this new play addressed a community with which he had now become all too familiar. *I Don't Have to Show You No Stinking Badges!* is unique in the development of Chicano dramaturgy as the first professionally produced Chicano play to deal with middle-class Chicanos rather than the usual working poor and working-class characters and situations that concerned most Chicana/o playwrights. The play centers on Connie and Buddy Villa, the self-proclaimed "King and Queen of the Hollywood Extras," who have forged a comfortable life for their two children and themselves playing (silent) maids and gardeners and other stereotypes for Hollywood. The major conflict arises when their son, Sonny, a Harvard honor student, drops out of the Ivy League to pursue a career in Hollywood. The parents, whose daughter is a medical doctor, are appalled and try to dissuade their brilliant son from "ruining his life," but he is intent (as is the playwright) to break through the wall of Hollywood racism and indifference. In typical Valdezian fashion, Sonny (and the audience) begin to hear voices and he imagines events that take us into a surreal or even expressionistic mode as we ponder whether this is all a dream/nightmare he is having. The set (and, if possible, the theatre) must look like a sit-com setting, complete with working appliances and running water in the sink, but with the inevitable television monitors and illuminated signs used for a live studio audience. There is even a laugh track under Sonny's "visions," to enhance the feeling that this is all a sit-com gone awry.

---

[30] As I was finalizing this book, Valdez was directing *Bandido!* for the San Diego Repertory Theatre with his brother, Danny, as the Musical Director. The play began previews in September of 1999.

[31] *I Don't Have to Show You No Stinking Badges!* is in Valdez, *Zoot Suit*, pp. 156–214.

Sonny is the central character in this play, a young, confused Chicano searching for his identity with parents that have lived invisible, silent identities all their professional careers. When Sonny chides his mother for always playing maids she counters with: "As Hattie McDaniel used to say: 'I'd rather play a maid than be one'" (Valdez, *Zoot Suit*, . . . p. 174). As if in response to the types of roles he will be offered, Sonny robs a fast-food restaurant dressed as a "cholo," or Chicano street punk. Sonny's response to Hollywood is to give producers what they expect and he fulfills their fantasy/nightmare by becoming a thief rather than a lawyer. When the police try to communicate with Sonny through megaphones outside, we do not know if this is real, although his girlfriend, Anita, also hears their voices. But the initial set-up, the theatre-as-television-studio, has left all options open and we soon find ourselves on another level of reality with the director's face and voice coming on over the monitors as it would in a real studio situation. But the Director looks and speaks exactly like Sonny.

The audience is thus plunged into what appear to be multiple realities, similar to the juxtapositions discussed in reference to *Bandido!* But while *Bandido!* transposed melodrama with realism, here we have the "real" in contrast to and in negotiation with the video "reality," which is, of course, not real at all. Yet, there are live actors on that stage and live audience members sitting next to you in the auditorium-cum-studio. All of this is designed to confuse and conflate realities we live with daily. Early in the play Sonny asks: "Is it real or is it Memorex?" A question that reverberates throughout the play.

Once the play becomes a live taping, anything can happen and it does. As the play/sit-com comes to a close, off-stage, Sonny and Anita are lifted in a space ship that is described as a giant Mexican *sombrero* (hat) as Connie and Buddy revel in their Son's decision to return to Harvard. In reality, the "Happy Ending" is neither. Having entered the realm of the sit-com, we are left to ponder whether any of this represents real people in real situations and the intrusion of the fantastical exit leaves more confusion than conclusion.

Still, Valdez's play raises issues that are ultimately crucial to him and, by extension, to any other Chicanas and Chicanos – Latinas and Latinos who are fed-up and frustrated with Hollywood's indifference to Latina-themed programming and Latino characters. By giving Sonny an existential moment of angst, the playwright raises themes that do not go away. Sonny tells his parents he did not belong at Harvard because he doesn't know where he belongs. In a major monologue on identity Sonny tells his parents:

"You see, in order to ACT TRULY AMERICAN, you have to kill your parents: no fatherland, motherland, no MEXICAN, Japanese, African . . . old-country SHIT!" (207) Sonny is speaking metaphorically, but the declaration is real to many people struggling with their place in this society. Survival has always been at the core of Valdezian dramaturgy, whether economic, cultural or spiritual, and this play is no exception to that commitment.

Going Hollywood: La Bamba

In 1987 Valdez's most successful motion picture to date, *La Bamba*, was released, making him the most visible Chicano director in Hollywood at the time. In response to criticism that he was selling-out to Hollywood, Valdez told an interviewer, "I'm not selling out – I'm buying *in*."[32] That same year he adapted an earlier piece, the *Corridos* for public television, re-titled "Corridos: Tales of Passion and Revolution."[33] Valdez described this project thus:

> What the program is attempting to do is open up new possibilities with respect to theater. Much of what theater is, is still locked in 19th century approaches. The whole idea of adapting theater for a mass audience is an artistic one that can push the limits of the way [stage] images are presented, which is what we have tried to do.[34]

Valdez's extensive interview with Ken Kelley in 1987 appears to signal a turning point for the playwright-turned-film maker. Early in the interview Kelley had asked Valdez if it had been difficult to make the transition from stage to screen. Valdez's response was telling: "It's hard to contain what I want to do in the box of the proscenium stage. And the theatre is one permanent long shot, camera-wise, whereas with film, you can do so much more . . . When I hit the movies, I thought, This is what I am. This is what I've been trying to *do* . . . "(Kelley, "The Interview," p. 53).

When Kelley asked Valdez about his commitment to the theatre, he answered: "I'll never abandon theatre. But I feel always constrained by the

[32] Ken Kelley, "The Interview: Luis Valdez," *San Francisco Focus* (September 1987), 52.

[33] Valdez's staged and televised productions of *Corridos* created much controversy, especially for its depiction of women. See Yolanda Broyles-González, "What Price 'Mainstream'? Luis Valdez's *Corridos* on Stage and Film," *Cultural Studies* 4 (October 1990), 281–93; and her later, revised version of this article in her *Teatro Campesino*, pp. 154–63. See also, Carlos Morton, "Critical Response to 'Zoot Suit' and 'Corridos'."

[34] Victor Valle, " 'Corridos' moves from stage to KCET," *Los Angeles Times*, October 5, 1987, n.p.

kind of tastes that prevail in theatre in America today. Europe is a lot more free. Consequently, Teatro was a hit in Europe for many years, but never here" (53). Despite the critical and especially the financial success of *La Bamba*, Valdez was still swimming upstream in Hollywood. He continued to work on other Hollywood projects while the Teatro continued to produce the Christmas pageants and sporadic productions during the rest of the year. In 1994 Valdez's adaptation of "The Cisco Kid" aired on the TNT television network. Valdez wrote and directed this movie which starred Jimmy Smits and Cheech Marin as the hero and his side-kick.

In 1995 Valdez began to divide his time between the teatro, his film career and a full-time position as head of the Performing Arts Department at the newly founded California State University, Monterrey Bay. He hoped that this position and the support from the university would enable him to develop a new form of dramatic event which he calls "tele-dramatics," combining the latest cyber-technology with living performers.[35] Still managing several projects at a time, Valdez was working on the screenplay of the life of Cesar Chávez while also developing his pilot program at Monterey Bay. He then took a two-year leave from teaching between 1997 and 1999 in order to focus more on his film work.

But Valdez's decision to work in Hollywood had affected his ability to effectively run his theatre company and it had also impeded his playwriting. In effect, by 1999, no completely new play had come from Luis Valdez's pen since the premiere of *I Don't Have to Show You No Stinking Badges!* in 1986. Frustrated by the slow-moving Hollywood machine, Valdez had told me in 1997 that he was eager to work on a play he had been developing for several years. The following year the San Diego Repertory Theatre received a major grant to commission Valdez as an Artist-in-Residence for two years, while he wrote that play, titled *The Mummified Fetus*. According to the Theatre's newsletter, the play would "explore five hundred years of California history through the lives, issues, and day-to-day decisions of a contemporary family."[36]

> Regarding his trajectory to 1998, Valdez commented:
> For me, it's always a question of the path less traveled. I have to be, like

---

[35] In an interview for "Necessary Theatre," my UCSD-TV television series, taped November 20, 1997, Valdez discussed his idea of "tele-dramatics," as live theatre beamed via the internet to audiences at their computers wherever they were. A kind of cyber-interaction employing the technology of cyberspace and digital imaging with live actors.

[36] From "The REPorter," Fall, 1998, p. 3. [The San Diego Repertory Theatre's subscriber newsletter].

Che, in the mountains. So I live in an isolated place (San Juan Bautista...). My focus is on trying to create pieces and plays. Theatre can only happen if there are enough pillars, and the pillars are the plays. That's what we pass on to the next generation. So when we get the play done, in any way possible, we continue to build a future."

(*REPorter*, 1998: 3)

Although Valdez's teaching and film projects had taken him away from the theatre company he had founded a generation earlier, the organization had not stopped functioning. By the mid-1990s the Teatro Campesino was being guided by the next generation of Chicana and Chicano theatre artists, the Valdez sons and other grown children of some of the earlier core members of the Teatro Campesino. In an interesting homage to the very roots of Chicano theatre, in the spring of 1999 the Teatro Campesino produced *The Shrunken Head of Pancho Villa* in San Juan Bautista and toured the production to San Diego, California, as well.[37] The Teatro Campesino was now following in the tradition of earlier Mexican theatre companies composed of extended families who produced and performed theatre in and of their communities for generations.[38]

Valdezian neo–aztec/Mayan mythology: mitos

To discuss Luis Valdez's mythos, we must return to the beginning of his work with the Teatro Campesino. Even as he and his troupe were creating the *actos* in the mid-1960s, the playwright/director had begun to investigate a complementary and contrasting form, which he termed the "*mito*," or myth, exploring the Chicanos' roots in Pre-Columbian philosophy, science, religion and art. This was his response to philosophical Eurocentrism as well as to realism in the theatre. In 1971 Valdez wrote: "Our rejection of white western European (gabacho) proscenium theatre makes the birth of

---

[37] The Teatro Campesino's production of *The Shrunken Head of Pancho Villa* in San Diego was excellent, directed by Kinán Valdez in the exaggerated style of the early Teatro Campesino. The cast included Kinán, his brothers Anáhuac and Lakín and other members of the Teatro Campesino's extended family, Maria Candelaria, Gustavo Manrique, Seth Millwood, Jeff Mirione, and Katrina Valdez.

[38] For more on the Mexican theatrical families of the late nineteenth and early twentieth centuries, see Nicolás Kanellos, *A History of Hispanic Theatre in the United States: Origins to 1940*; Elizabeth C. Ramírez, *Footlights Across the Border: A History of Spanish-Language Professional Theatre on the Texas Stage* (New York: Peter Lang, 1990; and Tomás Ybarra-Frausto, "I Can Still Hear the Applause. *La Farandula Chicana: Carpas y Tandas de Variedad*," in Nicolás Kanellos (ed.), *Hispanic Theatre in the United States* (Houston: Arte Publico, 1984), pp. 45–61.

new Chicano forms necessary, thus, los actos y los mitos; one through the eyes of man, the other through the eyes of God."[39] The Valdezian *mito* is a very personal inquiry into Aztec, Maya and Native American philosophy that the author has maintained to this day. It is Valdez's conflation of Christian and indigenous spirituality that gives the playwright poetic license to do whatever he wants with his characters and plots as he explores and recreates a Chicano mythos.

According to Valdez, the Chicano will find her/his balance through a respect for both indigenous and Christian beliefs. Thus he developed the "Theater of the Sphere;" what Yolanda Broyles-González terms "an alternative and native Chicana/o performance theory and practice."[40] Broyles-González' discussion is the first and only analysis and explication of the "Theater of the Sphere" in published form. Her examination is invaluable to anyone who wishes to gain a better understanding of Luis Valdez and his Teatro members' indigenous philosophy and practice, especially during the 1970s. Basing her analysis of this process on interviews, participant observation and members' notebooks, Broyles-González defines this system rather succinctly in the following passage:

> The Theater of the Sphere consists of a sustained attempt to restore "the totality of the Indio's vision," to affirm the submerged collective memory while making it the foundational training for a Chicana/o pedagogy and life performance.
>
> . . .
>
> . . .one very real dimension of this endeavor rests in its effort to counteract the human fragmentation and deformation inherent in capitalist society.
>
> (Broyles-González, *Teatro Campesino*, p. 87)

This "life performance" became a basis for the Teatro Campesino's work between 1970 and 1980, enabling the troupe to collectively create a variety of *mitos* only a group of believers could achieve. This was an effort to reclaim the Mechicanos' indigenous spiritual heritage and to give their people a sense of their own history as Mestizos: Euro-Native Americans.[41] Leftist

---

[39] Luis Valdez, *Luis Valdez – Early Works: Actos, Bernabé and Pensamiento Serpentino* (Houston: Arte Publico, 1990), p. 11. Originally published as *Actos* (San Juan Bautista, CA: Cucaracha Press, 1971), p. 5.

[40] Yolanda Broyles-González, *Teatro Campesino*, Ch. 2.

[41] I do not include African in this conflation (Euro-Native American), not because there were no African influences in Mexico, but because the Campesino's works do not reveal these. In contrast, Cuban and Puerto Rican culture is permeated with African influences, from the religious

critics would have none of this. For them, Valdez had lost touch with the working-class struggle of his original theatre troupe. In 1973, in response to those who criticized him for turning to what they perceived of as spiritual rather than concrete, material solutions, Valdez wrote an epic poem titled "Pensamiento Serpentino." In this bilingual poem, Valdez attempted to characterize his spiritual beliefs as inseparable from his political foundation. In the words of Professor Broyles-González, this poem expresses the concept of "the fundamental unity or fusion of all human action and performance, theatrical and other; of the fundamental unity of all living beings and of all races" (Broyles-González, *Teatro Campesino*, p. 94).

Valdez was basing his philosophy on the Maya-Quiche origin myth, *El Popol Vuh*, as well as on the influences of Mexican anthropologist, Domingo Martinez Parédez and Andrés Segura, ritual Conchero dancer and Aztec elder.[42] Valdez hoped that the *mitos* would encourage other Chicanos to study the Maya view of life in order to understand their role(s) in the cosmos, their place in the greater scheme of things. In an effort to explain the power and energy of the indigenous Spirit, Valdez wrote:

> El indio baila [The indian dances]
> he dances his way to truth
> in a way intellectuals will
> never understand[43]

Either you believe in miracles or you do not. But do not try to rationalize the experience any more than you can reason with rapture. For Valdez, the indigenous American dance evokes and affirms a belief in unseen powers that come from the cosmos. In Broyles-González' words, "In general, ritual dance seeks to promote a cosmic integration of the cosmic planetary movement, the individual, and the immediate and larger community" (Broyles-González, *Teatro Campesino*, p. 117). Valdez was not anti-intellectual in the above reference from "Pensamiento Serpentino," he was simply stating what is not palpable to the casual observer, but which is, to the indigenous dancer, Truth.

---

beliefs to the music and cuisine. See my article "Negotiating Borders in Three US Latino Plays," in Michal Kobialka (ed.), *Border Crossings: Theater, Theory, Practice* (Minneapolis: Minnesota, 1999), pp. 154–83.

[42] For more on Martinez Parédez 's interpretation of the Popol Vuh, see Domingo Martinez Parédez, *El Popol Vuh Tiene Razon* (Mexico: Editorial Orion, 1968).

[43] Luis Valdez's "Pensamiento Serpentino" was first published in a magazine titled *Chicano Theater One*, primavera, 1973, 1–19; later re-issued by the Teatro Campesino's in-house publishing arm, Cucaracha Press, in 1973. These two publications are now collector's items and the poem can be found in Luis Valdez, *Early Works*, pp. 168–99.

A contemporary Chicano savior: Dark Root of a Scream

Valdez's first *mito, Dark Root of a Scream* was initially produced by the Teatro Campesino in Fresno, California, in 1967, directed by the playwright.[44] This *mito* is an important example of Valdez's early attempt to educate his audiences about indigenous myth, in this case, the figure of Quetzalcóatl. According to Valdez's stage directions, the setting is "a collage of myth and reality. It forms . . . a pyramid with the most real artifacts of barrio life at the broad base and an abstract mythical-religious peak at the top" (*West Coast Plays*, 19/20, p. 3). This is a very ritualistic and expository play in which we learn about Quetzalcóatl Gonzales, a young Chicano nicknamed Indio. It is Indio's wake, for he is a fallen Vietnam veteran whose body lies in a flag-draped coffin. As the characters discuss Indio, the audience learns a great deal about him and how his life paralleled that of the mythical figure for whom he was named, Quetzalcóatl. Two conversations about Indio, one at the wake and another on the street corner, eventually merge into one, explosive confrontation.

Stylistically, this *mito* is unique in Valdezian dramaturgy for it is almost a dramatized lecture about the dead soldier's life. Also, in his attempt to reveal some differences between Christian theology and indigenous beliefs, Valdez locates the play on several levels of mythical and material reality. On the material plane, the pyramidal set includes three major locations: the wake in "someone's living room" (presumably Indio's mother), a street corner, and the apex of the pyramid, where the coffin rests. On the spiritual plane the *mito* sets up a clearly non-realistic metaphor; the street scene is Any Barrio, USA. When the "*vatos*" (street youths) end up at the wake they disrupt the proceedings and eventually open the coffin to discover an Aztec feathered headdress and Indio's still-beating heart. Indio/Quetzalcóatl is not dead.

For the first several scenes, the mourning mother and girlfriend are discussing Indio's life with the priest at the wake, while the "*vatos*," are on a street corner, also discussing Indio/Quetzalcóatl. By having the characters discuss the dead soldier's past, the playwright reveals Indio's character as well as the young Chicano's frustrated political objectives. We learn about Indio through a curious and effective technique in which the conversations

---

[44] Published in Lilian Faderman and Omar Salinas (eds.), *From the Barrio: A Chicano Anthology* (San Francisco: Canfield, 1973), pp. 79–98 and in *West Coast Plays* 19/20 (Los Angeles: California Theatre Council, 1986), pp. 1–19. For a complete discussion of this mito, see Betty Diamond, "Brown-eyed Children of the Sun: The Cultural Politics of El Teatro Campesino" (Ann Arbor: University Microfilms, 1977), pp. 160–71; and Huerta, *Chicano Theater*, pp. 97–103.

on the street corner and the wake – geographically distinct locales – blend into one another as if the characters were all in the same place. As an example of this technique, the Priest asks Dalia, Indio's girlfriend, a question about Indio and one of the "*vatos*" answers it, as though he were in the same room. Almost a call and response, as if in a temple or church.

Although there are no stage directions to this effect, in the 1971 and 1985 productions, the three "vatos" on the street corner were made-up to resemble their nick-names. Gato had cat-like features; Lizard had a reptilian appearance and Conejo resembled a rabbit. Therefore, from the moment the audience sees the setting and these characters they know that they have entered another level of reality. When blood begins to drip from the coffin, they can be certain that they have crossed into the realm of myth.

The climactic moment in this play is when the three youths disrupt the wake, chasing the priest out. Indigenous drums begin to beat ominously as Lizard, now dressed in an Aztec cloak and feathered headdress, reaches into the coffin. Having seen the blood dripping from a supposedly dead man's coffin, we do not know what to expect when suddenly Lizard lifts Indio's beating heart out of the coffin and it glows in the descending darkness. End of play. Having just heard (learned) that Quetzalcóatl was expected to return one day and bring peace to earth, the inference is that Indio is not dead. Perhaps his spirit will rescue the Mechicano from the darkness of oppression both at home and in Vietnam.

Perhaps the ending of this play leaves most contemporary audience members with more questions than answers. Yet, for those who believe the Mesoamerican philosophy, there is no death, only life-as-struggle, represented by Indio's pulsating heart. Perhaps Indio had to die, a sacrificial victim of late Capitalism and what was called the "military-industrial-complex" in the 1960s. What Valdez invokes with this young Chicano's death is the uselessness of war in general and that war in particular. Although Indio's life has been cut short, his fate must remain a lesson to other Chicanas and Chicanos not to go blindly into conflicts that will result in useless death and destruction. With this *mito* the playwright was taking a very anti-American position at a time when many Americans, of every stripe and color, were not proud of what the government was doing in the name of "America" and "freedom."

By combining contemporary situations with mythical figures, Valdez was expanding his audiences' awareness of indigenous thought and culture, hoping to alert them to the gross injustices of the war as thousands of Chicanos were being drafted and disproportionate numbers were being wounded and killed.[45] Although the Vietnam War is now a part of history, conflicts continue throughout the world and the play is still an important philosophical and artistic statement. *Dark Root of a Scream* signals the beginning of Valdez's fascination with Aztec and Maya mythical iconography re-configured within a contemporary Mechicano setting.

Learning to love and respect La Tierra: Bernabé

In 1970 the Teatro Campesino produced Luis Valdez's second *mito, Bernabé,* about a thirty-five-year-old retarded Chicano farm worker named Bernabé who is in love with *La Tierra,* Mother Earth.[46] Set in a Central California farming town in the dead heat of summer, this play is an exploration of man's relationship with the natural forces, especially the sun, the moon, and the earth. On the material plane everyone calls Bernabé crazy, laughing at his declarations of love for La Tierra. On the spiritual plane he meets La Luna (the Moon), a 1940s zoot suiter, who introduces him to his sister, La Tierra. When their father, El Sol (the Sun) rises, Bernabé asks for his daughter's hand. El Sol grants his wish and La Tierra asks Bernabé if he will love her *"Hasta la muerte"* (until death). She then turns to him to reveal a death mask. Bernabé repeats the phrase, *"Hasta la muerte,"* and the two embrace in a symbolic union between Man and Earth.[47]

In the next and final scene we see Bernabé's relatives carrying his "dead" body which they discovered in his hiding place, a hole in the ground in which he would symbolically copulate with La Tierra by masturbating. They believe he was smothered by a cave-in, but according to the playwright's neo-Maya philosophy, as with Indio in *Dark Root of a Scream,* Bernabé is only dead on the material level, not on the spiritual plane. Bernabé, a Chicano Everyman, has been granted his wish. He "marries" La Tierra and becomes a complete man. For Valdez, Death is merely a passing from one reality to another. This thought permeates his *"Pensamiento*

---

[45] Ralph Guzman, "Mexican-American Casualties in Vietnam," *La Raza* I, 1 (1970), 12–15. For more on the Chicana/o experience in Vietnam and on the home front, see Jorge Mariscal (ed.), *Aztlán and Vietnam: Chicano and Chicana Experiences of the War* (California, 1999).

[46] The text of *Bernabé* in Spanish is in Garza, *Contemporary Chicano Theatre,* pp. 30–58. The English version is published in Robert Hurwitt (ed.), *West Coast Plays 19/20* pp. 21–51, and also in Luis Valdez, *Early Works* pp. 134–67. The *West Coast Plays* version states that *Bernabé* was first produced in 1970 (p. 22), while Broyles-González, (*Teatro Campesino,* p. 242) places the first production in 1969. In what was a scholarly error, I wrote that *Bernabé* was Valdez's first *mito* (Huerta, *Chicano Theater,* p. 195), however *Dark Root of a Scream* was first produced in 1967 according to The Editor's notes in the *West Coast Plays 19/20* version, p. 2.

[47] All references to the text are from Valdez, *West Coast Plays, 19/20.* This reference is to p. 51.

Serpentino" as well as his own philosophy as adapted from the Maya. As he informed a group of *teatristas* (teatro artists) in 1973, the Maya word, *mucnal*, means "to plant corn" and also means "to bury a body." [48] Thus death produces new life in the universal cycle of birth, growth, death and rebirth common to all living things.

In *Bernabé* Valdez creates his own mythology, based loosely on the Aztec pantheon but adjusted to meet his political and creative needs. In the original Aztec myth, Huitzilopochtli, the sun, is born of Cóatlicue, Mother Earth, a virgin birth. However, before he is born, his sister, Coyoloxhaqui (the Moon), outraged that their mother is pregnant without a husband, gathers her brothers, the Four Hundred Gods of the South (the stars) to kill the newborn child. But Huitzilopochtli is born fully prepared for war and dismembers his sister, scattering her limbs and leaving her head on the slopes of a nearby mountain as he destroys his cowardly brothers, thwarting their attempts to flee on their southward journey.[49] This is a metaphor for the daily struggles between night and day, with the all-powerful rising sun ever victorious over the vanquished light of the moon and the stars. As Miguel Leon-Portilla also states, the legend gave the Aztec people license to wage war against any opponent.[50]

In his contemporary adaptation, Valdez changes the mythical family to Sun/father, son/Moon and daughter/Earth. Further, the moon, La Luna, is dressed as a zoot suiter and the earth, La Tierra, is described as an Adelita, the popular name given to the women who fought alongside and nurtured the men during the Mexican Revolution. The only one of these three characters that remains Aztec in nature and costume is El Sol. By reclaiming a Chicano icon (the rebel pachuco), and a Mexican icon (the Adelita), and making them the children of Huitzilopochtli, Valdez conflates both time and space and meaning.

With few experts among his audiences to challenge him on Aztec mythology, Valdez could adjust mythical relationships as he wished. By making La Tierra and La Luna symbols recognizable to Chicano audiences, the playwright gives the spectators historical and political reference points

[48] Valdez took this concept from Domingo Martinez, Parédez 's *El Popol Vuh Tiene Razon*, p. 153.

[49] The narrative of the birth of Huitzilopochtli is in Miguel Leon-Portilla *Pre-Columbian Literatures of Mexico* (Norman: Oklahoma, 1966), pp. 42–48. For an adaptation of this Aztec poem into a Chicano farce, see my play, "El Renacimiento de (Rebirth of) Huitzilopochtli," in Jorge A. Huerta (ed.), *El Teatro de la Esperanza: An Anthology of Chicano Drama* (Goleta: El Teatro de la Esperanza, 1973), pp. 98–123.

[50] For an account of the Mexica (Aztecs), Huitzilopchtli and war, see Miguel Leon-Portilla, *The Aztec Image of Self and Society* (University of Utah, 1992), pp. 99–104.

even as he fuses these with icons that have little meaning beyond the so-called "Aztec Calendar." It is as if the playwright chose not to go too far in his attempt to get his audiences to contemplate their indigenous roots. One Aztec god, one figure from the Mexican Revolution and one twentieth-century Chicano icon would be enough to span the centuries as Valdez searched for truth in myth. Or, in the words of Donald H. Frischmann, "*efectuando un sincretismo de lo mítico y de lo cotidiano*" ["Effecting a syncretism of the mythical with the everyday"].[51]

In his analysis of *Bernabé*, Frischmann sees this play as Valdez's and the Teatro Campesino's response to the violence that Mechicanas and Mechicanos face daily. "*La justicia social era ya una cuestión de armonía entre hermanos, y este rótulo ahora abarcaba ambos opresores y oprimidos*" ["Social justice was now a question of harmony between brothers, and this concept now included both the oppressors and oppressed"] (Frischmann, 264). Frischmann then supports this contention with a quote from Valdez himself: "We respond to a hating society by non-hating: much more can be done through the humanizing power of the arts than the gun in *this* America."[52] It is Bernabé, the so-called "simpleton," that is the wise man among men, for he understands what his ancestors knew from time immemorial: you cannot buy and sell Mother Earth. Further, you cannot disrespect Her as the rich continue to do.[53]

Cleansing evil spirits: Baile de los Gigantes

Perhaps the most symbolic and non-Western piece performed by the Teatro Campesino was *El Baile de los Gigantes* ("Dance of the Giants"), which was first presented publicly in 1974 at the inauguration of the TENAZ "*Quinto Festival de los Teatros Chicanos: Primer Encuentro Latinoamericano*" ["Fifth Chicano Theatre Festival: First Latin American Encounter"], at the pyramids of Teotihuacan outside of Mexico City. In reality, the Teatro did not "create" this dance-drama, but adapted it from the Chorti dance-ritual which is, according to Broyles-González, "a physicalization of the mythic portion of the . . . *Popol Vuh*" (Broyles-Gonzales, *Teatro Campesino*, p. 118).

---

[51] Donald H. Frischmann, *"El Teatro Campesino y su mito Bernabé: un regreso a la madre tierra,"* *Aztlán* (Autumn 1981), 264–65.

[52] *Ibid.* Frischman is quoting Valdez in Carlos Morton, *"La Serpiente Sheds Its Skin: The Teatro Campesino,"* *Drama Review* 18 (1974), 73.

[53] For more on *Bernabé* see: Diamond, "Brown-Eyed Children," pp. 146–59; Frischmann, El Teatro Campesino," pp. 259–70; and Huerta, *Chicano Theater*, pp. 195–99.

Historically, the dance is performed on the day of the Summer Solstice in an effort to cleanse the participants of potential evil caused by the high concentration of solar energy. According to Valdez, speaking to an interviewer in 1974, the *Baile de los Gigantes* is "a purification for the performers and for the whole tribe as well."[54]

In the words of Betty Diamond, this piece "is not a play but a ritual" (Diamond, "Brown-eyed Children", p. 183). Diamond writes about a "performance" she witnessed and eventually participated in, at the Teatro's headquarters in San Juan Bautista, California, in 1975:

> The members of the Teatro who are taking part in the dance are not now performers but participants, believers . . . Luis' [Valdez] voice, the music, the dance combine to lead the spectator into a world that is pre-conscious. I am drawn in . . . Something magical has happened . . . In the way that honest people can touch you, can reach your open place, El Teatro Campesino has reached that audience. They created a moment when people were open, but it was just a moment.
>
> (Diamond, pp. 184–85)

The sometimes cynical Diamond cannot help but affirm that something "Magical," something powerful, took place within this ritual dance. However, it must be noted that the experience Diamond relates happened in the Teatro's rehearsal space, a "safe place," cleansed and blessed by the "High Priest," Valdez. In other words, this was not an impersonal, public arena. Diamond was drawn in symbolically and literally, when she was invited to take part in the final moments of the dance along with about "a hundred people," dancing and singing. However, she was an outsider, a doctoral student researching her dissertation and as such could never participate fully in either the dance or the ritual of the Teatro. In effect, by terming the experience "magical," Diamond falls back on observation rather than lived experience. She returned to her typewriter to record what she had seen and felt, and although she would never be the same, neither did she join the dance.

Diamond's experience – objectively subjective – is what many of us who participated in Campesino's workshops and performances felt: a temporary thrill, soon to be replaced by the harsh realities of daily living. Few people experienced the Valdezian/Campesino philosophy as a way of life but many audience members who witnessed their mitos could not ignore the power that moved and motivated the believers. Indigenous dance had great

54 Theodore Shank, "A Return to Mayan and Aztec Roots," *Drama Review* 4 (1974), 62.

significance for Valdez and other members of the Teatro Campesino and for the community-at-large. In Valdez's words, the dance-ritual, *Baile de los Gigantes,* "shows the good forces fighting against bad force . . . it is cathartic" (Shank, "Return to Mayan," 62).

Broyles-González discusses the *Baile de los Gigantes* as central to the Theatre of the Sphere but notes that after its initial public performance at Teotihuacan in 1974, "the Teatro continued to perform the dance, although rarely in public" (Broyles-González, *Teatro Campesino,* 119). Although few subsequent playwrights or teatros would continue to re-create actual Pre-Columbian rituals such as the *Baile de los Gigantes,* the music persists; the drums and flutes continue to underscore many of the plays that I will discuss in this book.

Alurista's poetic ritual cleansing: Dawn

One of the first Mechicano poets of the 1970s to introduce indigenous cultures and icons into his writings was Alurista, nom de plume of Alberto Baltazar Urista, born in 1947 in Mexico City and brought to the United States at the age of eight. By the early 1970s, Alurista was well known in the Chicano Movement as someone who urged Mechicana/os to look to Native-American philosophies in their quest for spiritual, political and economic liberation.[55] In his published poems and in his public readings of those poems, Alurista became an impressive advocate of both political awareness and indigenous re-birth in the *barrios.*

Although he is best known for his poetry and especially for his readings of that poetry, Alurista's play, *Dawn,* published in 1974, is another early example of a play that incorporates Nahuatl gods and philosophies in a contemporary Chicano context.[56] In actuality *Dawn* is a ritual more than a play, a poetic narrative written during the last gasps of the Vietnam war that exposes the military-industrial-complex in a symbolic call for Chicana/o resistance and unity. This play is written in a three-act structure, but the entire published text, composed in narrow lines of verse, is only twenty-nine pages in length. Thus this play is not really a full-length drama, although

---

[55] For more of Alurista's indigenous-themed poetry see: *Floricanto en Aztlán,* (Los Angeles: Chicano Cultural Center, UCLA, 1971); *Nationchild Plumaroja* (San Diego: Toltecas en Aztlán, 1972).

[56] *Dawn* is published in *El Grito* (June–August 1974), pp. 55–84, and also in Garza, *Contemporary Chicano Theatre,* pp. 103–34. All references to this play are from the first published version in *El Grito,* 1974.

dances, songs and other ritual elements could add to its length in performance.

Through *Dawn*, Alurista introduces the audience to Nahuatl gods and
goddesses, such as Quetzalcóatl and Tezcatlipoca, and contrasts these with
gods of his own creation, named Pepsicóatl and Cocacóatl, "lord of imper-
ial racism" and "lady of blood money" (Alurista, *Dawn*, 56). Each act is
titled, giving the audience/reader an entry to the theme being explored:
"The Hunt," "The Tribunal," and "The Labor." A Council of Elders oversees and narrates the action, which leads to blood sacrifice and re-birth,
recalling the rituals of Pre-Columbian peoples.

As indicated by the titles of each act, the indigenous gods and goddesses
hunt for the villains, Pepsicóatl and Cocacóatl, allegories of the military-
industrial-complex. Once the evil pair is captured, they are put on trial for:

> crimes committed
> against bronze people
> and bronze land
> genocide
> genocide
> killer of children
> biocide
> biocide
> polluter of earth
> waters and sky
> (Alurista, *El Grito*, pp. 64–65)

During the Tribunal, Cocacóatl kills a Mexican who is about to kill her
husband, Pepsicóatl. Moments later an archetypal Chicano, called simply
"Chicano," enters and lists the evil these two have committed upon his
people:

> you are a murderer
> and a thief ese
> you too esa
> colonized
> our minds
> wanting us
> to be like you
> tell us
> we'd fare off well
> forgetting
> our mexican blood

you tried to rinse
our skins
with spain
while we worked
in your factories
slaved
in your mines
and died in your pesticide fields
we fought your wars
and came back
to the yankee occupation
of our barrios   (69)

Chicano speaks in the street vernacular of the barrios, disrespectfully calling Pepsicóatl "ese," or "dude," and his wife "esa," or "chick." Chicano's line, "you tried to rinse our skins with spain," refers to the common practice of Anglos calling Mexicans "Spanish" so as to European-ize them and rid them of the Indian. Cocacóatl responds to the Chicano's litany of accusations by seducing him. The two have sex under the table and then Cocacóatl kills the Chicano – a not infrequent result of the worker's seduction by consumerism: an early death. However, in an interesting twist, Cocacóatl also kills Pepsicóatl after being brought to wisdom by Chimalma, the wise woman who makes Cocacóatl recognize her own oppression under Pepsicóatl's rule.

It seems that the indigenous gods have their plans for Cocacóatl: she must bear the twins she carries in her womb and then she must die. The twins, the children of the Chicano and the transformed Cocacóatl, will be the new Lord and Lady of the Dawn. Once the twins are born and Cocacóatl is symbolically buried, the warrior god, Mixcóatl, speaks to the gathering of Elders and to the audience:

with the dawn
the tree of life
blooms
and
the tree of thorns
withers
thirteen heavens
begin
august 1987
the birth

the new man
the birth
the new woman
the birth
the new world
. . .
the blooming of humanity
of brotherhood
of sisterhood
of justice
of beauty
of labor
and of peace   (81–82)[57]

I remember Alurista commenting in the early 1970s on how the long arm
of global capitalism was made very clear to him when he visited the furthest
reaches of some Mexican jungle, trying to escape commodity culture only
to find discarded Coca Cola cans in the river. This image stayed with him
and appears in this play as the two allegories of capitalism, Cocacóatl and
Pepsicóatl; a satirical and conscious play on words and economic symbols.
These two United States-based soft drink companies are arch rivals, constantly fighting for the larger share of the global market and are thus the
perfect partners in a marriage of crime and convenience. When the one
murders the other it is wishful thinking and symbolically very satisfying to
anyone who fights against the menace of unbridled capitalism.

Alurista's use of "Cóatl" to designate the evil ones is curious because
Quetzalcóatl, the Feathered Serpent, was the "good" god, the one who gave
mankind Life. Quetzalcóatl's brother, Tezcatlipoca, represented evil, darkness and war. These two were binary opposites but both were revered by the
Aztecs, who believed that Good and Evil coexist in all of us; a constant
tension between the two symbolizes Life. I am sure the choice of the "cóatl"
was conscious, for if the playwright had used the last two syllables of
Tezcatlipoca, "poca," his villains would have been "Pepsipoca" and
"Cocapoca." While "poco," which means "little" in Spanish, could also be a
satiric comment, the playwright judiciously chose the term "cóatl" because
it is clearly a Nahuatl word without real meaning to most people other than

[57] Alurista echoes Luís Valdez, who was also reading Domingo Martinez-Parédez's *El Popol Vuh
Tiene Razon*, in which the Mexican anthropologist relates that August 16, 1987 marked the end
of the nine hells which began the day Cortez and his troops arrived to Mexico. See Valdez's
"Pensamiento Serpentino" in his *Early Works*.

the strange sound. Further, the playwright knew that "cóatl" means snake, thus he could have been employing the Old Testament trope of the snake as evil and thus a signifier of capitalism. However, although most people in the audience would not know what "cóatl" means, when tacked-on to icons of consumerism, the effect is highly comical.

Because it is a ritual rather than a "traditional" play, *Dawn* serves as an interesting and compelling contrast to the plays of Luis Valdez and Estela Portillo-Trambley.[58] What makes *Dawn* so interesting is the language; the poet's free verse and his concise and biting imagery that can be beautiful one moment and shatteringly violent the next. Ultimately, *Dawn* is more of a tone poem than a play and it remains a unique example of a contemporary Chicano verse drama written as ritual in the early stages of the Chicano Movement.

Portillo-Trambley's Mayan vision: Blacklight

Estela Portillo-Trambley is also one of the first playwrights to explore pre-Columbian mythology within a contemporary barrio setting. In her play, *Blacklight*, published in 1983, Portillo-Trambley dramatizes the economic and cultural struggles of an impoverished Chicano family.[59] What distinguishes *Blacklight* from most other Chicano domestic dramas, however, is the playwright's overt use of indigenous myth. While Valdez credits the Highland Maya book, the *Popol Vuh*, for his neo-Maya inspiration, Portillo bases her interpretation on the writings of the Maya of the Yucatan, the books called *Chilam Balam*. The term, *Chilam Balam*, translates freely into "the book of the soothsayer of hidden things," which are accounts of mythico/historical events as well as prophecies of the future.[60] It is the nature of those "hidden things" that fascinates our playwright, who incorporates prominent Yucateca gods into her play. Portillo-

---

[58] Alurista has not published any more plays to date and I know of no productions of *Dawn*. The absence of productions could be because *Dawn* is rather static, written in the tradition of the only extant pre-Columbian verse-drama, *Rabinal Achi* (*Warrior of Rabinal*), in which the two adversaries, Quiche Warrior and Rabinal Warrior verbally duel until the Quiche Warrior is sacrificed. *Rabinal Achi*, translated by Richard Leinaweaver, is in *Latin American Theatre Review* 1 (Spring 1969), 3–53. See also *Rabinal Achi: Teatro indigena pre-hispanico*, prologo por Francisco Monterde (Mexico: Ediciones de la Universidad Autonoma, 1955).

[59] *Blacklight* is in Portillo-Trambley, *Sor Juana and Other Plays*, pp. 100–42.

[60] According to Sylvanus G. Morley, there are fragments of "ten or twelve" books of *Chilam Balam*. Sylvanus G. Morley, *The Ancient Maya* (Palo Alto: Stanford, 1956), pp. 254–55. For one of the most detailed and important books, see Ralph L. Roys, *The Book of Chilam Balam of Chumayel* (Norman: Oklahoma, 1967).

Trambley introduces her audiences to Itzamná, Lord of the Heavens and also Lord of Day and Night; the rain god, Chac; and Ixchel, wife of Itzamná and patroness of pregnancy (Morley, *The Ancient Maya*, pp. 94–96). Portillo-Trambley resuscitates these gods for her modern interpretation of ancient myths.

Blacklight is a naturalistic drama that centers on an impoverished Chicano family living on the edge of the railroad tracks in a desert border town "whose larger population consists of Mexicans who crossed the river into the United States" (Portillo-Trambley, *Sor Juana*, p. 103). Most of the action takes place in the backyard of a very run-down house, with the usual outdoor clutter common to homes that suffer the proximity of railroad tracks: crates, old tires, used furniture, and the like. Even the people who inhabit the house and yard have been "thrown away" by an industrialized society that cares only for profit. But amid the clutter we also see a post with carvings of the face of Itzamná above "four faces representing the wind gods right below, then the face of the goddess Ixchel" (103). The faces are painted in fluorescent colors – the only color in the yard – and thus stand out amidst the drab surroundings. Visually, the colorful faces, though unfinished, evoke a sense of mystery to the scene, always looking out, silent observers of the people's actions. We can also see into a bedroom, obviously a young person's hangout, distinguished by walls covered with drawings of discs, insects and two huge eyes that dominate the small space. The playwright hopes to create the sense that the gods are both inside and outside of the house with these images. Images that will "come to life" later in the play.

The play opens with a brief prologue in which Foco, one of Mundo's friends, tells the audience that this yard and house are where everything happened: "Ancient gods came and went, forces that mingled with the sorrows and fears of Mundo's family. [to the "stick"] You were the master here a year ago. You're nothin' now" (104). Foco has returned to burn down the stelae, what he calls a *"palo maldito"* ("cursed stick"), but first he will relate the story of what happened in this house and yard. The playwright is thus letting us know that Mundo and whoever else inhabited this space no longer live here. By bringing-in the gods, Portillo-Trambley adds a certain mysteriousness to the scene, a mystery that will unfold shortly. The action then moves back one year in time and the story begins, when the face of Itzamná was still unfinished.

As indicated by Foco, the central figure in this story is Mundo, the eighteen-year-old son. From the inception of the play we see that Mundo is in conflict with his defeated, alcoholic father, Nacho. The playwright is attempting to create an archetypal Father–Son paradigm of conflict and forgiveness. Mundo's very name, "world," implies that he is a Chicano Everyman. Mundo's story is the sad tale of a family's disillusionment and defeat ultimately redeemed through sacrifice and re-birth. Portillo-Trambley's symbolism contrasts Nature with The Machine, in the form of the railroad train that thunders through the family's backyard with grotesque and intimidating frequency.

Nacho is determined to summon the Maya gods; to bring them back in order that he can "face the iron monster" and deliver the family from the industrial pollution and blight that surrounds them. It is he who carved the pole, which is his version of the Maya stelae, carved stone monuments that recorded important individuals, ceremonial occasions and other aspects of life significant to the Classic Maya. As Nacho attempts to relive his ancestors' struggles, he even renames his daughter Ixchel (goddess of pregnancy), in order to bestow her pregnancy with mythic status. Initially, Nacho is alone in his beliefs; the other characters humor him. While everyone in this play wants a way out, to escape to another, better place, only Nacho sees the gods as his saviors. Initially, Mundo seeks his escape through marijuana, acid rock and sex. But by the second act he, too, senses the presence of the gods and seeks redemption through them.

In the words of Maria Herrera-Sobek, both Mundo and Nacho "seek to connect to their mythic past."[61] In Herrera-Sobek's analysis, "Mythic space and time, together with Nature's assertive presence envelops the lives of the characters"(Herrera-Sobek, p. 17). What finally brings father and son together is that presence and their (eventual) common belief in the power of the unseen gods. Early in the play, Nacho tells his daughter, Ixchel, "Right here, now, the men of Itza are all around us. I feel the heaviness of their sorrow" (Portillo-Trambley, *Sor Juana*, p. 106). At the conclusion of the first scene, Nacho prays to the unfinished face of Itzamná, calling on the god for strength.

Ironically, although Mundo is a non-believer when we first meet him, it was he who re-introduced Nacho to their ancestors' beliefs by showing him a book about the Maya. However, Nacho tells Ixchel: "I knew them before I saw that book. Mi mamacita . . . used to tell me stories about our ancestors, the Mayans" (106). Later in the play, Mundo tells Foco: ". . . suddenly he's Ah Na Itz . . . [now he] comes up with the wierdest things . . . chants, dreams . . . Who's putting them there?" (116). The playwright implies a col-

---

[61] Maria Herrera-Sobek, "Systems in Conflict: Myth, Family and Industrial Society," Program note for the Hispanic Playwrights Project, July 6–12, 1987, 18.

lective unconscious; an instinctive understanding of the mysterious forces of nature that exist in all indigenous peoples. It is Foco who feels the gods' presence before Mundo does. He tells Mundo: "This place, it's special. The way the moon lights up those faces on the stick. There's special feelings in this place . . . I touched that piece of stick. It had a heartbeat." The still incredulous Mundo tells Foco, "You're as bad as my old man" (117). Although Foco has been characterized as "loco," crazy, he is more rational than Mundo's other friends, recalling Luís Valdez's assertion that "There is divinity in madness" in his description of his character, Bernabé.[62]

Portillo-Trambley's play is not simply a discussion of the gods. She brings them onto the stage as living, dancing images of Mayan deities long forgotten by most Mexicans outside of the Mayalands, and certainly unfamiliar to most Chicana/os. At the end of the first act, Nacho falls asleep and in his dream, four dancers dressed as the wind gods enter the yard while the voice of Itzamná fills the air, asking for a sacrificial offering. As the second act builds in intensity, the gods envelop the environment, unseen by the characters, but visible to the audience and evident to those characters who believe. It is a very dramatic and theatrical device that the playwright employs to add mythical depth and a sense of the sacred to a commonplace backyard full of useless debris and society's even more "useless" inhabitants.

As the play approaches its inevitable climax, Mundo has been transformed and he, too, calls on the gods to cleanse the house. The youths are smoking marijuana and enjoying the blacklight on a large rock which Mundo refers to as his "mountain," painted in fluorescent colors like the stelae. Mundo had planned to run away to California with his Anglo girlfriend, Shirley, who is married to the redneck, Charlie. Outside, the gods dance and Nacho and Amelia come together, reunited in a ritual mating and enter the house. The all-seeing Foco tells Mundo to escape because he senses that the gods want Mundo, not Nacho for their sacrifice. As part of the purification, Mundo has come to realize that he cannot leave because he loves his father and now sees that his father loves him. It seems that the cleansing is taking place, but at the conclusion of these rituals, the second act ends with the voice of Itzamná demanding human sacrifice: "Sacrificio. Son for Father. Fire killing fire . . ." (Portillo-Trambley, *Sor Juana*, p. 136).

Throughout the play, we are led to believe that Nacho will sacrifice himself to the "Iron Monster." Indeed, Mundo had to fight with him the

---

[62] Stan Steiner and Luis Valdez, *Aztlán: An Anthology of Mexican-American Literature* (New York: Random House/Vintage, 1972), p. 364. Valdez was referring to the title character in his *mito*, *Bernabé*, discussed earlier in this chapter.

night before to keep him from running onto the tracks when a train approached. Energized by his love for his father and in order to keep him from the tracks, Mundo ties Nacho to his stelae, which now shows the completed face of Itzamná. Nacho finally sees that his son really loves him and swears to him that he will not run onto the tracks again, but Mundo leaves him tied and retreats to his room, exhausted and nearly paralyzed from the strain. The detested Charlie comes into the yard carrying his shotgun and despite Nacho's pleas for his son's life, Charlie shoots and kills the now incapacitated Mundo. It then starts to rain and we hear the "first, lusty cry of a newborn baby," coming from the house and the play ends (142).

As we have seen, Portillo-Trambley has demonstrated a fascination with and respect for indigenous thought and culture since her first play, *Day of the Swallows*. In 1981, while discussing Chicanos and assimilation, she told an interviewer: "I don't think it's an evolvement [sic] to become too much a part of the Anglo world . . . they've forgotten their senses to a great extent. Their spontaneity, their freedom, their openness." She recognizes that a certain amount of "assimilation" is inevitable, but she hopes that Chicanos can "keep a part of them that is still the earth people . . . I hope they still relate to seasons and to plants and to colors and to the wind, and to the Indian in them, or the element that is closest to the earth."[63]

Portillo-Trambley may be romanticizing the ancient Maya, but her intentions are clearly to imbue the contemporary Mechicana and Mechicano with a sense of their own rituals and myths; a proud contrast to western European, Greek and Roman myths that permeate our learning systems. By giving the gods corporeal presences, she hopes to educate her audiences about the nature gods and their importance to their creators. By changing Maria's name to Ixchel, Portillo-Trambley is simply replacing one virgin mother with another. The Judeo-Christian God the Father becomes Itzamná and his consort, Ixchel, dual natures and dual god and goddess, as all indigenous gods were perceived. The four directions, too, are given anthropomorphic presence in the form of the dancers, representatives of the invisible but all-pervasive winds. Finally, the rain god, Chac, second most represented deity in the Maya Yucateca pantheon, is finally appeased by the sacrifice of Mundo and the rain begins to fall at the play's end. But what does it all mean?

It is very difficult, when a playwright attempts to educate an audience about myths that are not in their conscious learning, and Portillo-Trambley

---

[63] Richard A. Abrams, "Chicana playwright struggles" p. A24.

walks the thin line between didacticism and obscurity in this play. For some observers, perhaps, the symbolism is too obvious; for others, she may not reveal enough about the Chilam Balam gods to fully appreciate their meanings. For example, according to Morley, Itzamná was also "the inventor of writing and books," but we do not learn this in this play (Morley, *Ancient Maya*, p. 195). What we do learn, is that Nacho's ancestors were Mayan, not Aztec or any other native peoples and that they had a powerful connection to their natural environment. We also learn that the Mayan gods, like so many others, do, indeed, demand some sort of sacrifice.

Mundo becomes Christ and Quetzalcóatl in Portillo-Trambley's vision, for he must be sacrificed for both the rains and the new-born child to emerge. But another difference in this ritual sacrifice is that Mundo is not killed by a Maya priest, highly honored members of indigenous cultures, but instead, by an evil, ignorant Anglo on a mission of vengeance, not renewal. Charlie becomes an agent of death, not rebirth, for the Anglo represents the intrusive conqueror of the Southwest. In this conflation of history and myth, the historical conqueror gets his revenge once again, killing the Chicano.

Conclusions

This chapter has focused on the works of Luís Valdez and Estela Portillo-Trambley (with a brief look at Alurista's *Dawn*) because they were the first Chicana and Chicano to publish major works. They are also the two playwrights most committed to recovering an indigenous philosophy in their plays, attempting to give the Chicana and Chicano a place in the cosmos from an indigenous perspective, thus interrogating a Chicano mythos. Although Portillo-Trambley and Valdez employ ritual elements in their indigenous plays, unlike Alurista, they construct their plays in the western European traditions of rising and falling action, character development and linear plots that lead to a climax and resolution. They both employ elements of realism, surrealism or even expressionism as they explore long forgotten myths.

Each of the plays, *mitos* and rituals discussed in this chapter invites the audience to enter into their mythical worlds, not as anthropologists, but as active participants in the myths. "These are your myths," the playwrights are telling Mechicanas and Mechicanos, "these are the worlds you should know about." Thus, the authors "Chicano-ize" their myths, placing what seem like ordinary people in extraordinary situations that challenge traditional concepts of the Chicanos' history and evolution as a people. The language, the faces, the communities look familiar, but they are permeated with symbols, both visible and invisible, that place the characters and the audience in the realm of myth.

Sometimes, as in *Dawn* or *Bernabé*, the gods interact with the characters on stage, becoming a part of the Chicanos' living reality, however distorted that reality may be. In *Blacklight*, the gods are a presence, unseen by the characters but visible to the audience. In *Day of the Swallows* the nature gods are discussed and felt by Josefa, but they remain invisible to other characters as well as to the audience. In *La Gran Carpa de los Rasquachis* Jesucristo/Quetzalcóatl and the Virgin of Guadalupe appear to everyone but only to draw the play to a close while affirming the audiences' faith. And although we never actually see Quetzalcóatl in *Dark Root of a Scream*, this god's presence is felt constantly, through the dead Chicano named after him, and in the palpitating heart at the close of the play.

In the most ritualistic of the pieces discussed here, the *Baile de los Gigantes*, the audience is watching the gods dance as they interact with one another as forces of Nature. This is a ritual that relies on a very strong belief in the Chorti Creation myth by both the participants and the observers, who eventually become part of the ritual as well. But only if they Believe. As Betty Diamond observed, the moment was magical but she could not take the feelings she had discovered during that ritual home with her. *Baile de los Gigantes* is the extreme example of a non-scripted ritual performed by a Chicano theatre group whose members were in their own spiritual training under the tutelage of Luis Valdez and other *indigenistas* familiar with the dances and myths. Audiences could only enter into that realm for the duration of the dance.

I believe that one of the reasons for these playwrights' fascination with indigenous thought and cultures is that they are attempting to impose a mythos where there was none before them. They know that their audiences will have little or no knowledge of the Mayan, Aztec or other gods and mythologies they bring into their stories, so they are compelled to follow in the tradition of Spanish religious folk theatre and create dramas that will both educate and entertain.

By exploring their indigenous, Native American mythos within a specifically contemporary Mexican and Chicano context, the playwrights give the Mechicanos some entry into their mythos. Further, in Mexicanizing their mythos, these playwrights are rejecting a strictly Western European pantheon of icons and symbols, replacing these with indigenous concepts or conflating indigenous theologies with the Christian. In each case, the playwrights' mythos becomes a negotiation between the distinct cultural iconographies they investigate. Such is the case when Alurista names his villains Pepsicóatl and Cocacóatl, fusing consumerism with a Nahuatl snake; Valdez transforms "La Tierra," into an "Adelita" in *Bernabé*, conflating history with myth; or when Portillo-Trambley transforms Ixchel into a Chicana unwed mother.

In distorting what their audiences have been taught to believe for generations, if not centuries, these playwrights are metaphorically expressing their own displacement as Chicanas and Chicanos. Thus, their mythos is in constant flux, temporal and transient. It is a mythos-in-process as these playwrights attempt to give their audiences a sense of community through new icons based on ancient symbols of life and death, birth and renewal displaced long ago by Christian icons and mythologies. Of the three playwrights discussed in this chapter, Alurista did not continue to write plays, but Portillo-Trambley and Valdez pursued their strong belief in the power of indigenous forces and Christian teachings to form the basis of their lives and work.

It is significant that the two playwrights most dedicated to creating a mythos employing indigenous belief systems were also the first playwrights, a man and a woman, to publish plays about the Chicana/o reality. Estela Portillo-Trambley and Luís Valdez are the pioneers in the realm of Chicana/o playwriting, but few people followed in their footsteps to present Quetzalcóatl or Itzamná within a Chicano context on stage. Other teatros and playwrights invoke indigenous gods in their productions, but these examples are not as visible and accessible in print, especially, as are Portillo-Trambley and Valdez. As discussions of other plays in this book will reveal, however, the indigenous gods are not too far offstage in many other plays; proof that these two pioneers have left their indelible marks and will always be the starting point for any discussion of Chicana/o drama and a Chicana/o mythos.

Mystery or miracle:

bodiless heads and conversations with the dead

"You are the miracle people too, for like them the same blood runs through your veins. The same memory of a time when your deaths were cause for reverence and celebration, not shock and mourning."

Cerezita, *Heroes and Saints*[1]

"And even though my grandmother
had died, she didn't really go away.
I saw her often and she kept
Telling me things.
Even though it wasn't usually
what I wanted to hear."

Marta Feliz, *My Visits*
With MGM[2]

"Those people we saw crossing the river: They're our moms and dads and they drank dirty water for us. They died for us."

Tomás, *Santos & Santos*[3]

Challenging notions of reality: bodiless heads

Introduction

From the beginning of contemporary Chicano theatre, Chicana and Chicano playwrights have questioned and subverted notions of reality as they explored their mythos through "*el misterio*," those incidents or circumstances that have

---

[1] Cherríe Moraga, *Heroes and Saints and Other Plays* (Albuquerque: West End Press, 1994), p. 148.
[2] Edit Villareal, *My Visits With MGM (My Grandmother Marta)* in Linda Feyder (ed.), *Shattering the Myth: Plays by Hispanic Women* (Houston: Arte Publico, 1992), p. 178.
[3] Octavio Solis, *Santos & Santos, American Theater Magazine* (November 1995), 43.

no rational explanation. In the previous chapter I investigated the nature of the indigenous myths Alurista, Estela Portillo-Trambley and Luís Valdez attempted to revise and revitalize as a Mechicana/o Cosmic Reality. However, no matter how much these playwrights believe in their mythos, their stories are usually centered on the mystery of unseen forces. Those forces may have motivated, inspired and encouraged the believers on stage and in the audience, but the plays' dramatic interest lay in the fact that they were, after all, mysteries. In this chapter I will look at plays that evoke a mythos of mystery through distortion and death, perhaps the greatest "*misterio*" of them all. From the mystery of bodiless characters to appearances of the dead, the plays in this chapter also define a Chicana/o mythos, as the playwrights search for a greater understanding of our relationship with the Life Forces. In most of these plays, the playwrights continue to invoke indigenous symbols as well, continuing in the tradition begun by Alurista, Portillo-Trambley and Valdez.

The plays in this section are the playwrights' responses to the often distorted realities of the Chicano condition, distortions which are an integral part of "El Misterio." In his investigation of the representation and re-vision of history in Chicana/o theatre, W.B. Worthen cites a variety of sources as he attempts to situate Chicana/o playwrights in the broader context of "postmodern subjectivities." Quoting José Limón's reading of Fredric Jameson, Worthen describes how the Chicana/o does not fit into the customary precepts of postmodernism: "Indeed, if the 'cultural logic' of the postmodern . . . is the logic of Euro-American hegemony, Chicana/o representation necessarily employs the rhetoric of 'postmodern' expression with a *difference* . . . to Limón, 'the ideologically flattening, decentering effects of the postmodern' that Jameson takes as representative have been for some time (since the 1960s) the everyday living condition of working-class Mexican Americans, a *Mexicano* working-class postmodernity."[4]

Again referring to Limón, Worthen discovers that "But to consume and dispose postmodern culture, postmodern identity, requires class, status, or financial access to dominant culture – a room at the Bonaventure [hotel], cable television, pocket money for first-run movies, English" (Worthen, "Staging America," 105). Admittedly, Worthen is citing Limón's study of South Texas Mechicanos, a poor, working-class, rural population, but

---

[4] W. B. Worthen, "Staging America: The Subject of History in Chicano/a Theatre," *Theatre Journal* 49 (May 1997), 104. The Limón citation is from José Limón, *Dancing with the Devil: Society and Cultural Poetics in Mexican–American South Texas* (Madison: University of Wisconsin Press, 1994), p. 109.

Limón's thesis can also reflect the dislocation and alienation of the urban Chicano working class. What Worthen takes from Limón's evaluation is the idea of "fragmentation." In Limón's words: "In this south Texas context, postmodernism may be seen as the gradual decentering, fragmenting transformation of this identity into something else – a difficult version of global culture palpable but difficult to verbalize" (Limón, *Dancing With The Devil*, pp. 111–12). I believe that Limón's assessment can be used to describe the Mechicano's fascination with "*el misterio*," something that is palpable but difficult to verbalize. Crucial to this *misterio* is the concept of fragmentation and the ongoing process of cultural transformation that mediates and marks a Chicana/o mythos.

Luis Valdez explores Chicana/o distortions

Dis-membering the past: *The Shrunken Head of Pancho Villa.*

Dislocation and a concomitant search for identity have always been at the center of Chicano playwriting, serving as a recurring leitmotif for the majority of Chicana/o playwrights to date. Indeed, the search for identity within a hostile and insensitive society has been central to all immigrant plays in this country.[5] For most Chicano playwrights this search has usually been set in the home, representative of a private space which is free from society's harm. Unfortunately, however, very often the home is not a refuge for characters attempting to escape from one another. The dislocation of class struggle, racism and other problems that plague Mechicanas and Mechicanos too often leads to domestic violence, both physical and psychological – and this is reflected in many plays. The idea of the conflicts and struggles of a domestic drama may produce images of psychological realism, but, as we discovered in the previous chapter, in the Chicanos' plays the realism of the barrio is usually mediated by events that defy logic.

Luis Valdez's *The Shrunken Head of Pancho Villa* takes place in a humble Mechicano household that symbolizes immigrant disenfranchisement through distortion.[6] This play was written while Valdez was a student at San José State College (California), and first produced there in 1964 under his

---

[5] See Maxine Schwartz Seller (ed.), *Ethnic Theatre in the United States* (Westport: Greenwood, 1983), for discussions of immigrant theatre, from "Armenian" to "Yiddish."

[6] *The Shrunken Head of Pancho Villa* is in *West Coast Plays 11/12* (Berkeley: California Theatre Council, 1982), 1–61; and in Jorge Huerta, *Necessary Theater: Six Plays About the Chicano Experience* (Houston: Arte Publico, 1989), 142–207. For more about this play see Diamond (1977), 129–46; and Huerta (1982), 49–60.

direction. In his prefatory "Note on style," Valdez prepares the reader and production team for the style he envisions: "The play therefore contains realistic and surrealistic elements working together to achieve a transcendental expression of the social condition of La Raza en los Estados Unidos [Mexicans/Chicanos in the United States]. . . In short, it must reflect the psychological reality of the barrio" (Huerta, *Necessary Theatre*, p. 154). This play revolves around the central figure of Belarmino, a character *who has no body* and claims to be the lost head of Pancho Villa. For Valdez, the Chicano reality could only be expressed through the surreal (a bodiless head) juxtaposed with characters and situations that are also extensions of reality.

One of the most perplexing images in this play is created by the cockroaches that grow ever larger, crawling all over the walls, in true expressionistic fashion. Worse, Belarmino's sister, Lupe, feeds these repulsive creatures to him and eventually eats them as well. Audiences gasp and gag at this exaggeration, literally voicing their displeasure with audible "ughhss"and "yuks" at such an idea. This is precisely what the young playwright intended – you do not have characters eating cockroaches in your play without expectations. Expectations that your audience members will not soon forget the imagery, and the hope that they will think about what they have just witnessed. I believe this is Valdez's metaphor for what he terms "the psychological reality of the barrio": confusion created by displacement.

The young writer employed exaggeration for political reasons. Belarmino (the decapitated revolutionary) politicizes the hero, Joaquin, who represents the (revolutionary) Chicano. Joaquin is the most sympathetic character, the misunderstood "vato loco," a disenfranchised street youth in constant trouble with the authorities and in conflict with his brother Domingo, who transforms into "Mr. Sunday" in his total rejection of Mexican and Chicano culture. After spending time in jail for robbing supermarkets to feed the poor, Joaquin comes home without a head. The juxtaposition of the bodiless head and the headless body is clear: combine them for a complete, revolutionary man. It is the playwright's hope that the confusion he perceives in the barrio will be replaced by a political consciousness, his "psychological reality" more informed by an awareness of marginalization than by Freudian analysis. Valdez's characters and the situations in which they find themselves are representative of the playwright's dislocation, which, he believes, is universal to working-class Mechicanos.[7]

---

[7] As seen in his later play, *I Don't Have to Show You No Stinking Badges* (1985), discussed in chapter 1, Valdez believes dislocation affects middle-class Chicanos as well. While he was a student, however, Valdez's references were to the working-class Mechicanos of his immediate experience.

Although the characters never break the fourth wall to speak directly to the audience, the comic theatricality of *The Shrunken Head of Pancho Villa* leaves no room for realistic portrayals. The comedy of this play derives from the exaggeration as well as from the audience's awareness of the problems revealed. When Domingo rejects his culture the audience laughs at the ridiculousness of his actions because they know people like him. In order to heighten the effect, Domingo might wear white makeup on one side of his face and brown on the other, thus objectifying the concept of acculturation while heightening the theatricality of it all. Belarmino has the last word, calling for unity as an end to the Chicanos' cultural/political confusion.

In Valdez's early vision, the *misterio* of Belarmino's condition is not determined by supernatural forces, but, rather, by the playwright in his attempt to educate, to entertain and to horrify. Years after the first production of the play Valdez admitted that he had not exactly succeeded in each of these intentions. In a keynote address Valdez delivered in 1983, he told his audience that his older brother was the model for Mr. Sunday and that he (Luís) is represented in the character of Joaquin. He then admitted: ". . . people didn't exactly get it . . . the horror, the horror of watching a brother become a stranger and the horror of watching somebody get their head cut off."[8] Thus for the young playwright this play was a visceral response to the loss of a brother to total acculturation through denial of his Mexican roots and the loss of cultural identity through brainwashing/decapitation. In many ways, this experiment in playwriting set the tone for all of Luis Valdez's later works, none of which can be termed realism or realistic.

Cherríe Moraga challenges the patriarchy

Luís Valdez's bodiless character in *The Shrunken Head of Pancho Villa*, was in part responsible for inspiring Cherríe Moraga to create a central character without a body in her play, *Heroes and Saints*, first produced in 1992. Writing almost thirty years after Valdez's first play was produced, Moraga represents the next generation of Chicana playwrights, following in the footsteps of Estela Portillo-Trambley by writing in a variety of genres. Born in Los Angeles, California in 1952, Moraga is the daughter of a Chicana mother and an Irish Catholic father. She attended parochial schools and graduated from Immaculate Heart College in 1974 with a B.A. in English Literature. After teaching English at Providence High School in Burbank,

---

[8] Luís Valdez, "Keynote Address," n.d. (*c.* 1983) "Eighteen years after the founding of El Teatro Campesino." An unpublished typescript in my collection.

California, she moved to San Francisco where she earned a Master of Arts degree in Feminist Studies from San Francisco State University in 1980. Moraga assumed a self-imposed "exile" to the Northeast from 1981 to 1985, during which her publications began to appear while she worked in a variety of positions, from editorial consultant to founding editor and publisher of Kitchen Table/Women of Color Press in New York City.

Preceding by several years Chicano (male) scholars' discussions of homosexuality in literature, in 1981 Moraga and Gloria Anzaldúa co-edited the groundbreaking anthology, *This Bridge Called My Back: Writings by Radical Women of Color.*[9] Anzaldúa and Moraga were motivated to bring together the writers in this collection as a response to their perception that the women's movement in the United States was dominated by an Anglo agenda; women of color were seldom included in the equation. With this goal in mind, most of the contributors address their feminism and their cultural distinctions but with the hopes of creating "bridges" of communication between all women. Positive critical response was immediate, especially from women of color, and Moraga began to gain a national profile. Two years after the publication of *This Bridge Called My Back*, Moraga published another important work, her semi-autobiographical collection of essays and poems, *Loving in the War Years: lo que nunca paso por sus labios (what never passed through her/his lips).*[10] This collection is profoundly moving in its declaration of what it means to be a woman, a Chicana and a lesbian. But this self-revelatory book is not only about sexuality, it is also about cultural identity and displacement, a theme Moraga will explore in her dramatic works as well.

Moraga began writing for the theatre when she was selected to participate in Maria Irene Fornes's playwriting Lab in New York City in 1984.[11] The first reading of Moraga's first play, *Giving Up the Ghost,* discussed in chapter 4, was in 1984.[12] After a year with Fornes, Moraga returned to

[9] Gloria Anzaldúa and Cherríe Moraga (eds.), *This Bridge Called My Back: Writings by Radical Women of Color* (New York: Kitchen Table, 1981).

[10] Cherríe Moraga, *Loving in the War Years: lo que nunca paso por sus labios* (Boston: South End Press, 1983).

[11] Through her inspirational and motivating workshop, which INTAR (International Arts Relations, Inc.) operated from 1981 to 1992, Maria Irene Fornes can be termed the "Godmother" of many of our most successful contemporary Chicano and Latino playwrights. Fornes's alumni roster is a virtual "Who's Who" of Latina and Latino playwrights and includes several of the people discussed in this book.

[12] The first staged reading of *Giving up the Ghost* was at Foot of the Mountain Theatre in Minneapolis, in 1984.

"Aztlán," in effect reclaiming her identity as a Chicana.[13] Moraga moved to
San Francisco in 1986 and taught Writing and Theatre in Chicano Studies
at the University of California, Berkeley, from 1986 to 1991. All the while
she continued to write plays, prose, essays and poetry. Moraga's second play,
Shadow of a Man, was premiered in San Francisco in 1989 and in 1991 she
became Artist-in-Residence and Instructor in Writing for Performance at
Brava! For Women in the Arts, a nationally recognized women's artistic collective. In 1992 Moraga's third play, *Heroes and Saints*, was premiered in San
Francisco.[14]

Moraga's second volume of prose and poetry, *The Last Generation*, published in 1993, is just as personal as her first collection. In this book, too, she
is equally committed to creating a better understanding between men and
women, gay and straight, Latinas and Latinos, Latino and Anglo.[15] Like
her first collection, this book is written out of a kind of poetic desperation.
In her Introduction, Moraga compares the state of the Chicana and
Chicano to the recently conquered Aztecs, whose gods were all dead and
whose codices "lay smoldering in heaps of ash." She continues:

> I write with the same knowledge, the same sadness, recognizing the full
> impact of the colonial "experiment" on the lives of Chicanos, mestizos
> and Native Americans. Our codices – dead leaves unwritten – lie smol-
> dering in the ashes of disregard, censure and erasure. *The Last Generation*
> emerges from those ashes. I write it against time, out of a sense of urgency
> that Chicanos are a disappearing tribe, out of a sense of this disappear-
> ance in my own family.
>
> (Moraga, *Last Generation*, p. 2)

Concluding her Introduction to *The Last Generation*, Moraga writes:
"Truth must be expressed in 'Flower and Song,' the [Meso-American] sages
professed. In metaphor. So these are not essays as much as they are poems
and these are not poems as much as they are essays. Possibly the distinction
no longer matters – between the poem and the essay, between my art and
my activism" (4).

The same can be said about Moraga's playwriting, which is inseparable
from her activism. Perhaps because she was first a highly visible essayist and

---

13 Cherríe Moraga, *The Last Generation: Prose and Poetry* (Boston: South End, 1993), 2. As men-
    tioned in the Introduction, Chicana/os employed the term "Aztlán," as homage to the Nahuatl
    (Aztec) belief that they (the Aztecs) descended from a mythical region to the north, called
    Aztlán.
14 *Shadow of a Man* is discussed in chapter 4 and *Heroes and Saints* is discussed in chapters 3 and 4.
15 Cherríe Moraga, *The Last Generation: Prose and Poetry* (Boston: South End, 1993).

spokesperson for gay and especially lesbian voices, Moraga came into play-writing with the radical's agenda tempered by the poet's spirit. But then again, for her, as for the sages to whom she refers, there is no difference between art and politics, religion and science. These words echo Alurista, Luís Valdez and Estela Portillo-Trambley's beliefs based on indigenous thought and culture, as discussed in chapter 1.

Moraga is unique among the new generation of playwrights that emerged in the 1980s because she was a well-known poetess and essayist before she became known as a playwright. Thus her non-dramatic publications gave her a much broader visibility than most emerging playwrights could enjoy outside or inside the world of theatre.[16] Further, her personal writings also set her apart because they allow the reader entry into her persona, the inner thoughts that reveal an author in a way that her plays cannot.[17] Moraga, the theorist, is impossible to separate from Moraga the playwright or from Moraga the activist.

In 1997, Moraga was appointed Artist-in-Residence in the Department of Drama at Stanford University. Also in 1997, Moraga published another very personal memoir in which she discusses her (and her lover, "Ella's") decision that she would bear a child.[18] Subtitled "Portrait of a Queer Motherhood," *Waiting in the Wings* is more than a "portrait"; it is a fractured mirror in which some shards are sharper than the others, in which the images may be distorted but the messages are still there. Close to the end of this book, Moraga writes about the impending death of an older uncle: "I am trying to write about the impossible, the ordinary beginning of one life and the passing of another. Watching a life enter and another exit within the same brief moment of my family's history" (118). In this book Moraga recounts how she has been touched by the mystery of death too many times and that perhaps she will find a play in it all.

Moraga's dramaturgy is the product of a creative mind in the process of evolving thematically and aesthetically. In her inquiry into the genre of theatre Moraga took deliberate steps, beginning with a series of poetic monologues in the first version of *Giving up the Ghost*, and continuing

---

[16] Recall that Estela Portillo-Trambley published short stories (not essays or poems) before she published her first play, capturing the attention of literary critics, just like Moraga.

[17] Although there are more references to Moraga available in the bibliographies than to any of the newer generation of playwrights in this book, the majority of reviews and articles are about Moraga the poetess and essayist. See especially Yvonne Yarbro-Bejarano's study, *A Right to Passion: Collected Essays on Cherríe Moraga* (Austin: University of Texas, forthcoming).

[18] Cherríe Moraga *Waiting in the Wings* (Ithaca: Firebrand Books, 1997).

through her subsequent plays. The sequel to *Heroes and Saints, Watsonville*, and an apocalyptic version of the Medea/Llorona myths, *The Hungry Woman: Mexican Medea*, were unpublished at this writing.[19] The first three plays will be discussed in this book, beginning here with a play that recalls and re-constructs the first play written by a contemporary Chicano.

When a bodiless head speaks Flor y Canto: Heroes and Saints

Heroes and Saints received its world premiere production in 1992, produced by Brava! For Women in the Arts at the Mission Cultural Center in San Francisco, California. This production, directed by Albert Takazaucus, won several *Dramalogue* Awards, a major recognition from the Los Angeles-based entertainment media publication. In the fall of that same year the play was produced by the Guadalupe Cultural Arts Center in San Antonio, Texas, under the direction of Argentine, Susana Tubert. Both productions proved the skill of Moraga's writing, challenging the production teams and leaving audiences enthralled, delighted, entertained, educated and angry. The play has been produced by a number of theatres across the country.

Like the family in *The Shrunken Head of Pancho Villa*, the main characters in *Heroes and Saints* are farm workers living in the San Joaquin Valley. But, unlike Valdez's surreal, often exaggerated interpretation of the Mechicanos' condition, Moraga chose to write a play about real people, not archetypes or stereotypes. Both plays contain a bodiless character as central metaphor, but one is seen through the eyes of a Chicano student activist writing in the early 1960s and the other through the eyes of a nationally known Chicana author and activist writing in the early 1990s. The two plays are separated by a generation in time, by gender and by his-story.

Moraga was motivated to write *Heroes and Saints* following several incidents surrounding the efforts of Cesar Chávez and his United Farm Workers' Union in 1988. Less than a month after Chávez's 36-day fast ended, Dolores Huerta, the Vice-President of the Union, was brutally beaten by a San Francisco policeman while holding a press conference out of concern about pesticides in the fields and to protest President George Bush's disregard for the Union's grape boycott. When Valdez wrote his first

---

[19] Maria Teresa Marrero discusses a draft of *The Hungry Woman: Mexican Medea* in "Out of the Fringe: Desire and Homosexuality in the 90s Latino Theatre," *Latin American Theatre Review* 32 2 (Spring 1999), 96–98. *The Hungry Woman: Mexican Medea* will be published in Caridad Svich and Maria Teresa Marrero (eds.), *Out of the Fringe: Contemporary Latina/Latino Theatre and Performance* (New York, TCG, 1999).

Figure 1. Heroes and Saints, by Cherríe Moraga. Brava! For Women in the Arts, San Francisco, California. Directed by Albert Takazauckas. L. to R. Hector Correa and Jaime Lujan. © 1992

Figure 2. Heroes and Saints, by Cherríe Moraga. Brava! For Women in the Arts, San Francisco, California, 1992. Directed by Albert Takazauckas. L. to R. Juanita Estrada, Jennifer Proctor, Viola Lucero.

play in 1964, the harm from pesticides had yet to be documented.[20] Over thirty years later, it is now clear that certain pesticides are creating diseases in the workers, yet few people are even aware of this or of the fact that the grape boycott continues.

Moraga was also motivated by the Union's video documentary, "The Wrath of Grapes," which exposes the fact that the town of McFarland, California, has been identified as a "cancer cluster" in which a disproportionate number of children and adults are either dying of cancer, developing skin diseases, or are being born with birth defects. The Union blames the indiscriminate use of pesticides for this horror, showing how the chemicals permeate everything, including the ground water. *Heroes and Saints* is an angry, passionate appeal for support of the farm workers' cause that identifies a very specific, humanitarian reason for that support.

"The Wrath of Grapes" documentary shows a child born without limbs to a woman who had worked in the fields while pregnant. Moraga took this image to its extreme, borrowing from Valdez to create the central figure of an eighteen-year-old girl, Cerezita, who, like Belarmino, has been born without a body. Moraga is interested in several issues in this play, but the main theme, I believe, is the devastation wrought upon the farm workers and their families by pesticides, thus the bodiless Cerezita. Adding to the issue of pesticides in the fields, the playwright also exposes the dangers of toxic waste and AIDS as equally critical issues demanding attention.

Moraga creates a family that has other problems as well: Cerezita's sister, Yolanda, is nursing a dying child; her father abandoned the family long ago; her gay brother will eventually contract HIV; and her mother refuses to let her out of the house. Dolores, the mother, does not believe that any good will come from protests and union organizing, unlike her *comadre*, Amparo. It is Cerezita, the miracle child, who knows the cause of their suffering and it is she who must sacrifice herself for the good of all. Ultimately this play is an expiation leading to a cleansing through fire, just as indigenous cultures practice annual ritual fires to cleanse their lives and signify a new beginning.

Cerezita, the mystery child, speaks eloquently. She is a precocious reader who observes everything and who knows that there is a reason for her misfortune. She is the character-as-metaphor who speaks the poetry that distinguishes Moraga. The following soliloquy gives an idea of the author's prose:

---

[20] It is interesting to note that Alurista exposed the threat of pesticides in the fields in his play, *Dawn*, first published in 1974. *Dawn* is discussed in chapter 1.

The sheep drink the same water we do from troughs outside my window. Today it is an orange-yellow color. The mothers dip their heads into the long rusty buckets and drink and drink while their babies deform inside them. Innocent, they sleep inside the same poison water and are born broken like me, their lamb limbs curling under them . . . I watch them from my window and weep.[21]

Heroes and Saints successfully demonstrates a very specific problem faced by farm workers in particular areas such as McFarland. Framing the action, a television newscaster "reports" to an invisible camera as the events unfold. Also, during the course of the action, the family discovers that the entire housing tract, which was built with federal subsidies, is built on a toxic waste site. The characters' objectives are to end the suffering by seeking federal assistance in order to relocate and by getting the growers to acknowledge the pesticides as the cause of the diseases. The first image we see in this play is the silhouette of a lone cross in the middle of a vineyard with "the barely distinguishable figure of a small child hanging from the cross" (Moraga, *Heroes and Saints*, p. 92). Children are dying and someone is placing their bodies on these crosses in protest. Amparo, the character inspired in part by Dolores Huerta, agrees with this extreme measure, saying: "If you put the children in the ground the world forgets about them" (94).

From the beginning, then, the people are not sitting by helplessly, unable to do anything about their problems. By the end of the play the people finally take to the fields and torch them. The final image of the play recalls the first, but now it is Cerezita sacrificing herself as "the Virgin Saint" in a blazing grape field, her head atop a cross silhouetted against the red flames. Unlike the helpless head in Valdez's play, Moraga's bodiless character takes action, assisted by the people, as she sacrifices herself in an effort to bring more attention to their cause. She has known all along that this will be her destiny and she accepts it willingly, hoping to provoke social justice. Motivated by Amparo, the political activist who has been "wounded in battle," but not deterred, Cerezita, too, takes action; two women of distinct generations re-write their own her-stories.

Moraga's play is written in the style of Maria Irene Fornes, a cinematic, episodic "montage" of scenes, monologues and dramatic images. The play is divided into two acts, with sixteen scenes in the first act and thirteen scenes in the second. Some scenes are less than a minute long and each move the

---

[21] Cherríe Moraga, *Heroes and Saints and Other Plays* (Albuquerque: West End Press), 1994, p. 99. This play is also in Kathy A. Perkins and Roberta Uno (eds.), *Contemporary Plays by Women of Color* (Routledge, 1996), pp. 230–61. All subsequent references are to the Moraga, 1994, edition.

action forward as they develop the situation between the family members, the community that surrounds them, and the power structure that refuses to acknowledge the problem. The action moves rapidly from place-to-place, sometimes underscored by slide or video projections of images relevant to the action, such as the face of a gaunt Cesar Chávez on the day he ended his fast. The Union's efforts on behalf of the farm workers are discussed minimally within the text, for this is not a documentary. This is a play about real people, including the bodiless Cerezita. Moraga combines socio-political, spiritual and cultural struggles in this play in such a way that they are interconnected, as inseparable as life and death in the Mayan cosmic world view. With a bodiless head as central figure, *Heroes and Saints* takes the audience into the realm of *el misterio*.

The metaphorical woman without a body is not really alone in her struggle; Cerezita represents all women as Everywoman. Those people who have analyzed the role of a woman's body in our society will see the metaphor of the bodiless woman immediately – even with bodies, women have little control over them. Moraga believes that this is particularly true for Chicanas and Mexicanas. Responding to an article I wrote about this play, Moraga wrote me: "What I missed. . .was any analysis regarding Cerezita's struggle to wholly embody herself as female . . . Within the confines of her culture, she is restricted by her femaleness as well. [Cerezita's] bodilessness represents la Mechicana condition."[22]

Moraga's use of a bodiless character is extraordinary – beyond the realm of what we might call "reality." Yet there is something very natural about Cerezita's presence. The weak, infirm, aged and disabled have always been a part of the *barrio* experience, for Mechicanos do not put their loved ones in institutions regardless of the sacrifice. Thus, when Cerezita first appears, following the image of the crucified body in the opening tableaux, we accept this convention. Certainly, the audiences I have observed have understood Cerezita's condition as peculiar to her world and have followed her journey with interest and total involvement. The general observer will see Cerezita and feel the emotions such an image stimulates. Some might feel pity, others empathy; few in the audience will be unmoved. Cerezita's poetic language, what the Aztecs called "*flor y canto*" ["flower and song"] adds to her already extraordinary situation. She is a brilliant and sensitive young woman who reads voraciously and wishes only to get out, both metaphorically and

[22] A personal letter to me from Moraga dated January 29, 1992 following the publication of my article, "Moraga's 'Heroes and Saints': Chicano Theatre for the '90s'," *TheatreForum* (1992), 49–52.

literally. It is Cerezita's extraordinary condition that elevates her above all the others, indeed, above all of us.

By moving the action in a cinematic fashion Moraga gives the audience a camera's gaze into the thoughts and actions of her characters. The episodic nature of the play allows the audience members entrance to the various themes Moraga is addressing while challenging the production team to creatively fill-in the many blackouts required by such a technique. A well-equipped facility can provide the production with video projections as well as sound effects and music to keep the tension mounting as the climax of the play approaches.

Finally, it is the character as Miracle, Cerezita, who inspires the previously reluctant Juanito to join her in the final act of expiation as well. The bodiless woman takes responsibility and action as she faces the certain death that awaits her when Juanito wheels her into the fields, sacrificing themselves in an effort to bring more attention to their cause. Cerezita has known all along that this will be her destiny and she accepts it willingly, hoping to provoke social justice. When gunshots are suddenly heard, the dying Mario shouts, "Burn the fields!" inciting the people to do just that (Moraga, *Heroes and Saints*, p. 149). We can only assume that both Juanito and Cerezita have been killed.[23]

The final image of the play recalls the first, but now it is Cerezita and Juanito apparently sacrificing themselves. It must be made very clear to the audience that the people have set the vineyards on fire, taking direct action against the growers. Due to serendipitous technology, in the San Antonio production the video projections also appeared on the walls of the house; an uncanny image made all the more impressive because the house itself also seemed to be engulfed in flames. Everything in the town is being destroyed and cleansed, again recalling the indigenous fire ritual.

Heroes and Saints is a complex play that is based on facts that are irrefutable, intermingled with fictional characters and the extended reality of a bodiless head. The deaths, illness and misfortunes revealed in this play are documented fact. Cerezita's condition, of course, is metaphorical and miraculous. When Cerezita reads from a Mayan book, it is clear that the indigenous gods are also prominent in this play, although we do not see them. The playwright's activism mediates her spirituality, inspiring her to create a play in the tradition of the best miracle plays and agit-prop theatre.

---

[23] In the (unpublished) sequel to this play, *Watsonville*, it is revealed that Cerezita was killed but Juanito survived.

Thus, audience members are given a clear objective: take action from the Miracle.

Conversations with the dead

Introduction

In this section I wish to look at how Chicana and Chicano playwrights dramatize and explore the idea of death through deceased characters who become a presence among the living. As I stated earlier, perhaps death is the greatest *misterio* of them all, and certainly, it is the most universal theme any writer can address. In the case of the Chicana/os, this fascination with death is undoubtedly related to the Mexican attitudes as expressed in the Dia de los Muertos (Day of the Dead), November 2. On this day families commune with their dearly departed, cleaning and decorating their grave and then eating a meal "with the dead." Although non-Mexicans may find this practice rather morbid, to the Mechicanos it is a responsibility and an honor. In Mexico, street vendors sell skeleton toys, sugar candies in the shape of skulls and other reminders that we all look alike, rich or poor, beneath the skin.

As seen in the engravings of José Guadalupe Posada, the Mexican sees Death as comic, as tragic, as just another state of being.[24] In their earliest posters, the Teatro Campesino used Posada's delightful engravings of skeletons and in later productions staged entire plays with characters dressed as calaveras (skeletons), causing one confused critic to refer to their play as a "Halloween program."[25] But death has a special meaning to the Mexican. As Octavio Paz stated many years ago:

> The word death is not pronounced in New York, in Paris, in London, because it burns the lips. The Mexican, in contrast, is familiar with death, jokes about it, caresses it, sleeps with it, celebrates it; it is one of his favorite toys and his most steadfast love. True, there is perhaps as much fear in his attitude as in that of others, but at least death is not hidden away: he looks at it face to face, with impatience, disdain or irony.[26]

[24] For samples of Posada's prints, see Roberto Berdecio and Stanley Applebaum (eds.), *Posada's Popular Mexican Prints* (New York: Dover, 1972), pp. 2–19.

[25] Dan Sullivan, "El Teatro Campesino in a Halloween Program," *Los Angeles Times*, November 3, 1970 Sec. IV, p. 9.

[26] Octavio Paz, *The Labyrinth of Solitude: Life and Thought in Mexico* (New York: Grove, 1961), pp. 57–58.

What most of us will not experience, however, are visitations from the dead, apparitions or life-like appearances that place us in a very special relationship with *El Misterio*. The plays in this section are each concerned with dead characters who return to interact and participate in the lives of the living characters on stage. In some instances, the living recognize the dead as dead, in other plays, neither we nor the characters are aware that another character is not alive. The idea of Death is explored through the interventions of the deceased who sometimes appear to be real. In some plays, the dead appear to the living in an almost casual manner – neither the dead character nor the live one are upset by the interaction. In other plays, the dead are not friendly and have a sinister, medieval quality about them. In all instances, however, the living characters are ordinary people caught in extraordinary circumstances caused by *El Misterio*.

Edit Villareal's visits with the dead

Edit Villareal has always been fascinated with the idea of characters who come back from the dead, beginning with her most produced play, *My Visits With MGM (My Grandmother Marta)*. Villareal was born in Brownsville, Texas, in 1944, a fourth-generation Chicana on her mother's side. Her father was born in Matamoros, Mexico, the town directly across the border from Brownsville, making Villareal a "paradigmatic border child." For the first six years of her life, Villareal's grandmother looked after her; a positive and loving relationship that she has never forgotten. She was into her pre-teens when her family moved to Los Angeles; her later memories of her grandmother come from summer visits. In Los Angeles, Villareal attended public schools and graduated in 1967 from the University of California, Berkeley, with an A.B. in set and costume design. Following her undergraduate education Villareal worked as a carpenter, medical social worker and held assorted jobs "in and around theatres" in the Bay Area for five years.[27]

In 1981 Villareal participated in Maria Irene Fornes' Hispanic Playwright's Lab and, with Fornes' encouragement, applied to the graduate program in playwriting at the Yale School of Drama. She was accepted into this prestigious program, perhaps the first Chicana ever admitted in Playwriting, and completed her M.F.A. in 1986. Immediately after graduate school, Villareal joined the faculty of the Theatre Department at the

---

[27] n.a. "Profiles: Edit Villareal," *Los Angeles Times*, February 14, 1993, pp. 72, 74.

University of California, Los Angeles, and began teaching courses in playwriting and Chicano theatre. She became the second Chicana or Chicano to be hired by a Theatre or Drama department in the University of California (state-wide) system and thus we had much to talk about. When my undergraduate Teatro Ensemble de UCSD toured Spain, France and (then) West Germany in the summer of 1988, Villareal came along to chronicle the first international tour by any Chicano student troupe.[28] Villareal is now an associate professor, Head of Playwriting and Vice-Chair of Graduate Programs for the Theatre Department at UCLA. She has written several full-length plays and one-acts as well as screenplays.

In 1993 Villareal collaborated on the screenplay of *La carpa* with film maker, Carlos Avila, who also directed the piece for PBS's *American Playhouse*. *La carpa* is a narrative drama that takes place in the 1930s in a California farm worker community. As the title suggests, the film is about the impact of a troupe of Mexican performers (*carperos*) who come to town and change the lives of the people there.[29] Reviewing the program for *The Los Angeles Times*, Ray Loynd wrote: "For a non-Latino viewer, this quaint bittersweet story about racism, young love and a travelling Chicano tent show . . . is a refreshing slice of social history." Mr. Loynd then adds the astute observation that the program "dramatizes what, in effect, is the political legacy of Cesar Chávez and the theatrical legacy of Luis Valdez."[30]

Romeo and Juliet meet the day of the dead: The Language of Flowers

For a look at Villareal's treatment of *el misterio*, I turn to two of her plays. Her full-length play, initially titled *R & J* then re-titled *The Language of Flowers*, is a contemporary adaptation of Shakespeare's *Romeo and Juliet*. This play was produced at California State University, Los Angeles, twice, in 1991, both versions directed by José Cruz González, and also at the University of California, Los Angeles, in 1994, directed by Norma Saldívar. The playwright's decision to adapt Shakespeare's classic is certainly not a

---

[28] For more on the 1989 Teatro Ensemble de UCSD tour of Spain, France and West Germany, see Edit Villareal's two articles, "El Teatro Ensemble de UCSD: First International Tour," *Americas* 17 (1989), 73–83; and "Johnny Tenorio by Carlos Morton and Los Vendidos by Luis Valdez," *Theatre Journal* 41 (1989), 231–33.

[29] As noted in chapter 1, the Mexican *carpas*, or tent shows, had a great influence on the communities they served. Avila and Villareal's *La carpa* gives a wonderful "picture" of the period and of a *carpa* in action.

[30] Ray Loynd, "TV Reviews: 'La Carpa': Bittersweet Love and Chicano Social History," *Los Angeles Times* June 16, 1993, F7.

new idea.[31] However, Villareal set the play during the three days that begin with Halloween and end on November 2, the Mexican *Dia de los Muertos,* or, Day of the Dead, placing the play within a Mexican/Chicano context. Several characters are dressed and/or masked as *calaveras* (skeletons), in a theatrical and mythical extension of the Halloween party that initiates the young lovers' tragedy.

The adaptation attempts to bridge the schism between the Euro-American fear of death and the Mexican celebration and even mocking of the Afterlife. Further, Villareal's version of the tragedy takes the young couple beyond death. They rise from their tombs and dance in one another's arms, thus experiencing "death in life and life in death," as the indigenous forebears would say. In her analysis of the first version of the play, Susan Mason wrote: "Contrary to audience expectation, the conflict . . . is not between an L.A. version of the Sharks and the Jets, but is a class and cultural struggle within the Latino community."[32] Mason also points out that the second version "further emphasized the class conflict and the struggle of illegal immigrants" (92). What interests us here, however, is the playwright's portrayal of death, which, in Mason's analysis "is the central image in the play" (88).

In the program notes for the first 1991 production of (the then titled) *R & J,* Villareal stated:

> . . . a careful reading of *Romeo and Juliet* reveals a Shakespeare consumed with thoughts about the nature of death. Setting my adaptation during Day of the Dead made me also think about the nature of death, but from a Mesoamerican point of view. . . . Ancient Mesoamericans believed that life and death are different expressions of a continuous energy. In other words, life and death are both present in the world equally and simultaneously. If this is so, maybe the living, in certain situations, can actually see the dead. Maybe the dead continue to help the living. Maybe the dead have the same foibles that they had while alive.[33]

---

[31] Lynne Heffley, "Shakespeare in Baggy Pants," *Los Angeles Times,* July 10, 1997, Calendar, 42. In July of 1997, the East L.A. Classical Theatre produced an abridged, zoot suit version of Shakespeare's *Romeo and Juliet* set in Los Angeles in the 1940s, cut to seventy minutes for young audiences. The adaptation was directed by Elina DeSantos.

[32] Susan Mason, "Romeo and Juliet in East LA," (Yale) *Theater* (Spring 1992), 88.

[33] Typescript dated November 1991 in my files.

Figure 3. My Visits With MGM (My Grandmother Marta), by Edit Villareal. Milwaukee Repertory Theatre, 1993. Directed by Norma Saldívar. L. to R. Maricela Ochoa, Renee Victor, Feiga M. Martinez.

Dancing with the dead: My Visits With MGM

Meso-American philosophy also informs and inspires Villareal's *My Visits With MGM (My Grandmother Marta)*, a play in which the dead do, indeed, return to the living.[34] The professional world premiere of this play was directed by Peggy Shannon, Artistic Director of the San José (California) Repertory Theatre in 1992. In this memory play Villareal explores the relationship between Marta Feliz, the central narrator of the story, and her grandmother, Marta Grande, who returns in the second act as a ghost to guide her in her path towards liberation from her past and towards fulfillment. This is, therefore, an example of a dead character who exists as a living entity on stage, although she is visible only to Marta Feliz and to the audience.[35]

---

[34] Published in Linda Feyder (ed.), *Shattering the Myth: Plays by Hispanic Women* (Houston: Arte Publico, 1992), pp. 143–208.

[35] In the Spring of 1999 the San Diego Repertory Theatre produced the world premiere of Villareal's latest (unpublished) play, titled *Marriage is Forever*. In this play, too, the dead come back from the past to educate the living.

Figure 4. My Visits With MGM (My Grandmother Marta), by Edit Villareal. Milwaukee Repertory Theatre, Milwaukee, Minnesota, 1993. Directed by Norma Saldivar. L. to R. Feiga M. Martinez, Thaddeus Valdez, Maricela Ochoa and Renee Victor.

My Visits With MGM is Villareal's most produced play to date, with several staged readings and over twenty-five fully staged productions in a variety of venues: universities, community and professional teatros and "mainstream" theatres. *My Visits With MGM* explores the lives of three generations of Mexican and Chicana women. Spanning seventy-five years, the play follows the trials and tribulations of Marta Grande, her younger sister, Florinda, Grande's daughter, Marta Chica, and her granddaughter, Marta Feliz, who narrates the story. Two other characters come into their lives on stage: the grandfather, Juan, and a young Chicano priest, Father Ernesto.

My Visits With MGM is written to be performed on a set that allows for flexibility in staging. Because it is a memory play the action goes back-and-forth in time, narrated by Marta Feliz in a story theatre, transformational style. Since everything in the play is a memory, the actors and the designs must be adaptable to instant transformations in character's ages, and also adaptable to multiple locations. The settings and costumes cannot change as often as a realistic play would require, nor should they because, ultimately, this is a play about character. In the playwright's words, "I wrote *My Visits With MGM* as an homage to my grandmother, Marta Garza Cortinas."[36] Thus Marta Feliz speaks for the playwright, a somewhat autobiographical character who takes the audience back and forth in time as she exposes the stories of three distinct and strong-willed women in her life. Although Marta Feliz is narrating the events, the play is really about her grandmother and the lessons she taught her granddaughter about love, strength and survival.

The play opens in the present with a setting that should suggest the remains of a burnt-out house. The playwright sets the tone of her play from the very beginning with Marta Feliz rummaging through the remains of the house as the voice of her aunt Florinda reverberates throughout the theatre. Then we see her grandmother. Two ghosts. We do not know that these characters are dead yet but we definitely know by the theatricality of their "appearances" that we are in the realm of *el misterio*. We also know immediately that there is a special bond between the two Martas. After Florinda's voice and the vision of Marta Grande have disappeared, Marta Feliz looks at the audience and says, "After my Ama, my grandmother, died, I threw away clothes. And I stored away photos, green cards, letters and bills. The only thing I kept for myself was her coin purse" (Feyder, *Shattering the Myth*,

---

[36] Edit Villareal, "Thoughts From the Playwright," Milwaukee Repertory Theater *Prologue* (September, 1992), 4.

p. 148). From the beginning of this play we discover that the dead are speaking to the living.

In the stage directions, the playwright tells the reader, "The play calls for the actors to play a wide range of ages, age need not be played realistically. In fact, youth, age and death should be treated as temporary states" (145). After the brief prologue just described, Marta Feliz takes us back in time to when Marta Grande and Florinda were girls escaping the Mexican Revolution. In the readings and productions I have seen, the actors playing the two sisters have been mature women. Once the women begin behaving like girls, the audience is happy to go along with the convention. We see all of the characters in various stages of their lives, from childhood to adulthood or even old age. Transformational theatre of this kind encourages the audience to take greater leaps away from traditional realism, inviting them to enjoy the transformations as well as the story. When an adult actor takes-on the persona of a teenager, for example, the audience can take pleasure from the incongruity. This kind of theatre also invites fantasy and fantastical occurrences, such as ghosts that speak.

When the play opens, the only characters that are not dead are Marta Feliz and Father Ernesto, whom we do not meet until the second act. As Marta Feliz narrates, maintaining an on-going dialogue with the audience, Grande corrects her, reminds her of certain details, never addressing the audience herself, almost like a Greek chorus. Grande also generally keeps the play upbeat with her humorous remarks and vulgar tongue. When Feliz asks her if all Mexicans speak with such vulgarity, Grande responds, "Only the women" (160).

Through the course of the first act, Feliz narrates the progression of Marta Grande and Florinda's odyssey once they leave Mexico and emigrate to Texas. We see Grande's courtship with the delightful Juan, a native of the United States. He tells Grande and Florinda: "I'm Tex-Mex honey. American. And proud of it" (152). By the end of the first act, both Juan and Marta Grande have died. When Marta Feliz is rushing to the hospital to see her grandmother, Grande appears to her, as real as a living person, and tells her she has died. This is the beginning of the other-worldly relationship that will flourish in the second act, when Marta Feliz is in real need of guidance.

Confirming the playwright's belief that death is "only a stage," towards the end of the first act (Scene fourteen), when we know that she has really died, Marta Grande is dancing with Juan, ostensibly in heaven. She tells Marta Feliz: ". . . he never took me dancing. But now, M'ija (my daughter),

I can dance" (176). Villareal's Heaven is a place where one can finally dance, just as the young lovers do in her play, *The Language of Flowers*. For this playwright, there is no death, but there is the dance.

Throughout the first act, Marta Grande appears to Feliz, we believe, because she is a part of Feliz's memory, along with her aunt Florinda and grandfather Juan. But when Grande talks to Feliz at the end of the first act, and announces her own death, the playwright is taking her audience on a different kind of journey. When the second act begins, Feliz tells us: "And even though my grandmother had died, she didn't really go away . . . I saw her often and she kept telling me things. Even though it usually wasn't what I wanted to hear" (178). The second act definitely takes us into the realm of *el misterio*.

The major action of the second act is about Marta Feliz's liberation. Liberation from her past, from her Aunt Florinda and even from Texas. Feliz now has two objectives: to get her grandmother's house and to settle her third divorce. Feliz's situation is complicated further by Father Ernesto, who comes into the story, as discussed more fully in chapter 3. We first meet Father Ernesto as he blesses Grande's house, going from room to room to sprinkle Holy Water, as Florinda attempts to gain his favor and that of the Church. The parody of this practice is complete when Florinda asks him to bless the garage and Feliz comments "Up until now I didn't even know garages could sin" (185). Aunt Florinda has taken her religion very seriously and in her desire to be a kind of Mother Teresa of the barrio, decides that she must have Grande's house. "I need this house! For my work with the poor" Florinda tells Feliz, who responds: "But tia (aunt) I am the poor" (188). Throughout Feliz's interactions with both Father Ernie and her aunt, Grande is always around, seen and heard only by Feliz and the audience.

In Villareal's interpretation of what the dead can do for the living, help is limited to offering advice. Grande warned her granddaughter after her death that her aunt would fight her for the house and she does. Yet Grande, who knows where the will is, cannot reveal the hiding place to Feliz and the wretched aunt wins title to the house. But in matters of love and life, Grande is full of other-worldly wisdom. While Father Ernie has believed that Florinda put a curse on Feliz because Feliz feels sick, it takes the dead Grande to inform her that she is only pregnant. Finally, before she leaves forever, Grande tells Feliz that she must move away, an act that changes her granddaughter's life forever. The dead really can help the living. What begins as a play in which the dead are recalled as memories, transforms into a remembrance of ghostly appearances and intercessions in Villareal's poignant and loving tribute to her grandmother.

The Latino theatre lab revives a modern Chicano hero

Although officially credited to a fictitious author, Violeta Calles, *August 29th* was collectively created by the Latino Theatre Lab, a group of Chicana and Chicano theatre artists, under the direction of José Luis Valenzuela, in 1990.[37] This play explores and exposes police brutality both in the past and in the present by bringing the ghost of an actual Chicano journalist, Rubén Salazar, into the life of a fictional Chicana history professor who is writing a scholarly book about the slain journalist. She is caught between her efforts to achieve tenure and pressure from community activists to denounce police brutality involving one of her Chicano students. The Latino Theatre Lab entered into the realm of *El Misterio* in order to draw attention to an important historical and political event, the Chicano Moratorium of August 29, 1970. By focusing on Salazar's death and martyrdom twenty years after the fact, this play gives a human face to a defining moment in Chicano history, the day tens of thousands of Chicana/os marched in East Los Angeles to protest the War in Vietnam.[38]

The Los Angeles Theatre Center's Latino Theatre Lab, directed by José Luis Valenzuela, was the only group of its kind, an ensemble of professional Chicana and Chicano theatre, television and film artists, working in a mainstream theatre company.[39] During his tenure with the Los Angeles Theatre Center, from 1985 to 1991, José Luis Valenzuela and his staff were responsible for more professional Chicano/Latino theatre productions, readings and workshops than any other mainstream or Latino theatre company in the country.

The evolution of the Latino Theatre Lab was unique, having been initiated by a mainstream theatre company before securing its autonomy

---

[37] The group attributed the play to a fictitious author because they feared that the critics would treat the piece differently if they knew it was a collective creation, focusing on the process rather than the production and the play.

[38] For more on the Chicano Moratorium of 1970, see: Rodolfo Acuña, *Occupied America: A History of Chicanos* 3rd edn., (Harper and Row, 1988), pp. 345–49; Jorge Mariscal (ed.), *Aztlán and Vietnam: Chicano and Chicana Experiences of the War* (California, 1999); *La Raza* 3, Special Issue (1970) features Raul Ruiz's photo essay of the Moratorium, documenting police repression.

[39] Because *August 29th* was written collectively and there is no single author to credit, I focus here on José Luis Valenzuela, as the director who made it happen. With few exceptions the director is ultimately responsible for all that the audience eventually sees. In terms of the writing process, each of the people involved can take responsibility and credit.

outside of the theatre establishment. In 1985, Bill Bushnell moved his Los Angeles Actors' Theatre into an impressive 80,000 square foot former bank building in downtown Los Angeles which became known as the Los Angeles Theatre Center. Soon after, Bushnell appointed Valenzuela Director of the Latino Theatre Lab. Almost immediately, Valenzuela put out a call for Latina and Latino actors to join his workshop in Chicano/Latino theatre. After auditioning "every actor in LA," he chose twenty-four men and women of varying ages and rehearsed four plays with them for a year. At the end of that year Valenzuela staged workshop productions of the plays in an effort to influence Bushnell to produce one. Bushnell chose El Teatro de la Esperanza's historic docu-drama, *La víctima*, and the Latino Theatre Lab went public with a revival of this play in 1986. The production was greeted with tremendous critical and popular acclaim, a major new force in Latina/o theatre was launched, and outside funding soon followed.

Because he was born and raised in Mexico, he does not claim to be a "Chicano," but, ironically, José Luis Valenzuela is probably the most important director of his generation directing, teaching and producing theatre by and/or about Chicanas and Chicanos. Valenzuela was born in 1953 in Los Mochis, Sinaloa, Mexico, where he attended primary and secondary schools before studying business and theatre arts in the Universidad Tecnológica de Mexico in Mexico City from 1968 to 1972. He came to the United States in 1973, interested in the Chicano Movement he had heard about as a student in Mexico. In fact, ironically, the Chicano Moratorium of 1970 had made a great impression on him, only two years after protesting students had been massacred at Tlatelolco (Mexico City), in 1968.[40] After observing the Teatro Campesino for a short while, Valenzuela moved to San José, California, to, in his words, "study Chicanos." He enrolled in a theatre class being taught by Adrian Vargas at San José State University and became involved with the Teatro de la Gente.[41]

Valenzuela's work with the Teatro de la Gente (Theatre of the People), co-directed by Adrian Vargas and Manuel Martinez, was an excellent training ground in both the early Chicano theatre aesthetic as well as in the

---

[40] In 1968 student protesters were massacred at Tlatelolco by government forces – an infamous attack that few people outside of Mexico knew immediately about. Nobody knows for certain how many people were killed, but reports vary from a few hundred to several thousand, depending upon whom you read. The Summer Olympics were to be held in Mexico City in a few weeks and the Mexican government did not want the world to see protests of any kind.

[41] From my UCSD-TV interview series, "Necessary Theatre," taped February 24, 1995.

politics of the Chicano Movement. Both Martinez and Vargas were students in the graduate directing program at the University of California, Davis, working closely with Theodore Shank, an expert on people's theatre and a close observer of the Teatro Movement.[42] Valenzuela worked with Teatro de la Gente until 1978, when he joined the Teatro de la Esperanza in Santa Barbara, California. He performed with this group for several years, participating in local, national and international tours.[43] All these years, Valenzuela was learning everything he could about the collective process, how to direct and write as an ensemble. While in Santa Barbara, Valenzuela worked with actor and future playwright, Evelina Fernández, whom he would subsequently marry.

Fernández and Valenzuela left the Teatro de la Esperanza in 1984 and moved to Los Angeles where they formed a company of professional actors eager to perform in a play that spoke to their community. In 1985 the group produced Teatro de la Esperanza's collectively created play, "*Hijos: Once a Family*," in El Teatro Jorge Negrete, a small theatre space in East Los Angeles, to popular and critical success. Valenzuela directed this domestic drama about a Mechicano family that disintegrates as the family members struggle to survive.[44] Valenzuela's professional future was confirmed with that brilliant production, for which he earned a *Dramalogue* Award for Best Direction. This production helped Valenzuela get into the Los Angeles Theatre Center.

Although he was officially the "Director" of the Latino Lab, Valenzuela's experience with other Chicano theatre groups gave him an understanding of the collective process not taught in any theatre training programs in this country. A natural-born teacher, Valenzuela is a director who knows how to collaborate in every sense of the term, guiding the creation of a play from its inception to the final production. Valenzuela listens to the other members of the collaborative team, especially the actors/playwrights. Having been an actor and performer, this man understands the tremendous responsibility that rests on the shoulders of the people who face the audi-

---

[42] See Theodore Shank, *American Alternative Theater* (Grove, 1982), as well as his article about the Chicano Theatre festival in Mexico City, "A Return to Mayan and Aztec Roots," *Drama Review* 4 (1974), 56–70.

[43] For an interesting account of the evolution of Teatro de la Esperanza, from its inception to 1990, see Mark S. Weinberg, *Challenging the Hierarchy: Collective Theatre in the United States* (Westport: Greenberg, 1992), Chapter 3.

[44] The Teatro de la Esperanza's play, *Hijos, Once a Family*, is unpublished. For an account of this play see Weinberg, *Challenging the Hierarchy*, pp. 81–83.

ence each night. Valenzuela also knows how to bring a group of talented people together in mutual purpose, regardless of individual egos and agendas.[45]

When Bill Bushnell and Diane White hired Valenzuela to head the Latino Lab, he was, in effect, hiring a company. Along with Valenzuela, the founding members of the Latino Lab were (in alphabetical order) Enrique Castillo, Evelina Fernández, Sal López, Angela Moya, and Lupe Ontiveros. Each of these actors had been in Valenzuela's production of *Hijos: Once a Family* and each had an impressive resume of acting experience in Hollywood as well as in Chicano theatres, having worked with such groups as the Teatro Campesino, Teatro de la Esperanza and other community-based groups. Like many other Latina/o actors working in Hollywood, Castillo, Fernández, Moya and Ontiveros had all been in Luis Valdez's *Zoot Suit*, either in Los Angeles or New York (or both), as well as in the film of that play. They each brought a knowledge of professional theatre and film to the Lab and were crucial to the success of the company, acting in almost all of the plays the Lab produced.[46]

In 1991 the Los Angeles Theatre Center lost its funding and the organization had to vacate the (city-owned) facilities. Seeing that the Latino Lab was now without a home, Gordon Davidson invited Valenzuela to direct the Latino Theatre Initiative for his company, the Center Theatre Group, better known as the Mark Taper Forum. Hopeful that this new arrangement would be beneficial to all concerned, Valenzuela moved the short distance to the home of *Zoot Suit* in 1992. While at the Taper Valenzuela again began to commission new writers and he also directed new works or revivals. He directed the Chicano comedy trio, *Culture Clash*, in a piece titled *Carpa Clash*, in 1993, followed by a production of Luis Valdez's *Bandido* in 1994.[47]

---

[45] I speak from intimate knowledge of Valenzuela's creative process. We first worked together in a collective creation, *El Pulpo (The Octopus)*, which I directed for the Teatro de la Esperanza in 1980. Further, Valenzuela directed the collective creation of "*Un puño de tierra*" (*A Handful of Dirt*), with a group of Latina and Latino graduate actors and directors at UCSD in 1990. The (unpublished) production was a highlight of this graduate program.

[46] Valenzuela's influence in the development of Chicana and Chicano playwrights has also been very important. As Director of the Latino Theatre Lab, Valenzuela was responsible for commissioning plays from some of the most prominent and promising Chicana and Chicano playwrights of the 1980s, including Cherríe Moraga, Milcha Sanchez-Scott and Octavio Solis, all of whom are discussed in this book.

[47] It is interesting to note that despite negative reviews and a budget approaching one million dollars, *Bandido* was the most (financially) successful production at the Mark Taper Forum that season. The name, Luis Valdez, continues to attract audiences.

Valenzuela was appointed a professor of theatre in the School of Theatre, Film and Television, University of California, Los Angeles in 1995, where he currently heads the Graduate Directing Program. That same year Valenzuela and the ensemble of theatre artists, left the Center Theatre Group and re-named their company the Latino Theatre Company. The company relocated to the Plaza de la Raza in East Los Angeles, and inaugurated their new independence and their new, community-based venue with a very successful revival of *August 29th*. The company continued to produce new works, including Evelina Fernández's two one-acts, *How Else Am I Supposed to Know I'm Still Alive?* and *Premeditation*, which opened at the Plaza de la Raza's Margo Albert Theatre in 1996 and then toured in 1996 and 1997.[48] Valenzuela also directed a motion picture of *How Else Am I Supposed to Know I'm Still Alive?* in 1992. In 1996, Valenzuela directed Evelina Fernández's play, *Luminarias*, which was produced at the reconstituted Los Angeles Theatre Center and in 1998 he directed the full-length motion picture of *Luminarias*, premiering the movie in 1999 at various film festivals in the United States and abroad.[49]

Evelina Fernández's *Luminarias* is an important play for many reasons, but perhaps mostly because it deals with the Chicana/os internalized and externalized racism, challenging notions of culture and stability. Further, this play is about four professional Chicanas, and focuses on their middle-class problems rather than the usual working-class themes that predominate in most Chicana and Chicano plays. Fernández wrote this play as a vehicle for herself and other Latina actors, but also for the feminist themes it addresses even as it critiques both male and female chauvinism within and without the Mechicano communities. *Luminarias* is a result of the Latino Theatre Company's dedication to producing plays that reflect the totality of the Mechicana, Mechicano and Latina/o experiences in the United States. By 1999 the Latino Theatre Company had gone full-circle, moving back into offices at the Los Angeles Theatre Center, their original home.[50] The

---

[48] Evelina Fernández's one-act, *How Else Am I Supposed to know I'm Still Alive?* is in Kathy A. Perkins and Roberta Uno (eds.), *Contemporary Plays by Women of Color* (Routledge, 1996), pp. 158–67. In the playwright's words: "How Else. . . was written for my friends Lupe Ontiveros and Angela Moya. Two extremely gifted actors who are rarely given the opportunity to play leading roles" (Perkins and Uno, p. 159). *Premeditation* is not published.

[49] As of this writing, the producers had not found a distributor for the motion picture of *Luminarias*.

[50] No longer under the leadership of Bill Bushnell and Diane White, the Los Angeles Theatre Center is operated by the City of Los Angeles and offers performance and office spaces to independent groups.

ensemble remains the most important group of its kind, paying professional artists to produce and create important works for the theatre, film and television.

An affair to remember: August 29th

I believe that *August 29th* was one of the major theatrical achievements of the decade of the eighties.[51] This play brought the audience members to their feet when it premiered on August 29, 1990 at the Los Angeles Theatre Center on the twentieth anniversary of the Chicano Moratorium. Many of the people in the audience had participated in that fateful march and cried and cheered at the play's dramatic conclusion. Rubén Salazar's widow, Sally, two of their children, and other family members were there, as well as veterans of the Chicano Movement, adding a pathos that we can only hope for in the theatre. A new classic in Chicano theatre was born that night and the play was so well received by the public and the press that it was extended to November.

Once again demonstrating that reality mirrors art, just weeks before the opening of this play, Los Angeles policemen had killed a fourteen-year-old Chicano just blocks from the Plaza de la Raza, under suspicious circumstances, causing two days of civil unrest. The parallels between the death of Rubén Salazar, who was killed by a sheriff's tear gas projectile, and the wrongful death of this boy did not go unnoticed by the local audiences. Ironically, the plot of *August 29th* turns on the question of whether the Chicana professor, Lucero, will speak out against police brutality at an upcoming ceremony in which the mayor of Los Angeles will honor her as "Hispanic Historian of the Year." Just days before the action begins, Lucero's student was shot by the police as he attempted to protect his father from their beatings and the student now lies in the hospital in critical condition.

After scenes that establish Lucero's dilemma she goes to her apartment to finish her book about Salazar. As Lucero types into her computer, Salazar appears in the shadows. "She smiles at him, he smiles at her like old friends that haven't seen each other for a while." Rubén says "It's been a while" as Lucero simultaneously says "I missed you" (Fernández, *Luminarias*, I, p. 16). Apparently, Salazar began to appear to her as she wrote about him and there is a deep connection between the scholar and her subject. Indeed, it is soon

---

[51] *August 29th* is not published. All references are to a typescript, dated September 15, 1990.

apparent that Lucero is in love with her subject, a love affair that challenges reality while it serves the narrative. She must complete her manuscript this night and as the two discuss and debate the past and the present, we learn about the real person and his fictitious champion, how similar their lives and goals were and are.

Through dialogue, flashbacks and scenes highlighted with film and slide projections of the Chicano Moratorium, we learn about that event. Salazar asks Lucero questions about current conditions for the Mechicana/os and is appalled at how things have not changed for the better. Salazar's ghost is contrasted with Lucero's living colleagues and friends, who are urging her to make her acceptance speech an act of defiance, to bring public attention to continuing police brutality. Lucero does not want to jeopardize her chances of getting tenure, fearful that her university would punish her for her political actions, prompting a colleague to call her a "sellout," an accusation familiar to Salazar.

In various flashbacks that inform much of the conversations between Salazar and Lucero, we learn that she had been a student activist during the 1960s and seventies, the daughter of a proud veteran of Korea who supported the war in Vietnam and hated "those radicals." We also learn that Lucero's brother was killed in Vietnam, adding to her anger and defiance. Lucero and Salazar discuss one another's past and the parallels between the two successful Chicanos is telling. As he learns the facts about his death and the recent police shooting of Lucero's own student, Salazar urges her to take action. When she asks him why he went to the Moratorium, he tells her: "Because we care about each other. And like all human beings, we love." Rubén and Lucero hug each other and he tells her, "Finish your book. Then get on with your life!" (*August 29th*, II, p. 16A).

The creators of this piece, Enrique Castillo, Evelina Fernández, Angela Moya, Lupe Ontiveros, Sal López and José Luis Valenzuela, crafted a beautiful lesson in love. This play celebrates a love for Mechicanas and Mechicanos as they face daily battles against oppression of all sorts. The authors researched the events that led up to the Moratorium, the police violence, the murders and the trials that followed. They also interviewed people who had been there, people like Raul Ruiz who had taken the photos that proved that the police were lying about the facts behind the fatal shooting and who later testified in the subsequent trials. Ruiz and other real people became characters in the play, giving the drama a sense of déjà vu for those who had witnessed the events as history was being replayed.

The play builds in intensity, calculated to arouse anger and suspense as we watch the past unfold and wonder of the present: will Lucero make a political statement and confront the hierarchy as she had done as a high school student? The intermingling of the fictitious Chicana professor with historical figures and actual trial transcripts, slides and motion pictures of the March and the police riot are images that are not easily forgotten. In the penultimate scene Lucero types as Salazar recites his final monologue, a moving picture of the marchers that fateful day:

> We were like a river. A brown river. A river whose little streams had pushed their way through the rock and dirt and mud. Pushed and pushed for years. Each one trying to reach the other. A quiet but constant flow until they came together to create a huge river of brown faces. Full of hope and anger and hurt but mostly joy and pride and love. And the river was strong and as more streams flowed in, it became stronger and its rush could be heard for a long way. And when it crashed against the rocks it was the loudest. And by the time they knew it, the river was pushing its way through the mountains because it wanted to reach the ocean. It wanted to flow free . . . (RUBÉN stands center stage. A POLICE[MAN] aims a projectile at his head. He fires.).
>
> (II-19–21A)

From the image of the sheriff firing the projectile we move to Lucero standing behind a podium. She is at the ceremony. Her speech begins innocuously as she thanks the authorities for this honor, leaving us to think that she will not confront the System. But then her tone changes as she says:

> It's been twenty years since Mr. Salazar was silenced by a tear gas projectile in East L.A. and police brutality has not subsided but it increases by the day. I will not accept this award because it would be an insult to Rubén Salazar and to a student of mine, Ricardo Chávez, who was shot by a police officer, and who died last night. I demand a full investigation into his death. Who am I to make such a demand you might ask? I am a Chicana, a Mexicana, a woman, an American. And I have the right to demand that injustices taking place in my community be addressed by this City, this Government. It's time to demand a moratorium.

End of play. I wish I could recreate for the reader the emotions that this play aroused in its audiences night after night. Having been at the Moratorium in 1970, having watched as the trials made a mockery of justice, and knowing that police violence against Mechicanas and Mechicanos continues with impunity, the final effect of this play was overwhelming.

Tears flowed as people on stage and in the audience repeatedly chanted "Chicano!" "Power!" with fists raised in anger and pride.

August 29th becomes a romantic, political ghost story, full of anger and love, frustration and, perhaps, hope. The irony is that it takes the dead subject, not the living characters, to convince Lucero to take action against repression as she (and we) see how past events transpired and how the present repeats the past if you allow it to. Unlike classic ghosts such as Clytemnaestra or Hamlet's father, who begin the action of their plays by seeking revenge, Salazar's ghost does not know what happened after he was shot. Thus, he (and the audience) learn the truth of his and the community's fate through the course of this play. Further, it is the ghost of an actual person that brings Lucero to challenge the hierarchy, not a fictional ghost. Not only can we learn from the past, this play is telling us, we must learn and take care not to let history repeat itself.

Curiously, none of the authors of *August 29th* is an academic scholar, yet they unconsciously painted a very telling picture of the relationship between the scholar and his/her subject. In effect, the scholar does carry on a love affair with the object(s) of her/his investigation. You sleep with the book, you dream about the book, the project becomes like a demanding lover, always calling you from the deepest recesses of your mind, often interrupting your other activities. And, just as Salazar questions and challenges Lucero, so, too, does the subject challenge the scholar. And, in the best of circumstances, this lover changes your life, for in dissecting a subject, the scholar dissects her/himself.

August 29 of 1970 will live in my memory forever and so will the night of August 29, 1990. With their production of *August 29th* in 1990 and again in 1995, the Latino Theatre Company brought the Chicano Theatre Movement full-circle, recalling the early days when teatros collectively created politically committed actos and docu-dramas. But the difference in this instance, is the fact that this docu-drama was written and produced by professional Chicanas and Chicanos, no longer students or untrained community activists. They are a distinct breed of activists, however: people you see regularly on television and in films, sometimes as stereotypes, yet they are contesting the stereotypes and negative Hollywood images with the plays and films they produce. It is their work in the Latino Theatre Company that sustains them, for these artists continue to produce plays and films that present the Chicana and the Chicano as real people caught in circumstances that have relevance for the Mechicana and the Mechicano.

Octavio Solis' misterios

Another Chicano among the new generation of playwrights that also explores the mystery of death in his plays is Octavio Solis, who was born in 1958 in El Paso, Texas, where he was also reared. Solis studied theatre formally and holds a B.A. (1980) from Trinity University in San Antonio, Texas, and an M.F.A. in Theatre from the Dallas Theatre Center (1983). He studied playwriting with John O'Keefe and, like so many other Chicano and Latino playwrights, he also honors Maria Irene Fornes as an important influence in his training. Solis spent the ten years between 1980 and 1990 in Dallas studying and "paying his stage dues," by teaching high school and serving as co-Artistic Director of the Deep Ellum Theatre Garage. Because his plays have been produced by a number of Latino and regional theatres, as well as by universities throughout the country, and because some of his texts have been published, Solis is one of the best-known Chicano playwrights working today. His plays deal in one way or another with being a Chicano, reflected by the juxtaposed and sometimes conflicting realities of El Paso/Ciudad Juarez. I believe this constant image of Mexico permeates Solis' work, for he cannot forget his roots.

Solis' first play, *Man of the Flesh*, to be discussed later, was first produced by the Teatro Dallas, of Dallas, Texas, under the direction of artistic director, Cora Cardona in 1988. *Man of the Flesh* was followed by *Prospect*, first produced at the Deep Ellum Theatre Garage in Dallas in 1989, directed by Solis. *Prospect* revolves around a young Chicano named Scout, a self-identified "computer nerd," who has denied his Mexican heritage and rediscovers his cultural and linguistic roots when he finds himself in an all-night drinking, smoking and cocaine snorting binge with total strangers. The only Chicana in the play is Elena, a young woman who is dying of cancer and who reminds Scout of his grandmother. Scout's emotional encounter with Elena causes him momentarily to go back in time to fond memories of his Mexican grandmother who tried to teach him to speak Spanish – a language he has attempted to forget. This is Solis' most naturalistic play, with only two settings required. The action begins with a brief scene in a bar where Scout meets the people with whom he will spend the rest of the night. The action then moves to Elena's run-down house when her husband takes Scout and other people there to party. This play takes a harsh look at working-class people from various cultures while gently expressing the Chicanos' search for identity. The house and the people in it are metaphors for society at large, in this impressionistic reflection of a fractured Chicano identity.[52]

Solis' next play, *La posada mágica*, was commissioned by the South Coast Repertory Theatre, Costa Mesa, California, and produced there in 1994 under the direction of José Cruz González.[53] This play quickly captured the enthusiasm of the Rep's audiences and became an annual tradition for that theatre every Christmas. Solis' version of the traditional Mexican Christmas play centers on Gracie, a young Chicana whose brother's death has caused her to lose her faith in God. She rediscovers her faith on Christmas Eve when a traditional Mexican Christmas processional, *La Posada*, comes to her home. This play for young audiences is written as a play within a folk play, exposing multiple realities as the action shifts from narration to a meta-theatrical re-creation of Joseph and Mary's search for "*posada*," lodging. This is a play with music incorporating elements of the traditional Spanish and Mexican Christmas celebrations with contemporary dramatizations of the Chicano experience.

El Paso Blue was first produced in 1994 by the Intersection for the Arts in San Francisco, California, directed by Solis.[54] This play is much more complicated than any of Solis' other works. In this play he attempts to recreate archetypal struggles when a young Chicano's Anglo-American wife leaves him for his own father. Set in the Southwestern desert, the action shifts from site-to-site as the playwright exposes the characters and their conflicts. The play is accented with songs and much of the dialogue is written in free verse with code-switching that may confuse the non-bilingual audience member. Rich poetry permeates this abstract look at cultural, ethnic and generational conflicts.

All of Solis' plays are written in formal and informal verse, a bilingual poetry that manages to capture the spirit and the conflict of border existence. Imagery ranges from appearances of the dead to poetic descriptions of the human condition. The plays range from the playful comedy of *Man of the Flesh* to the deadly seriousness of *Santos & Santos*. Some of his plays employ live music and songs to enhance the celebratory nature of his writing; in each, the rhythms of the language provide a vivid score. Solis often contrasts his Chicano characters with non-Chicano adversaries and allies. Each of his plays investigates the cultural and spiritual nature of the

---

[52] *Prospect* is published in *TheatreForum* 5 (1994), 79–99.
[53] *La Posada Magica* is published in *Plays From South Coast Repertory* Vol. II (New York: Broadway Play Publishing 1998).
[54] *El Paso Blue* is not published.

Figure 5. Santos & Santos, by Octavio Solis. Campo Santo in Association with Thick Description, San Francisco, California, 1996. Directed by Tony Kelley. L. to R. Deena Martinez, Michael Torres, Luis Saguar, Maria Candelaria and Sean San José Blackman.

Mexican-American, from a traditional Christmas play to a play about a family of brothers whose last name is *Santos*, "Saints."[55]

Don't mess with the living or the dead: Man of the Flesh

One of Solis' most produced plays to date is *Man of the Flesh*, an adaptation of the Don Juan legend initiated by *El burlador de Sevilla* (*The Trickster of Seville*) around the year 1616 in Spain.[56] Solis bases his version of the

---

[55] Solis is one of the most sought-after Chicano playwrights to date. As of this writing he was working on commissions from San Francisco's American Conservatory Theatre, the Center Theatre Group in Los Angeles, and the Dallas Theatre Center. His project with the Center Theatre Group is a collaboration with composer Louie Perez, of the Chicano musical group, Los Lobos. Solis calls it an "East L.A. Orpheus story." E-mail from Octavio Solis, June 28, 1999.

[56] *Man of the Flesh* is published by the South Coast Repertory Theatre's SCR Publications, Vol. III, No. Two.

Figure 6. Santos & Santos, by Octavio Solis. Dallas Theatre Center, Dallas, Texas, 1995. Directed by Richard Hamburger. L. to R. Jennifer Griffith, Richard Chaves, Rene Moreno, Vilma Silva, Al Espinosa, Dolores Godinez, Bob Burrus, Toni Allen, Jimmie Ray Weeks.

timeless parable on the José Zorrilla y Moral version, *Don Juan Tenorio*, first produced in Mexico in 1844. The playwright places his Don Juan in the middle of not only a sexual clash but also a cultural and class conflict, to make his statement about class and racial strife in the United States. In Solis' vision, Juan is the reprobate son of Don Diego, a humble Mexican gardener for the Downey's, a rich Anglo family in the affluent part of town. Don Diego forces Juan to work for him at the Downey estate to pay for the illegitimate children he has fathered. But when Juan first sees Anna Downey, he sets his sights on her, assuring his skeptical friend that she is the only woman for him. The play takes place on the *Dia de los Muertos*, as is customary throughout the Spanish-speaking world. And as in the other versions of this Spanish and Mexican classic, Juan is visited by the dead. In this case, however, it is the ghost of Juan's mother, formerly the Downey's maid, who returns at the behest of Don Diego, who can no longer control his impetuous and lustful son.

Man of the Flesh is a fast-paced play that moves from place to place as if it were an Elizabethan comedy. The action must flow from the barrio to the mansion, from interiors to exteriors, in an almost cinematic way, as we follow Juan's attempts to reach the object of his desire. All the while, the ghost of Juan's mother permeates the action, appearing in the shadows as she places three female temptations in front of her inconstant son. Of course, Juan seduces the three women his mother has placed in his path, and, of course, he is condemned to Hell for all eternity at the conclusion of the play. In this case, however, Juan's mother transforms into La Muerte (Death) and gives him his final kiss, sending him to his just reward.

Solis has made important changes to the original text that reveal his deeper, more political purpose. The original Don Juan was a nobleman; this Juan is a working class Chicano. By juxtaposing a Chicano with an Anglo girl, Solis is pointing out the cultural differences as well. Solis also incorporates indigenous Mexican beliefs, enhancing his story and reminding the audience of their autochthonous past. Juan refers to the marigold as cempasuchitl, using Nahuatl to describe the traditional flower which is used to adorn the altars and invite the deceased to return to earth on the Dia de los Muertos. In a notably funny scene, Juan seduces Anna's lusty sister with a bouquet of cempasuchitl. This is a play about the many faces of seduction: the seductive powers of sex, money, life forces and even death. But this is, after all, a man's version of mythical powers and *El Misterio* of deadly visitations.

A dead paterfamilias watches his sons destroy his dreams: Santos &
Santos

In his play, *Santos & Santos*, Solis again explores *El Misterio* focusing on
the children of a dead Mexican immigrant, Don Miguel, whose gentle
spirit oversees the action. This play received its world premiere production
at the Dallas Theatre Center under the direction of Artistic Director,
Richard Hamburger in 1995.[57] The only other play by a Chicano to be published in *American Theatre* magazine,[58] *Santos & Santos* is a stunning and
troubling examination of a fictitious family of young, successful Chicano
lawyers. In reality, the play is based on actual events evolving around a
prominent El Paso family of Lebanese Mexicans. The events are real but
the characters are fictional. *Santos & Santos* is, I believe, Solis' most powerful play to date, an epic, sprawling montage of scenes that lead inexor-
ably to their tragic conclusion. The central figure is Tomás, the youngest
brother, who has returned to El Paso to join his two brothers in the law
offices of Santos & Santos. Tomás is the bright young prodigal son, a
former prosecutor in San Diego and the baby brother who will supposedly
bring a degree of integrity to the family's criminal law practice. But upon
his arrival, Tomás is appalled by the realization that his brothers, Fernie and
Mike, respected members of the community, have been making their
fortune dealing in illicit drugs. The entire family is destroyed by their
greed, leaving no one unharmed by the events that transpire. Multiple settings, flashbacks, monologues, poetic language and visions from the past
give this play a classic, epic scope as the playwright develops the characters
and their devastating downfall. Don Miguel's appearances leave no doubt
that we are in the realm of *El Misterio*.

   Santos & Santos is not an easy play to witness nor to stage. The theme
verges on Hollywood stereotypes of yet another drug dealing Chicano
family but the action and the characters are so well written as to be classical in scope, and not stereotypical unless the director and/or the actors
make them such. This play demands superior, trained actors to interpret
Solis' characters and language. When an interviewer asked Solis if
Shakespeare was a model for him, the playwright answered: "Absolutely.
Santos was a play I felt should have a kind of cinematic sweep, but I wasn't
thinking in terms of cinema, but in terms of Shakespeare. He was never

---

[57] *Santos & Santos*, is in *American Theatre Magazine* (November 1995), 35–57.
[58] The only other Chicana/o play published by *American Theatre* magazine to date is Milcha
   Sanchez-Scott's *Roosters*, and is in Elizabeth Osborn, *On New Ground: Contemporary Hispanic-
   American Plays* (New York: TCG Publications, 1987), pp. 244–80.

bothered by the fourth wall and realism, a thing I'm always trying to bust out of."[59]

With Shakespeare as his inspiration and in true renaissance fashion, many of Solis' characters recite inner monologues in language that is sensuous and dangerous at the same time. Very early in the play, Tomás's brother offers him a line of cocaine and Tomás recites the following inner monologue as he slowly approaches the drug:

> [A thin white scar on the table, my father's table, his memory, the sentences of all my suspects, powdered like sweet bread, symbols in search of symbols on the fine grain of the wood facing north, where all good things are, the best homes, the best clothes, the best laws, the best jails, the best kind of death, plunging downward, downward, falling toward heaven, oh what the hell, just once, just for them, my brothers, my family, mi raza.] *Tomás snorts up the line.*
>
> <div align="right">(Solis, <i>Santos & Santos</i>, p. 37)[60]</div>

Tomás's monologue above deftly contrasts a myriad of symbols even as it subverts symbolism in the words, "symbols in search of symbols." We see his Mexican past, his father's crossing north, hanging onto golden dreams of immigrants, only to fall to a certain death and now his sons are on another path toward self destruction, "Falling toward heaven." In this one monologue Solis is foretelling all that will transpire to the brothers and their families. They will fall but heaven will not be on their horizon. Tomás soon learns that his brothers are dealing in drugs and although he is shocked and repulsed, he initially cannot take action against them. His brother Mike reinscribes the American Dream gone sour when he tells Tomás: "This is how the world works, brother. It's what we do for the good of our bloods and our business. Sure it sucks, but it makes our charity work fly, it's enabled the education of our brothers and sisters, and reinforced our image as positive role models . . . Imagine what this could do in the hands of real criminals." To this, the other brother, Fernie, adds, "Tomás, this has given us power. Power to help our community"(40). Shortly after this revelation, the Judge who will eventually preside over the brother's trial and who will be assassinated by their hired killer, appears to Tomás. Tomás calls on his father's spirit for strength. "[La sangre [blood] crying crying legal or loyal, swelling in my head the old man crying for his sons falling over falling into

---

[59] Douglas Langworthy, "Customizing Culture: An Interview with the Playwright [Octavio Solis] by Douglas Langworthy," *American Theatre* (November 1995), p. 34.

[60] The playwright places all inner monologues in brackets to indicate that the characters are speaking their thoughts.

America]" (41). A few seconds later Tomás picks up the phone to call the authorities and everyone's fate is sealed.

The action in this play shifts so quickly from place to place, that the only necessary set prop is a "long polished conference table." I saw a brilliant production of this play in 1996, produced by the Campo Santo theatre company of San Francisco and directed by Tony Kelley. I can still visualize the production. The theatre was the typical alternative space, a rectangular room with about seventy seats on elevated rows facing the acting area. The walls were painted white and Don Miguels' Mexican wooden conference table dominated the whole. Nothing else but some chairs around the table and two small chairs up stage right. Tony Kelley's production trusted the play and his actors to allow the characters and the language to carry the evening and they did. Photographs of other productions reveal more spectacle, but Solis' text should not be obscured by designer pyrotechnics.

Although we do not see Don Miguel, the dead father, very often, his appearances frame the action. We first see him in the opening scene as Tomás calls upon his spirit. Tomás's invocation reveals the fact that his father brought his furniture making craft from Mexico a generation ago. It seems to be a solemn prologue to the play, a calling on the dead to bless the event. The father appears, polishing the table with a cloth, and tells his son: "Use only one thing, from this moment on and forever and forever until the stars cave in and the rivers run dry and the land refuses any seed. Use only this and nothing else, *mijo* [my son]." Tomás asks his father, "*¿Que, papa?*" (What, father?) and the father answers: "Lemon Pledge" (35). We laugh at this incongruity as the scene is shattered by the entrance of Tomás's brothers. The playwright has "played" with us, leading us to expect some Mexican revelation, when, instead, he makes a joke, turning our emotions on themselves. It is one of the few moments in the play that will make us laugh.

Don Miguel again appears to Tomás late in the play, after everything has fallen apart and Tomás does not know what to do next. Don Miguel is polishing his own coffin and tells his son: "Promise to betray me. When the time comes, promise to turn against your father. It is what anyone who wants to succeed in this land must do. I did it to *mis padres* (my parents) and your children will do it to you. But in the end, remember this. You are the first law" (55). As he fades away, Don Miguel blesses his son in his final act of expiation. Betrayal begets betrayal in this complex play, leading to gruesome murders until Tomás is left alone to ponder what he has done. Mike is in jail, Fernie is dead and the final scene is a flashback to the moment Tomás is holding a gun to his brother's head. Fernie taunts him to pull the trigger but a blackout ends the play before we know whether Tomás actually killed his brother.

Metaphorically, Tomás's call to the authorities kills everyone, for nobody is left untouched by that act. Just as his father had predicted, Tomás has taken the law of the land and converted it into his own law and there are no easy answers. This play is about the living, not the dead, yet Don Miguel's presence is literally felt by that long, hand-carved wooden table that serves the play so well. The wood is Don Miguel's heart and soul and we cannot look at it without seeing him, carving it from a beautiful piece of Mexican timber a generation ago. The table is Mexico, just as it is a corporate conference table on which cocaine is snorted and lives are decided upon.

There is another ghost in this play, Camacho, the brothers' henchman who is burned alive because they believe he called the authorities. Tomás tells the others that he was the informant, not Camacho, but they do not believe him and we sit in horror as Camacho is taken off by the hired killer and we hear his screams. It is a Renaissance moment of utter terror. At the beginning of Act 2 Tomás goes to the place where Camacho was immolated, calling out his name. Camacho appears and Tomás tells him, ["I don't understand what killed you, my brothers' law, or the law of the land."] To which Camacho replies ["What's the point? They both kill."](46) Then, Don Miguel appears and he and Camacho measure out a piece of wood for an unidentified piece of furniture. The two then fade into darkness as Tomás reflects on what is happening to him and to his family. The dead men can talk to Tomás but they cannot help him and he can no longer help himself.

Conclusions

In most of the plays discussed in this chapter, we find ordinary people in extraordinary circumstances, events that place them in the presence of *El Misterio*. While the dead characters are extraordinary because they are dead, of the living characters, the only truly extraordinary individuals are Belarmino in *The Shrunken Head of Pancho Villa* and Cerezita in *Heroes and Saints*. While it is their fragmented physicality that makes Belarmino and Cerezita extraordinary, Cerezita's intellect, her thought processes, also make her extraordinary. Further, the fact that Cerezita takes action and in so doing incites the entire town to follow her, places her in a category above the ordinary human being. Belarmino, on the other hand, remains powerless to the end of his story, waiting patiently for his mother to place his head on Joaquin's headless body. Cerezita shifts from fragmented inaction to subjectivity, from impotent victim to community sacrifice. The mystery of their condition, the question of how they can live without a body informs our responses to Belarmino and Cerezita. The closer we are to a Mexican view of life and death, the closer we can come to these two characters, their situations and their outcomes.

Questions of Life and Death permeate all of these plays. While we ponder what keeps heads without bodies functioning in the first two plays, we watch with either amusement or fear in the last four plays that bring the dead back to the living. In *My Visits With MGM, August 29th, Man of the Flesh* and *Santos & Santos*, we find two distinct functions for the dead characters, the benevolent spirit and the avenging ghost. In *Man of the Flesh*, Octavio Solis creates a mother whose ghost returns to test and then to punish her own son, when he fails her test three times. Thus, she becomes a spirit in the medieval tradition of the dead who return to punish the sinner, even if this sinner is her own son. She transforms into Death as allegorical character, gives Juan the Kiss of Death and drags him to Hell kicking and screaming, reminding us of the Spanish religious dramas that portrayed the disastrous fate that awaits all sinners. In his re-working of the Don Juan myth, Solis sees Death as many-faceted and with many faces, from benevolent mother to avenging devil.

In each of these plays, we are introduced to characters who return from the dead to guide the living in their daily struggles, to lead them to the correct decisions, or to watch helplessly as they destroy their lives. It is the dead who inspire the living to take their lives into their own hands and get out of their present condition. However, each of the dead characters has limited powers over the living. Juan's mother cannot change her son's behavior, although she tries and the ghost of the father in *Santos & Santos* does not and cannot stop his sons' deadly course. Camacho's ghost functions in Tomás's memory, perhaps to rid himself of his guilt, but nothing more. Marta Grande cannot stop her selfish sister from taking her house away from Marta Feliz. And the ghost of Rubén Salazar apparently cannot see the events that transpired after his assassination: he must be informed of what happened after his death. Thus, these playwrights do not romanticize death, they do not give the dead characters powers beyond the ability to return to the living until their job is done.

Most of the plays discussed in this chapter employ indigenous symbols as a means of evoking *El Misterio*, whether through the sounds of drums or indigenous flutes, or in visual examples as basic as the corn growing in a garden. Cherríe Moraga's Cerezita is most conscious of indigenous philosophy, especially the Maya, and her knowledge informs her greater purpose.

She is both Mayan sacrifice and Christian martyr, dedicating her life to her community. In *Santos & Santos* one of the brothers is constantly referring to his Aztec heritage in an effort to give himself greater significance. In contrast, Edit Villareal pokes fun at too much adoration of the Aztecs. The young Marta Feliz refers to the Aztecs as a refuge from the horrors of adolescence and tells her grandmother, "I'll kill myself and go to Aztec heaven with birds all around me." But the pragmatic Marta Grande responds, "Forget the pinche Aztecas, mi'ja" (stupid Aztecs, my daughter) (Feyder, *Shattering the Myth*, p. 157). Certainly, Villareal does not dismiss indigenous cultures, as she stated in her introduction to *The Language of Flowers*. But Grande's retort is a reminder of the grandmother's pragmatic and Protestant nature.

Another example of the indigenous influences upon these playwrights is the Dia de los Muertos as the setting for the plays. Villareal's *The Language of Flowers*, and Solis's *Man of the Flesh,* both take place on the Day of the Dead and both plays are suffused with a visible and invisible sense of the afterlife.[61] We see the ghost of Juan's mother throughout Solis's play and we sense the presence of death through the overriding imagery of *calaveras* (skeletons) cavorting about the setting in Villareal's parable. But the operative word here is "cavorting." The distinction between Solis' view of death in *Man of the Flesh* and Villareal's portrayal in *The Language of Flowers* and *My Visits With MGM* is that the former uses death as a punishment and the latter employs death as just another step in the mystical process of living. In Villareal's two plays there is joyous dancing in the afterlife. Whether it's an Aztec Heaven her characters go to depends upon the viewer.

Certainly, Mechicana/os are not alone in their fascination with death. What cultures are not concerned with the question of what awaits us when we leave this earth? In the plays I have discussed here, there is no singular vision of death, no common thread that binds the plays and playwrights in a "Chicano view of death." But what these playwrights do share is a conflation of Roman Catholic and indigenous beliefs and in those contradictions express a view of death that cannot be removed from the Chicana/o experience – the so-called post-modern experience of fragmentation, dislocation and alienation that comes from being marginalized in their own homeland. This fragmentation moves these playwrights to seek Mexican and indigenous symbols as they confront the universal mysteries.

---

[61] For another adaptation of the Don Juan myth, see Carlos Morton's *Johnny Tenorio* in his *Johnny Tenorio and Other Plays* (Houston: Arte Publico, 1992), pp. 25–52. Morton, too, invokes pre-Columbian thought and imagery in his contemporary vision of a Chicano libertine. Edit Villareals' reviews of my production of this play are cited above, note 28.

3

Redemption:

looking for miracles in a man's church

"But Florinda was not happy as a Holy Roller either. Living in the United States convinced her that here, voodoo was necessary."

Marta Feliz, in *My Visits With MGM (My Grandmother Marta)*[1]

Celestial sound as a white narrow shaft of light falls on Angela. She levitates, her wings spreading.

Roosters[2]

JUDGE   Are you saying nuns . . . do not have the same rights priests do?
BISHOP WESTERN   Yes.

La Guadalupe Que Camina[3]

Introduction

In this chapter I am interested in how Chicana/o playwrights are continuing the tradition of the Spanish colonial religious dramas by dramatizing representatives of the Church, miracles and other spiritual events. What brings these plays together is the playwright's interest in Christian doctrine, redemption, as taught by the Roman Catholic Church. However, with the exception of Milcha Sanchez-Scott, all of the playwrights I will discuss contest and subvert the historical influences of the Roman Catholic Church and individuals within that institution. I will therefore be looking at how the playwrights perceive the role of the Church, its teachings and influence as I attempt to identify those elements in their plays that also determine a Chicana/o mythos. Why has the Church been so important in the lives of

[1] Linda Feyder (ed.), *Shattering the Myth* (Houston: Arte Publico, 1992), p. 151.
[2] Milcha Sanchez-Scott, *Roosters,* in Elizabeth Osborn (ed.), *On New Ground* (New York: Theatre Communications Group, 1987), p. 279.
[3] Beverly Sanchez-Padilla, *La Guadalupe Que Camina,* unpub. ms., December 14, 1990, p. 31.

these communities and to what extent has the Church prompted the kinds of dramatic statements these playwrights are making? This discussion focuses on the Roman Catholic Church, because I have yet to read or see a Chicana/o play which includes ministers or other representatives of Protestant denominations on stage.

The only playwright I discuss in this book who was not raised in the Roman Catholic faith is Edit Villareal, who was born into a Mexican Protestant family. It seems that Chicana/o playwrights' religious background reflects the demographics of the broader Mechicano communities; the majority of Mechicanos continue to call themselves Roman Catholic. And although there is a very active movement of Protestant, evangelical churches in many barrios, they represent a small minority of the general Mechicano population. Thus, the plays I will discuss only portray priests or, in a few instances, nuns. In most cases the priests are major characters but in only one play is a nun the central figure. As might be expected, male religious figures dominate on the stage, as they do in real life. In most cases, the individuals represent more than their characters, for they are not depicted in isolation from the Church.

The role of the Church in the evolution of a Mechicano consciousness is well documented by scholars in various disciplines and has not been ignored by Mechicana/o teatros and playwrights. The Church and its teachings have engaged and enraged Chicana and Chicano dramatists because the Institution has fascinated, sustained and frustrated the people for centuries. There is a certain irony in looking at how the Church is represented by Chicana/o playwrights. As discussed in chapter 2 it was the Church itself that kept a theatrical tradition alive in the Spanish-speaking communities long before people began to call themselves "Chicana/o." Further, as discussed in chapter 1, I believe Chicano theatre has its roots in both the indigenous rituals practiced before the Conquest and in the Spanish-language religious theatre that the conquering Spaniards employed to proselytize the natives.[4] In the plays I will discuss indigenous gods and concepts keep cropping up where least expected, mingling with the Christian saints, just as they did in ancient times.

Long before the Conquest the Spanish Church fostered a form of religious drama, termed *autos sacramentales*, that were short religious presentations, usually based on biblical events as well as allegorical treatments of Christian doctrine. The autos were brought to the New World early in the

---

[4] See Jorge Huerta, *Chicano Theater: Themes and Forms* (Tempe: Bilingual Press, 1982), pp. 187–94.

sixteenth century by the Spaniards, who produced the plays as symbol and representation of Christian faith. Autos such as *Adan y Eva* (*Adam and Eve*) and *El sacrificio de Isaac* (*The Sacrifice of Isaac*) were successfully employed to convert the natives to Christianity; other autos often frightened the indigenous people with medieval images of devils, Hell and damnation.[5] The *autos* were later brought to the northern reaches of Nueva España and survive to this day in barrio churches throughout the United States.[6]

Many contemporary teatros are also reinscribing this tradition by producing plays such as *La Pastorela* (*The Shepherd's Play*) and *Las cuatro apariciones de la Virgen de Guadalupe a Juan Diego* (*The Four Appearances of the Virgin of Guadalupe to Juan Diego*) in churches and secular spaces to large, devout crowds. The latter play is probably the most produced Spanish religious folk play to date, confirming that the Miracle of the Virgin's appearances five centuries ago remains a potent force. In the words of Milcha Sanchez-Scott, "We believe in miracles. We need them."[7] Thus, in this investigation of redemption in Chicana/o drama, I will discuss those plays that demonstrate the strong influences of the Roman Catholic Church in the Mechicana/o communities.

Irreverent visions of God, the Devil, Heaven and Hell

Carlos Morton

One of the first Chicano playwrights to challenge Church doctrine and practice is Carlos Morton. Like Luis Valdez and Estela Portillo-Trambley, Morton is another playwright who has earned the rank of "*veterano*," for he has been writing and publishing plays, reviews and critiques of Chicano and Latino theatre since the 1970s. Morton was born in 1947 in Chicago but as the son of a military man, he grew up all over the world. Morton's initial interpretation of the Chicano was thus that of a citizen of the world, someone who had to recapture his Mexican identity almost as an outsider,

---

[5] For more on the early Colonial Church dramas see Marilyn Ekdahl Ravicz, *Early Colonial Religious Drama in Mexico: From Tzompantli to Golgotha* (Washington: Catholic University, 1970).

[6] For more on early religious folk theatre in the Southwest, see: Arthur Campa, *Spanish Religious Folk Theatre of the Southwest* (Albuquerque: University of New Mexico, 1934); and Aurora Lucero-White Lea, *Literary Folklore of the Hispanic Southwest* (San Antonio: Naylor Company, 1953).

[7] Jan Breslauer, "Southwest Passage," *Los Angeles Times*, May 23, 1993, *Calendar*, p. 3.

looking in. He began writing plays in the early 1970s, during undergraduate studies at the University of Texas at El Paso. By living and studying in
the Southwest, the peripatetic playwright initiated a re-connection with his
Mechicano and Spanish religious roots, leading him to write plays that
reflected a Judeo-Christian/indigenous view of man in his cosmos: *El jardín*
and *El cuento de Pancho Diablo*, plays that I will discuss below.

Morton was admitted into the graduate program in playwriting at the
University of California, San Diego, in 1976 and completed the M.F.A in
1978. After completing his M.F.A., Morton worked with the San Francisco
Mime Troupe and taught Chicano theatre courses at the University of
California, Berkeley from 1979 till 1981. From California, Morton and his
wife, Azalea, moved to San Antonio, Texas, where he worked with the
Theatre Program of the Guadalupe Cultural Arts Center. The following
year, the Mortons moved to Austin, Texas where he enrolled in the Ph.D.
program in Theatre. He completed his doctorate in theatre in 1987 at Austin
and taught for one year at the University of Texas, El Paso, before moving
with his wife and their two young sons to take a position in the Department
of Theatre at the University of California, Riverside, in 1990, where he is
currently a full professor of Theatre.

Morton's oeuvre is extensive and varied. He has published many articles
about Chicano and Latino theatre, published two anthologies of his plays,
and has also published individual plays in other collections. He published
his first anthology, *The Many Deaths of Danny Rosales and Other Plays*, in
1983 with *Rancho Hollywood*, *Los Dorados*, about the arrival of the Spaniards
to California, and *El jardín* complementing the title play. Morton is also
unique in that he has published an anthology of plays by Mexican playwrights in English translation.[8] He has written for television and also
created a very successful series of Spanish-language dramas for Mexican
radio. His plays have been produced by grass-roots and professional teatros,
universities and regional theatres all over the United States and Mexico.
Among his achievements, his *Many Deaths of Danny Rosales* won the New
York Shakespeare Festival's "Hispanic Playwrights Festival Award" in 1986
and his *Pancho Diablo* was honored with a fully staged workshop production at the same "Festival Latino" the following year. In 1988 I directed
Morton's version of the Don Juan myth, *Johnny Tenorio*, with undergraduate students at U C S D and toured this production to Spain, France and

---

[8] Carlos Morton (Trans.), *The Fickle Finger of Lady Death and Other Plays* (New York: Peter Lang, 1996).

(then) West Germany.[9] That same summer I directed a professional production of his *El jardín* for the Puerto Rican Travelling Theatre in New York City.

In 1992 Morton published his second volume of plays titled *Johnny Tenorio and Other Plays*. The other plays in this collection are *The Savior*, a serious drama about the assassination of Archbishop Oscar Romero in El Salvador in 1980; *The Miser of Mexico*, an adaptation of Molière's comedy; and *Pancho Diablo*. In 1995 I directed Morton's English translation of Mexican playwright, Eduardo Rodríguez Solis's comedy about death, *Las ondas de La Catrina* [*The Fickle Finger of Lady Death*] for the Puerto Rican Travelling Theatre.[10] In 1996 the prestigious *Compañía Nacional de Mexico*, in Mexico City, produced a Spanish-language version of *Rancho Hollywood*, translated and directed by Iona Weissberg.[11]

Morton's most produced play to date is one of his first, the docudrama titled *The Many Deaths of Danny Rosales*.[12] The first version of this play was created in collaboration with Morton's fellow first-year graduate students at UCSD, directed by Bennett McClellan in 1976 as an exercise in the collective creation process. The play was inspired by the apparent murder of a young Chicano, Richard Morales, by a Texas police chief in 1974.[13] Unfortunately, the theme of police violence against people of color and the economically challenged continues to plague our com-

---

[9] For an account of that production and European tour, see Edit Villareal, "El Teatro Ensemble de UCSD: First International Tour," *The Americas Review* 17 2 (Summer 1989), 73–83; and "Los Vendidos . . . Johnny Tenorio . . . El Teatro Ensemble de UCSD International Tour," *Theatre Journal* 41 2 (May 1989), 231–33.

[10] See my article: "Taking 'La Catrina' to the Streets: A Mexican Play About Death in New York City's *Barrios*." In Geneviève Fabre and Catherine Lejeune (eds.), *Cultures de la Rue: Les barrios d'Amérique du Nord* (Paris: Cahiers Charles V, Université Paris 7 Denis Diderot, 1996), pp. 77–89. The English translation of this play is published in Carlos Morton (trans.), *Fickle Finger*, cited above, pp. 57–82.

[11] *Rancho Hollywood* is in: Carlos Morton, *The Many Deaths of Danny Rosales and Other Plays* (Houston: Arte Publico, 1983), pp. 50–86; James Howe and William Stephany (eds.), *The McGraw Hill Book of Drama* (New York: McGraw Hill, 1995), pp. 978–98.

[12] Initially titled *Las Many muertes de Richard Morales* and published in *Tejidos* (Austin), Vol. 1, No. 3 (Spring 1977), 28–50. The play was subsequently revised and re-titled *Las muchas muertes de Richard Morales* [*The Many Deaths of Richard Morales*] and published in *Conjunto*, Casa de las Americas La Habana, Cuba, No. 44 (abril–junio 1980), 74–109. *The Many Deaths of Danny Rosales* is in Carlos Morton, *The Many Deaths of Danny Rosales*, pp. 7–49; Sylvan Burnet, Morton Berman, William Burto and Ben Draya (eds.), *Types of Drama* (R. R. Donnelley & Sons, 1997), pp. 809–32. The play has also been translated into Spanish, *Las muchas muertes de Danny Rosales*, and is in David Olguin (ed.), *Teatro Norteamericano Contemporaneo* (Mexico City: Ediciones el Milagro, 1995), pp. 324–95.

[13] See Huerta, *Chicano Theater*, pp. 167–73 for more on *Las Muchas muertes de Richard Morales*.

munities.[14] *The Many Deaths of Danny Rosales* is a penetrating indictment of the legal, judicial and police systems of this country and an important docu-drama that does not lose its topicality.[15]

Finding redemption after the Garden of Eden: El jardín

One of Morton's first plays, *El jardín*, was initially published in 1974 and directed by the playwright for the Mecha student organization at Harvard University in 1975.[16] Ironically, this play has a centuries-old predecessor, the Spanish *auto sacramental* titled "Adan y Eva," mentioned earlier in the introduction to this chapter. Unlike his sixteenth-century predecessors, however, Morton is not interested in devout or fearful tears. Instead, he takes an irreverent attitude in his comedy using the Old Testament tale of temptation and fall from Grace as a point of departure for a contemporary vision of the Chicanos' post-modern, post-colonial condition. Time is irrelevant in this quickly paced comedy which opens in The Garden and ends in contemporary Chicago.

By taking his audience back to The Beginning, the original Paradise, Morton is placing his characters in a theological context, reminding us of the teachings of the Church. He also contextualizes Adan and Eva as Mechicanos by having Eva crave Mexican foods and saying: "He's [Dios] the big ranchero. We're nothing but peons!" (Morton, *Many Deaths*, p. 108). Thus this Paradise represents the Americas before the arrival of the Spaniards and other western Europeans, while the playwright also exposes certain negative and topical aspects of contemporary society. And because the characters are allegories or archetypes, they gain a broader significance. Like the characters in the medieval mystery and miracle plays and the Spanish *autos sacramentales*, these people are not human individuals but concepts being dramatized. God and the Serpent are allegories for Good and Evil, and Adam and Eve become archetypal Chicana Mother and Chicano Father.

Although we never see the Church in this play, we do see and hear God the Father, the Serpent, and representatives of the Church in the form of

[14] For an interesting analysis of this play by a professor who also acted in a production in Texas, see Edith E. Pross, "A Chicano Play and Its Audience," *The Americas Review* 19, 1 (1986), 71–79.

[15] See my discussion of The Latino Lab's *August 29th* in chapter 2 as another important docu-drama about police violence.

[16] The first version of *El jardín* is in *El Grito* 7 (June–August 1974), pp. 7–37; a revised version is in Carlos Morton, *The Many Deaths of Danny Rosales and Other Plays* (Houston: Arte Publico, 1983), pp. 105–28. All references are to the 1983 version.

priests. Adapting the original narrative to a Southwestern context, Morton has the Serpent tempt Eva with a cactus apple. She is at first reticent to bite, but the Serpent then shows Eva the future of her people, telling her: "You live in Paradise worshipping the Lord who will one day come with the conquistadores" (110). The Serpent warns Eva: "the Europeans will use God's name to conquer our people and there will be centuries of oppression" (112). We then see Dios playing Columbus and Adan portraying the native in a "flashforward." Again, the playwright emphasizes the obvious connections between the past and the present, between the Church and the autocratic state.

The Serpent transforms into a variety of politically charged incarnations, such as Richard Nixon and "Padre Ladrón," a lecherous priest whose name means "thief." By purposefully having the Serpent take on other villainous types, Morton underscores his commentary on these (then) current politicians and (recurrent) wayward priests. Either God, or the Church, or both, have failed Humanity, Morton tells his audience. Morton employs Judeo-Christian archetypes within a Chicano context in order to challenge the Church and its custodians. However, like all of the other playwrights discussed in this book, Morton does not condemn spirituality. He maintains a positive attitude towards a Supreme Being even as he satirizes Chicano icons.

In fact, after He has vanquished the Serpent, Dios tells Eva that "The New Church has made a commitment to help those who need it the most" (124), obliquely referring to the Theology of Liberation which was gaining currency in Latin America when the play was first written. Dios blames the leaders of the Church for ignoring Latin America's problems. At the conclusion, the Serpent begs Dios for forgiveness and the Almighty says "Perhaps we can arrange a minor place for you in Purgatory," as the two walk off the stage, conversing like the old friends they are (128). Perhaps there is hope for Mankind in Morton's examination of the Fall, for Adan and Eva find redemption in Dios's own discovery of a world gone wrong.

The Devil resigns his post in Hell: El cuento de Pancho Diablo

Morton's sequel to *El jardín*, *El cuento de Pancho Diablo*, was first written in 1974 and published in 1976.[17] A revised version of the play was produced by

---

[17] Carlos Morton, *El cuento de Pancho Diablo* was first published under that title in *El Grito del Sol* 1 (July–September 1976), 39–85. It was subsequently published as *Pancho Diablo* in Carlos Morton, *Johnny Tenorio and Other Plays* (Houston: Arte Publico, 1992), 153–92. All references to this play are to the 1992 version.

the New York Shakespeare Festival's "Festival Latino" in 1987 with the shortened title of *Pancho Diablo*, directed by the late Marvin Felix Camillo. This play is a raucous, bawdy spectacle not based on any biblical referents, but inspired by Milton's *Paradise Lost*. In Morton's play the Devil resigns his post in Hell and ascends to Houston ("It reminds me of home, hot and steamy") where he founds a funeral parlor, called "Pancho's Palacio" (Morton, *Johnny Tenorio*, p. 166). Dios "descends" to earth as a Texas Ranger and confronts his nemesis, El Diablo, continuing the eternal struggle between Good and Evil. Again, the playwright's impiety is tempered with respect while he deconstructs Church dogma. Although other characters are apprehensive, Dios forgives El Diablo in the end, redeeming the Evil One while the playwright symbolically redeems God by making him a God who is aware of the problems in the world and ready to do something about them.

In both *El jardín* and *Pancho Diablo*, Morton creates a theatrical world of saints and sinners who reflect our own human foibles and weaknesses in a fantasy world. Both plays employ songs to further the narrative and both are anachronistic and episodic, travelling through time and space with abandon. These early plays serve as backdrop to the next generation of playwrights: Chicanas and Chicanos who also satirize and comment upon the Church and its representatives even as they believe in miracles.

Reinscribing the miracle play

Milcha Sanchez-Scott

One of the more visible playwrights who have written plays that affirm the Mechicana/os spirituality is Milcha Sanchez-Scott. Her best-known play, *Roosters*, is a modern miracle play and was the most produced Chicana/o play during the late 1980s, bringing much attention to the playwright and her works. Although Sanchez-Scott does not call herself a Chicana, she has captured the essence of the Chicano spirit in several of her plays and became the second Latina playwright (writing about Chicana/os) to gain prominence after Estela Portillo-Trambley.[18] Born in 1955 on the island of Bali, Sanchez-Scott's mother was Indonesian, Chinese and Dutch and her father a Colombian who was raised in Colombia as well as in Mexico. Her father's

---

[18] I use the term, "Latina," to describe Sanchez-Scott since she is not really of Mexican descent. By employing that term, however, I must acknowledge (remind) the reader that the first truly prominent Latina playwright was Maria Irene Fornes.

work as an agronomist took him all over the world and she spent much of her early school years in a Catholic girls school near London, where she learned to speak English. When she was fourteen her family moved to La Jolla, California, where she discovered what it means to be marginalized for the color of one's skin. While she was waiting for the school bus, an obnoxious boy threw a pebble at her and shouted: "This isn't the Mexican bus stop. You have to go to the Mexican bus stop!"[19] Fortunately, Sanchez-Scott was not dissuaded from her creative endeavors by young racists.

From childhood, Sanchez-Scott has displayed a vivid and creative imagination, inspired, in part, by her summers and Christmas holidays in Colombia with family members. Talking about her distinctly Latin American world-view, Sanchez-Scott recalled how "we say things in Colombia: 'Do you remember the day all the birds flew into the bedroom'?" (Osborn, *On New Ground*, p. 246). Images like this lent themselves to the concept of "magical realism," a genre the playwright has not denied, but rather, embraced. In fact, Sanchez-Scott is the only playwright discussed in this chapter who calls herself a "magical realist." In the words of director Peter Brosius: "For Milcha, magic realism is not a genre so much as it is a way of life . . . One isn't grafted onto the other. It's just part of the perceptual apparatus she brings to the world every day."[20] Initially, the playwright wanted to be an actress but the seeds of *el misterio* were firmly planted in her imagination and in time, she would find her writer's muses and a theatricality that reflected her particular view of Latina/o cultures.

Sanchez-Scott attended parochial schools and then entered the University of San Diego where she studied literature, philosophy and theatre. After graduating from college, she moved to Los Angeles to pursue an acting career. Discouraged by the paucity of roles in Hollywood for Latina/o actors, Sanchez-Scott turned to playwriting. Her first play, *Latina*, was based on her experiences working as a receptionist in a maid's agency in Beverly Hills while awaiting "the Big Break" all Hollywood actors dream of.[21] This play was first produced by the New Works Division of Los Angeles-based Artists in Prison and Other Places (Susan Lowenberg, Producing Director), in 1980. The play was written in collaboration with and directed by Jeremy Blahnik.

Latina is a realistic play set in the offices of the Felix Sanchez Domestic Agency. Sarita, the central (and autobiographical) character, narrates the

[19] Elizabeth Osborn, *On New Ground* (New York: TCG Publications, 1987), p. 245.
[20] Howard Allen, "Matadors and Mysteries," *American Theatre* (January 1995), p. 12.
[21] *Latina* is in Huerta, *Necessary Theater*, pp. 75–141.

story, breaking the fourth wall to comment to the audience as events unfold in a typical day in a Beverly Hills domestic agency. Although she was writing an ostensibly realistic play, distortions of reality crept into her playwriting from the beginning. The playwright uses images that only the audience and Sarita can see to reveal her inner thoughts and personal demons. In a nod to surrealism, mannequins come alive to speak to Sarita. We are also witnesses to flashbacks of the (Anglo) nuns that helped mold Sarita's personality. The flashbacks are very brief but establish the importance of early teachers in Sarita's development. One nun represents a Western European bias while the other encourages Sarita to appreciate her Mexican heritage rather than to deny her roots. These visions are captured within the conventions of selective realism in a microcosm of Latin American women seeking the "American Dream" while Sarita eventually learns to embrace her cultural roots.[22] The three appearances by the nuns are very brief but their impact on Sarita's character is important and telling. By showing one culturally insensitive nun and one nun who attempts to get Sarita to be proud of her Mexican roots, the playwright gives us a balanced picture of "The Good Nun" and "The Bad Nun."

Miraculous Latinas: Dog Lady and The Cuban Swimmer

After the success of *Latina*, Susan Lowenberg commissioned Sanchez-Scott to write another play, resulting in two one-acts which venture even further into the realm of mystery and miracles: *The Cuban Swimmer* and *Dog Lady*, first developed as a special project for Los Angeles Theatre Works in 1982. In 1983–84 Sanchez-Scott participated in Maria Irene Fornes' Hispanic Playwright's-in-Residence Laboratory, an experience she calls "the best thing that ever happened to me."[23] While in residence with Fornes, Sanchez-Scott was able to finesse *Dog Lady* and *The Cuban Swimmer*, and to begin work on *Roosters*, to be discussed more fully below.

Both of the one-act plays center on young Latina athletes as metaphor for all Latinas striving for success and recognition in this society as young women and as Latinas. *Dog Lady* is a delightful comedy that concerns Rosalinda, a young Chicana long-distance runner living in East Los Angeles.[24] Rosalinda is intent on winning an up-coming race and does so,

---

[22] For more on *Latina*, see Alicia Arrizon, *Latina Performance: Traversing the Stage* (Bloomington: Indiana, 1999), pp. 102–15.

[23] Elizabeth Osborn, *On New Ground*, p. 246.

[24] Milcha Sanchez-Scott, *Dog Lady*, TCG Plays in Process, 1984 (Dramatists Play Service, 1989; and Ramon Delgado, (ed.), *Best Short Plays of 1986* (New York: Applause Books, 1986).

with special assistance from one of her neighbors, the one everybody calls "the Dog Lady" because of her many dogs. The Dog Lady has special powers, it seems, and is able to give Rosalinda canine running abilities that enable her to run faster than her competitors. Rosalinda also acquires some very canine-like characteristics, which adds to the humor. Still, the play relies on the audience's willingness to believe in the Dog Lady's power. To believe, as does the playwright, in the Miracle.

Dog Lady is usually produced with its sister one-act, *The Cuban Swimmer*, about Margarita Suarez, who is swimming to Catalina Island, off the coast of Los Angeles, in a race.[25] Margarita's family is following her in their boat, with her father coaching her to win in order to bring recognition to the family of Cuban immigrants. While we do not actually see Rosalinda's unnatural powers during her (offstage) race in *Dog Lady*, in *The Cuban Swimmer* the playwright asks the audience to believe that the girl is actually swimming on stage, both above and under the water. In seven short scenes, we follow the family and Margarita, learning a little about them, their history and their dreams as the race drags on. Sanchez-Scott thus combines magic with realism in this first experiment with the literary genre and its challenges on stage.

An example of literary magical realism in *The Cuban Swimmer* is a brief monologue by the grandmother, in which she describes a supernatural event as though there is no question that it really happened. She is talking about an event that occurred on the island of Cuba, "home":

> . . . they say one day it rained blood. All the people, they run into their houses. They cry, they pray, pero [but] your great-grandmother Luz she had cojones ["balls"] like a man. She run outside. She look straight at the sky. She shake her fist. And she say to the evil one, "Mira . . . (Beating her chest) coño, Diablo, aqui estoy si me quieres" [Look . . . damn Devil, here I am if you want me]. And she open her mouth, and she drunk the blood.
> (Sanchez-Scott, *The Cuban Swimmer*, p. 9)

The grandmother's brief account is a literary technique rather than a theatrical one. In other words, instead of attempting to recreate this phenomenon on stage, the playwright has a character describe what happened. Since the event is narrated, not portrayed on stage, it functions on a mental level; the playwright is asking the audience to visualize the blood raining down, a special effect that could be difficult to stage. She is also asking the audience to believe in the Devil.

---

[25] Milcha Sanchez-Scott, *The Cuban Swimmer* (New York: Theatre Communications Group, Plays in Process, Vol. v, No. 12).

The grandmother's narrative works more easily on stage than the other "magical" event in this play when Margarita appears to drown and the stage directions tell us: "SHE becomes disoriented and falls to the bottom of the sea. Special on MARGARITA at the bottom of the sea" (15). This is a director's and designer's dream or nightmare, but so is the idea of staging Margarita swimming, her family on a boat and a helicopter overhead. Sanchez-Scott has always been fascinated by occurrences that defy logic and she delights in bringing these moments into her theatre. Margarita's rise from the bottom of the sea is another example of the playwright's vision of a world of magic and miracles. Apparently, the New York production at INTAR was quite effective, directed by INTAR's Artistic Director, Max Ferra. Elisa de la Roche describes that production as:

> . . . lyrical, magical, enchanted: a fantasy combining surrealism with naturalism . . . The striking sets by Ming Cho Lee had an exaggerated perspective which gave a wide angle spectacle, using hot orange and pink for the freeway and sunset in California, and blue on blue for the ocean, with a white boat and a red helicopter (red, white and blue are the colors of the Cuban flag. . .).[26]

Looking for miracles in the sky: Evening Star

Another important work in Sanchez-Scott's trajectory, *Evening Star*, was first produced by Theatre for a New Audience in New York City in 1988, directed by Paul Zimet.[27] In this extended one-act, Sanchez-Scott takes us into a day in the lives of two Latina/o families living next to one another in a barrio in Los Angeles. One family is Cuban and the other an unidentified nationality, probably Chicano. *Evening Star* is a coming-of-age play that revolves around three young people, two fourteen-year-old girls, Olivia and Lilly, and Lilly's sixteen-year-old brother, Junior Rodríguez. The elders are Olivia's Cuban grandparents, Tina and Juan, who have raised her since birth and Mrs. Rodríguez, whose husband abandoned the family several years ago. *Evening Star* is the most realistic of Sanchez-Scott's plays discussed in this chapter. The setting consists of two modest houses; in the foreground is the street, where the Vendor plies his trade and makes his observations of current events.

There are no miracles, per se, in *Evening Star* but the playwright gives us hints at *El Misterio* early in the action. The Vendor's voice opens the play

---

[26] Elisa de la Roche, *Teatro Hispano!: Three Major New York Companies* (New York: Garland, 1995), p. 46.

[27] *Evening Star* is published by Dramatists Play Service (New York, 1989).

with his off-stage lines, "¡Tengo mangos! . . . Mangos y papayas" [I have mangos and papayas], setting a tropical tone with images of the fruit and a definite Spanish rhythm (Sanchez-Scott, *Evening Star*, p. 5). A few lines later the (still unseen) Vendor says, "The sun is sinking. The hour of enchantment, the crack between night and day, the moment of magic is upon us. Are you prepared for the night?" Soon after, the Vendor enters and shouts out, "From the head waters of Rio Negro, I bring you the roots and barks of enchanted trees to guarantee sleep, tranquility and sweet dreams" (6). This again invokes indigenous customs and rituals, the "enchanted trees" bringing us closer to mystical environments and, perhaps, a miracle.

The Vendor adds to the Latino context of this neighborhood, selling herbs and love potions as well as produce. In his first interaction with Olivia's grandmother, Tina, she tells him she has seen a miracle. Tina is staring at a white rose in her garden, a rose she did not plant. "This thing has the scent of the white madonna," he tells her. She tells the Vendor about her vision: "the white rose became . . . the face of the white madonna . . . I could see it . . . growing out of the stem . . . a tiny baby with small thorny breasts" (7). Thinking this must be a sign that she is pregnant, the Vendor tells Tina to see the doctor, but she is too old to conceive. "If not birth," she asks the Vendor, "what could the white rose mean?" (8). The mystery has been established, her vision will be clarified in the course of the play.

Evening Star focuses on the three young people; the title comes from Junior's fascination with the stars and their promise. Junior, the realist, is contrasted with Olivia, the dreamer, while Junior's sister, Lilly, is squarely in the middle of this adolescent trio. Lilly has been acting very strangely and her mother is convinced that her peculiar behavior is caused by unseen forces. "Some spirit is trying to steal her," Mrs. Rodríguez tells Junior (18). We soon discover that Lilly has not been "bewitched," but is pregnant, unmarried and afraid to tell her mother of her condition. With the miraculous white rose as prelude, Lilly's pregnancy has been blessed by the Madonna. Saints and spirits are contrasted with harsh realities in this play that lovingly portrays the three young people and barrio life in general.

Most of Junior's scenes take place on the roof, where he looks for stars in a borrowed telescope. Olivia looks for the fantastical to escape from everyday life. As Junior searches the sky she tells him, "We have to be patient and expect miracles" (6). But Junior does not believe in miracles and tells her to "Look at reality, stop making everything so fantastic and phony." Olivia, responds: "I see reality, I see too much reality . . . It's all around me hard, ugly reality. I just have to turn it into something else or I'll die. . .or stop trying" (21). Just as the evening star will rise and set with the moon, so, too, will life go on in this barrio of broken dreams and bigger promises. The young people are the future and both Junior's practicality and Olivia's fantasy life will make it possible for the next generation to succeed. The miracle of the white rose is prelude to the miracle of all births as evidenced in Lilly's child, about to be born at the end of the play. Lilly, the unwed teenage mother, is redeemed and in her redemption, life will go on.

Not your everyday miracle play: Roosters

As demonstrated in the three one-acts discussed above, all of Sanchez-Scott's published plays written after *Latina* challenge conventional reality, as they evoke *El Misterio*, provoking miracles and affirming Christian faith. Further, her later plays are even more unreal, especially *Roosters*, which was first co-produced by I N T A R and the New York Shakespeare Festival in 1987, directed by Jackson Phippin. Since then the play has been produced by non-Latino and Latino theatres, college and university theatre departments all across the United States and abroad.[28] *Roosters* was also the first play about Chicana/os to be published by *American Theatre* magazine, which accounts for its broad visibility.[29] When it premiered, *Roosters* was the first Chicano play to be seen in New York since *Zoot Suit* (1979), impressing the non-Latino critics as magical realism, with its human dancers portraying fighting cocks and its climactic Ascension, a miracle. Critics have also interpreted *Roosters* as magical realism because of the heightened language, a poetic interpretation of the way working-class Chicanos speak.[30]

    Roosters is a delicately written piece about a Chicano family in crisis, the story of a father's return to a family after serving a seven-year prison term for manslaughter. The six characters in this play represent different types, even archetypes. Sanchez-Scott told an interviewer in 1988, "These people in this play are mythical, archetypal characters: mother/father, madonna/whore, son/daughter."[31] Complementing the immediate family of the

---

[28] *Roosters* was produced by the Bush Theatre Company in London in 1988. *London Theatre Record* 8:18 (1988), 1189–90.

[29] *Roosters* is published in *American Theater* (September 1987), 1–11. It is also published in Osborn, *On New Ground*, pp. 243–80. All references are to the Osborn edition.

[30] *Roosters* was made into a film for P B S in 1993 and had an unsuccessful theatrical release in 1994. The project took years to come to fruition and was fraught with problems. See Jan Breslauer, "Southwest Passage," *Los Angeles Times*, May 23, 1993, *Calendar*, pp. 3, 26–30, for a thorough report on the process. The film is available in video.

[31] Janice Arkatov, "Playwright Enters World of Cockfighting in 'Roosters'," *Los Angeles Times*, June 15, 1988, Part VI, p. 3.

father, mother, son and daughter are the aunt and a Mexican friend of the family, representative of the typical Mechicano extended family. The most significant conflict in the play is between Gallo, the forty-five-year-old father, and his twenty-year-old son, Hector, in a paradigmatic struggle between the old and the young, the man and the boy. Everyone wants Gallo's attention, but he only has eyes for his rooster. Central to the action, however, is Angela, the fifteen-year-old daughter who looks and acts twelve. It is her religious faith and creative imagination that carry the play to its surprising conclusion. Like everybody else in this family, Angela, too, wants to be released from a mundane life in the desert. She plays with dolls dressed as nuns and martyrs and wears tattered old wings in an effort to demonstrate her faith in God. But, according to the playwright, Angela's faith is not fanatical. In Sanchez-Scott's words:

> [Angela] has a whole interior life under the house with saints and angels. It's not that she's a religious fanatic; it's that fantasy is her escape from the harshness of reality: living in the desert with a very poor family and typical Latin role models – her mother is the long-suffering madonna and her aunt is a whore. So she's living under the house, not coming out of childhood.
>
> (Arkatov, "Playwright Enters World of Cockfighting," p. 3)

Gallo opens the play with a poetic monologue that immediately takes us into the realm of the extraordinary: "Lord Eagle, Lord Hawk, sainted ones, spirits and winds, Santa Maria Aurora of the Dawn . . . I want no resentment . . . I want no rancor" (Osborn, *On New Ground,* p. 249). By opening her play with Gallo calling on unseen natural forces and the Virgin Mary, conflating indigenous and Christian concepts, the playwright creates a sense of mystery, preparing us for the miracle that will happen. Gallo's monologue and interaction with the cock establish the beauty and the horror of cock fighting, giving exposition that tells us that he killed a Filipino who caught him borrowing his rooster to mate him in order to produce a winning cock.

Gallo's opening words reflect peace and harmony but the cock fight mirrors a macho vitality associated with strength, blood and chance. When Gallo speaks to Zapata, the product of those matings, played by a male dancer, the audience knows that anything can happen in the world of this play. And it does. After the various conflicts are established by the playwright and we get to know the characters' opposing goals, the inevitable fight between father and son occurs at the climactic moment of the play.

Hector overpowers Gallo and could easily kill him with his knife, but stops short when suddenly Angela levitates. The death fight between father and son is halted and peace envelops the scene. Gallo falls asleep in his wife's lap in a pieta-like pose while the other characters stare up at Angela and the lights slowly fade. In the words of the playwright, "The message is that we have the ability to grow, that we are better than our animal natures" (Arkatov, "Playwright Enters World of Cockfighting," p. 3). In the words of Harry Elam, Jr., "Like an angel, she levitates over her family, bringing about an abrupt end to her family's immediate social crisis . . . Angela's levitation is indicative of a particularly Latino, culturally organized Catholicism. A syncretic faith that unites Christian mythology and Indian mysticism and, as a consequence, accepts the presence of miracles in everyday life." [32]

Elam's assessment of *Roosters* is unique in the study of Chicana/o drama because he discusses this play in relation to an African-American play, August Wilson's *Fences*.[33] He looks at both plays in an attempt to show that "Wilson and Sanchez-Scott purposefully conform to but, also subvert the traditional structural principles and narrative tropes associated with American domestic realism in order to confront issues of familial, and cultural inheritance" (Elam, "Angels and Transcendence," p. 288). Elam concludes his study with the following observation: "The unexpected, non-realistic conclusions to their plays suggest that realism itself is problematic and inadequate to accommodate certain cultural experiences or expressions of the current postmodern condition" (299). Thus, Elam also feels that there is more to the Chicana/o experience than meets the eye. He argues persuasively that plays about the African–American and Chicana/o experiences of necessity enter into the realm of the unknown because that is an integral part of the cultural and spiritual landscapes these two groups occupy.

Along with Gallo's opening lines and Angela's continual references to God and the saints, the play's desert landscape is a constant reminder of *La Tierra, Nuestra Madre*, the Life Force that can give as easily as it can take. For Rachel Chipman Waite the environment takes on a life of its own. She points out that an example of magical realism occurs when Gallo enters the

---

[32] Harry Elam, Jr., "Of Angels and Transcendence: An Analysis of *Fences* by August Wilson and *Roosters* by Milcha Sanchez-Scott," in Marc Maufort (ed.), *Staging Difference: Cultural Pluralism in American Theatre and Drama* (New York, Peter Lang, 1995), p. 289.

[33] Harry Elam, Jr. is the only scholar of whom I am aware who compares and contrasts African-American and Chicano theatre. See his paradigmatic study, *Taking It to the Streets: The Social Protest Theater of Luis Valdez and Amiri Baraka* (Michigan, 1997).

scene for his homecoming. The stage directions read: "The stage darkens, as if smoke from the distant fire has covered the sun. Drum howls are heard. In the distance we hear a rooster crow and the sounds of excited chickens as the henhouse comes to life. Gallo appears" (Osborn, *On New Ground*, p. 260). In her reading of these stage directions, Waite writes: "Gallo's appearance has an effect not only on the members of his family, but a mysterious effect on the natural world."

Waite believes that Sanchez-Scott's parents were both "intimate" with the earth, her father as a botanist and her mother as a professional orchid grower. Thus, Waite concludes, "it is not unusual that earth imagery permeates her plays" (16). Waite believes that the earth images in this play are yet another reminder of the "power and mystery of the natural world" (90). As a vivid example of this imagery, Hector, who is the most poetic of the characters, describes "the daily war" that transpires in the earth, as he prepares to go to the fields to pick the crops:

> . . . the intimidation of violent growth. . .the expanding melons and squashes, the hardiness of potatoes, the waxy purple succulence of eggplant, the potency of ripening tomatoes. All so smug, so ready to burst with sheer generosity and exuberance. They mock me . . . I look to the ground. Slugs, snails, worms slithering in the earth with such ferocious hunger they devour their own tails, flies oozing out larvae, aphids, bees, gnats, caterpillars, their proliferation only slightly dampened by our sprays. We still find eggsacks hiding, ready to burst forth. Their teeming life, their lust, is shameful . . .
>
> (Osborn, *On New Ground*, p. 259)

The sensuous quality of Hector's description, mingling the grotesque with the sexual, the beautiful with the deadly, brings La Tierra and all that inhabit this earth into sharper focus. It is a reminder that we, too, will be food for worms. What separates us, the playwright is asking, from the worms? The answer lies in the miracle that eventually resolves the conflicts.

Blood imagery is also important in this play, beginning with Gallo's first monologue when Zapata draws Gallo's blood and "Gallo contracts in orgasmic pleasure/pain" (250). Later in the play we witness a cockfight portrayed by two male dancers which results in the death of an inferior rooster as Zapata "kills" him. Again blood is drawn and spilled on the ground as Hector narrates his memory of the night his father proved he was a master at cockfighting. Describing the cock, named Quasimoto, Hector says, "He was a whirlwind flashing and slashing like a dark avenging angel then like some distant rainbow star exploding he was hit." Quasimoto seems dead, but Hector's grandfather tells him, "get up. . .up here with me and you will see a miracle." Hector continues:

> You, father, picked up Quasimoto, a lifeless pile of bloody feathers, holding his head oh so gently, you closed your eyes, and like a great wave receding, you drew a breath that came from deep within your ocean floor. I heard the stones rumble, the mountains shift, the topsoil move, and as your breath slammed on the beaches, Quasimoto sputtered back to life. Oh, Papi, breathe on me (263).

In a scene that could only be narrated, as in a Greek tragedy, the images that Hector's memory provokes are stunning and allow the audience members to create their own pictures, enhanced by the two dancers in battle. In the narrative, the ocean is prominent, as a great natural force, but so is the topsoil, without which the desert would give no fruit. Also, as Waite points out, the phrase, "Breathe on me," is repeated three times. First by Hector to Gallo, as seen above, then by Hector to his aunt Chata, and finally to Angela as she ascends. The breath of life is also associated with blood. Blood is everywhere in the narrative and it represents the blood sacrifices of the ancient ones as well as the blood sacrifice of all Chicanas and Chicanos.

The life-giving blood is contrasted with two characters as "Shadows," dark, allegorical figures that represent rancor and resentment – the two forces Gallo renounces in his opening monologue. They are looking for Gallo, ostensibly to avenge the Filipino's death, but they are frightened away by Angela, proving that the evil that surrounds us can be warded-off with faith. The girl who repels evil with her faith becomes a miracle herself, an angel after all. This is what she has longed for and this is what she gets, redeeming herself and her belief in God. It is the playwright's belief as well, for Sanchez-Scott, who is a "child of the world," has found her home in her own Miracle.

Just before the fight between father and son, Angela studies a peach pit and envisions an entire world in miniature, a microscopic island paradise with a little man and a little woman, with halos, holding an even littler baby (Osborn, *On New Ground*, p. 268). It is a heavenly Garden that Angela conjures up, a magical world that only she can see. When she ascends soon after her vision of that paradise, we know that what Angela saw was not a fantasy but real. In both instances, Chata, the realist, reflects the practical side of human nature. When she looks at the peach pit, eager to see what Angela has so delicately described, Chata looks carefully, then retorts: "I can't see dick!" (268). When Angela ascends, it is Chata who once again is cynical. Her response is: "Shit happens . . . been happening all my life, that's all I know" (280). Some might agree with Chata, but Angela's miracle becomes our miracle, if we choose.

Regarding Angela's levitation, Elam compares her character to Cerezita in Cherríe Moraga's *Heroes and Saints,* discussed in chapter 2. He feels that Moraga "appropriates and redefines the image of *La Virgen de Guadalupe* as symbol of female activism and collective struggle," and that Sanchez-Scott's "use of levitation can be linked to that tradition" (Elam, "Angels and Transcendence," p. 298). Having argued that Angela has been marginalized throughout this play, Elam makes the following observation: "Angela. . .has sought transcendence, to be lifted out of the life that has imprisoned her and her family. Her levitation resurrects her faith and forces a reevaluation of her subjectivity by the audience as well as her family. She, who was marginalized, is now symbolically placed in the center of the action" (298).

Angela's levitation transports the audience into the realm of Spanish religious folk theatre, where people believe in miracles. Having seen various productions of this play, and various "solutions" to the technical challenge of staging an ascension, only one production moved me, the world premiere production at INTAR. I went to this play knowing nothing about it and certainly not expecting an ascension at the end. But the production came together for me as I watched Angela "lift" behind the house, above the roof. She only elevated high enough to conceal her feet, but she ascended and the moment was transcending. Although I knew she was being lifted up mechanically or by stage hands, it did not matter to me and I loved the spirituality of the moment. You do not look for the wires when a miracle occurs.[34]

Priests and nuns in a restrictive church

Martyrs and miracles: Heroes and Saints

By her own admission, Cherríe Moraga is a very spiritual woman, but hers is a spirituality removed from patriarchal hierarchies that have subjugated

---

[34] The motion picture of *Roosters* reveals a production team or producers who do not understand the nature of miracles nor of their importance to certain people(s). In the final moments of the film, the last image we see is of Angela jumping off a water tower. Freeze frame. She does not ascend, she does not fall. The believers will "know" that she will ascend, the non-believers will imagine her crashing to the ground, a suicide.

women and the economically oppressed for too long. Moraga's spirituality can be seen in a true reverence for human life, regardless of social standing or sexual orientation. Her spirituality is also inspired by activism. In her Preface to *This Bridge Called My Back*, Moraga writes: "I am not talking here about some lazy faith, where we resign ourselves to the tragic splittings in our lives with an upward turn of the hands or a vicious beating of our breasts . . . It is the faith of activists I am talking about."[35]

Moraga's particular brand of spirituality and faith is clearly reflected in *Heroes and Saints*, first discussed in chapter 2. In this play, Moraga combines the miracle of Cerezita's bodiless condition while also portraying a priest who is sensual, political and committed to the poor. Father Juan is a priest with limitations and desires not often reflected in other contemporary priests Chicanos have dramatized. When Cerezita asks him if he will always be a priest, Juan answers: "Yes. There's no choice in the matter . . . The priesthood is an indelible mark. You are bruised by it, not violently, but it is always felt. A slow dull ache, a slight discoloration in the skin . . ."[36] Still, throughout the play it seems that Juan is reconsidering his decision to become a priest and the consequent limitations on his personal, sexual and political choices.[37]

Juan is also, like the playwright, a "half breed," a character type that had not appeared in any previously produced Chicano play.[38] By making Juan a mixed-breed who can "pass" for Anglo, Moraga adds another dimension to his character. While it is clear that Juan could have ignored his community's needs, blending into the Anglo mainstream, he is a follower of Liberation Theology who chooses to return to his community to help the campesinos. However, the playwright clearly believes that this priest is the exception to the rule among the Church's ministers. When Cerezita's mother, Dolores, first meets Juan, she remarks: "*Pues*, I'm glad you came. Most a the priests, they not like you, they don' come to the house no more unless you got money" (Moraga, *Heroes and Saints*, p. 100).

[35] Gloria Anzaldúa and Cherríe Moraga (eds.), *This Bridge Called My Back: Writings by Radical Women of Color* (New York: Kitchen table, 1981), p. xviii.

[36] Cherríe Moraga, *Heroes and Saints and Other Plays* (Albuquerque: West End Press, 1994), p. 115. All references to the text are from this edition. The play is also published in Kathy A. Perkins and Roberta Uno (eds.) *Contemporary Plays by Women of Color: An Anthology* (London: Routledge, 1996), pp. 230–61.

[37] It should be noted that in Moraga's sequel to *Heroes and Saints, Watsonville* (unpublished), which premiered in 1996, Father Juan has left the priesthood.

[38] As mentioned in chapter 4, Oliver Mayer's play, *Young Valiant*, centers on a bi-cultural (Mexican-Anglo) child. His *Blade to the Heat* also features a bi-cultural Chicano and is also discussed in chapter 4. Like Moraga, Mayer's mother is Chicana and his late father was Anglo.

It was a photo of Cesar Chávez at the end of his 33-day fast that inspired Juan to return to the valley. He tells Cerezita, the central, bodiless character: "I came home to the valley that gave birth to me. Maybe as a priest it's vanity to believe you can have a home. The whole church is supposed to be your family, your community, but I can't pretend I don't get lonely" (115). The church is not enough for this revolutionary priest; he needs his Raza, his people. And they need him.

As a thinker, Juan also enjoys the intellectual challenges Cerezita offers. Early in the play Juan reads the following lines to Cerezita from the Maya book, *Balun Canaan,* establishing his political views as well as a debt to his indigenous, "pagan," ancestors: ". . . And they determined that the rich would care for and protect the poor in as much that through them, the rich had received such benefits" (101). To his surprise and delight Cerezita recites the verse from memory. Juan has met his intellectual equal. She then asks him: "Am I your *pobre,* Father?" (102). It soon becomes clear that Juan is looking for *his* redemption through his work with the poor.

This young priest is a complex character that embodies the multiplicity of the Chicano's search for identity. Juan's search for his cultural, sexual, political and spiritual identity reflects the broader community's confusion and displacement. Although he feels committed to the farm workers' cause and participates in the Union's demonstrations against the growers, Juan vacillates in his resolve. His inaction is contrasted with Cerezita's literal inability to move without her "raite," the machine that she manipulates with her tongue in order to move around the house. The play is about both of these characters taking action that will change society.

Juan takes on the burden of a man who wants a destiny. "I always wanted that kind of sixteenth-century martyr's death," he tells Cerezita. "To die nobly and misunderstood, to be exonerated centuries later by a world that was finally ready for me" (115). But later, when the police brutally attack Amparo as she addresses a political rally, Juan cannot do anything to stop the violence. "I got scared," he tells Cerezita (134). Juan wonders if Cerezita is his *pobre,* as he fights his vacillation between words and deeds, determined to find his true purpose. When the police beat Amparo, Juan, the intellectual, is moved to become Juan, the revolutionary. However, although Juan takes final political action, he cannot commit himself to sexual action. He tells Cerezita why he joined the priesthood: "It was the fabric that drew me, literally the cloth itself that drew me to be a man of the cloth. The vestments, the priest's genitals asleep underneath that cloth, the heavy weight of it pressing against him, tranquilizing him" (115). Thus it is the costume, the <u>performance</u> of the priest that attracted Juan to the role. With his sexual identity "tranquilized" under his ecclesiastic robes, perhaps that is why Juan chose the priesthood. When he first meets him, Mario tells his mother, "I was just helping the man. I mean, the priest" underscoring the distinction (98). Juan, the priest, longs to be Juan, the man.

Cerezita, the bodiless head, and Juan, the man with a body he is not supposed to "use," are in a game of intellectual and sexual foreplay almost from their first meeting. The irony is that while Cerezita has no body, Juan represents male power, an embodiment of the all-powerful Church, yet he has to suppress his body's sexual role. In a scene rarely witnessed in Chicano dramas, Cerezita tries to experience Juan sexually. Juan is standing behind her. He kisses Cerezita's hair, face and mouth, until, "Suddenly Juan's face takes on a distanced look. He grabs Cere's cheeks between his hands." Then she says, "I want to taste you, Juan." He hesitates, then kisses her again as she asks him repeatedly to move in front of her. He pushes his body against her "raite," and comes to orgasm (139–40).

Without undressing, with no truly intimate physical contact, Juan reaches orgasm and rushes out, leaving Cerezita unable to satisfy *her* sexual needs. It is a stunning moment; a curious scene that shocks and compels the audiences I have observed. No other Chicana or Chicano play has demonstrated the sensuality and sexuality of a priest in this manner; in all the other examples, the priests' sexuality is discussed but never shown. The uninhibited eroticism forces us to examine our responses to this act. It is after his orgasm that Juan rushes out to take political action, blending sexual tension, energy and release with political action. Now committed to placing the dead body of Dolores' grandchild on a cross to draw public attention to the children's deaths, he "glows" with excitement.

Cerezita's objective throughout the play has been to get out of the house, to force the world to see her in her condition and thus "speak" about the devastation of the pesticides. But her mother denies her the outside world in an effort to protect them both from ridicule and humiliation. Thus, Cerezita must become "god-like" to persuade her mother to let her go. Cerezita has the children transform her into "La Virgencita" by placing a blue veil over her head (like the Virgin of Guadalupe), causing her mother to let her out of the house and into her destiny. Although the devoutly Roman Catholic Dolores sees this as a miracle, in actuality, Cerezita orchestrates this transformation as her only hope for liberation. Cerezita becomes the bodiless Virgin seeking social justice. Her very life, her existence without a body is wondrous and when the people see her they bow in prayer and amazement. Cerezita *is* a miracle.

Motivated by her helplessness, Cerezita has urged Juan to use his body throughout the play. In reference to the unfulfilled love-making scene, Juan tells Cerezita: "I'm a priest, Cere. I'm not free. My body's not my own" (144). From the literal to the metaphorical, this bodiless-ness has kept both of them from doing what they discover they must. Finally, Juan grants Cerezita her wish. He gives Cerezita her mobility, her body, as he wheels her into the vineyards, fully aware that they could both be shot by the growers' helicopter patrols. Juan has called the television reporter to witness their actions, bringing their imminent slaughter to the eyes of the world. Juan's ultimate commitment to the cause of the farm workers, his own sacrifice, is contrasted with our virtual inaction. Both Cerezita and Juan offer to give their lives; not for the peoples' sins, however, but for the sins of a society that has ignored and abandoned them.

Moraga's priest becomes a man of action who works with and for his people against the forces of the hegemony, as he takes a deadly risk in his desire to be a martyr for the cause. The audience does not really know if Cerezita and Juan die at the end. The stage directions tell us that after he pushes her "raite" into the fields, out of sight, helicopters begin to shower the fields with gunfire, causing the people to rush after them and burn the fields.[39] Whether he lives or dies, Juan is a hero in the eyes of his community. Cerezita will always be known as the Miracle Child and Juan finally achieves his redemption.

Josefina López

Josefina López is unique among the playwrights discussed in this book for several reasons. She is the youngest person I am writing about and she was born in Mexico (1969), rather than the United States. Further, she was brought to this country illegally at the age of five, settling with her family in East Los Angeles. She started grammar school the following year and thus began the process of "Chicano-ization" in the school system and in this society. From her first day in school, López knew that although her parents had green cards, she was undocumented and therefore lived in fear of being deported. But she used her vivid imagination to get her through, living a

---

[39] It is in the (unpublished) sequel to *Heroes and Saints*, *Watsonville*, that we discover that Cerezita died in the final confrontation with the growers' goons. Juan survived to become a full-time activist.

kind of shadow existence for several years until she became a Temporary Resident through the Amnesty Program in 1987. The threat of deportation would inform several of her plays, becoming a kind of leitmotif in the lives of her characters. According to López, she "became a Chicana" at the age of twenty, ostensibly when she no longer feared deportation.

López first started writing plays in the fifth grade. However, her major influences were the televized version of the Teatro Campesino's *La gran carpa de los Rasquachis*, retitled "*El corrido*," and the live production of Luis Valdez's *I Don't Have to Show You No Stinking Badges*. She had seen "*El corrido*" when she was in the 9th grade.[40] "*El corrido*" was taped in part as a stage performance and López could see the possibilities in the staged version. Watching the program, the impressionable and imaginative author felt liberated from the constrictions of realism:

> I thought, wow, I didn't know that theatre could be this way ... that's how I think ... that's what I loved about it, that one moment you're in Mexico and the next [you're in the US] ... transitions and transformation – that's how I think; that it could be an epic, adventuresome ... it doesn't have to stay in one place.[41]

López saw *I Don't Have to Show You No Stinking Badges*, directed by Luis Valdez, at the Los Angeles Theatre Center in 1986, while attending the Los Angeles County High School for the Arts.[42] Yet, while Valdez's play was an inspiration to the young playwright, it also stimulated her emerging feminism. As she searched Luis Valdez's works for a monologue to perform, López discovered that Valdez's female characters "were very flat – all mothers and girlfriends."[43] It is important to remember that López was studying acting in high school with the intention of becoming an actress. Like many female actors who become playwrights, López decided to create her own vehicles to perform. If the male-dominated Teatro Movement was not going to satisfy López's desire to act, she would take matters into her own hands.

López participated in the Los Angeles Theatre Center's Young Playwrights Lab from 1985 to 1988, gaining valuable experience, writing and

[40] The televized version of *La gran carpa de los Rasquichi*, retitled "*El corrido*," was first produced and broadcast by PBS in 1976. López saw a re-broadcast version.

[41] From an unpublished interview with Josefina López in Chicago, Illinois, October 3, 1992.

[42] *I Don't Have to Show You No Stinking Badges* is discussed in chapter 1. It is published in Luis Valdez, *Zoot Suit and Other Plays*.

[43] Judith Green, "She's at that Stage," *San Jose Mercury News*, November 12, 1989, Arts and Books, p. 5.

watching all of the plays she could. Her playwriting career was initiated when *Simply Maria, or the American Dream* was produced as part of the California Young Playwrights' Contest in San Diego, California, in 1988. This simple, yet complex play, directed by a Mexican actor and director, Luis Torner, launched the young playwright on a trajectory that only she could have imagined. Shortly after the San Diego production López participated in Maria Irene Fornes' Hispanic Playwright's-in-Residence Laboratory in New York City in 1988.

A father returns from Hell: Food for the Dead

While in Fornes' workshop López wrote the first draft of her best-known play to date, *Real Women Have Curves*. She then enrolled in the undergraduate program at New York University's Tisch School of the Arts for one year. Whereas the Fornes workshop was a very positive experience for the young playwright, NYU was not as satisfying. Several years later, she wrote: "At that time I felt very alienated. I was the only Latina in my writing class and I felt like no one understood where I was coming from. I was experiencing so much cultural shock that I wanted to write something that celebrated my culture."[44] Roused by her feelings of alienation, López mined creativity out of adversity and began to write a one-act comedy titled *Food for the Dead*. But she had to come back to California to see Chicanas and Chicanos interpreting her characters.

In the fall of 1989 López entered the undergraduate theatre program at UCSD, eager to take advantage of the graduate actors and directors in the newly established graduate program in Hispanic-American theatre."[45] Laura Esparza directed an early draft of *Food for the Dead* in the fall of 1989 with Latina and Latino graduate and undergraduate actors. Although I briefly discuss *Food for the Dead* in chapter 4 for its treatment of a gay Chicano character, the play's real focus is on the liberation of a Mexican mother. Further, the use of devils, Hell and damnation, locate this play in the Spanish religious folk tradition as another modern morality play, complete with Lucifer and a Hells' Mouth spewing fire and smoke.

The action of *Food for the Dead* takes place on Halloween, the night

---

[44] Josefina López, *Food for the Dead (and) La Pinta* (Woodstock, Illinois: Dramatic Publishing Company, 1996), p. 7.

[45] The UCSD Graduate Program in Hispanic American Theatre graduated one class of eight actors and two directors in 1992. I headed the Program and Tony Curiel was also a principal faculty member. The three-year program did not continue due to lack of funding.

Candela is concluding her nine-year mourning period for her husband, Rubén. Her grown children come home for this special event and we learn about each of the characters through their interaction at the dinner table. Candela is finally letting go of Rubén's macho grip. "I am going to say good-bye to Rubén and hello to the new me" she tells her children (López, *Food for the Dead*, p. 13). Candela has only one more house payment, she is taking night school classes and she has even acquired her own credit card. Candela's children, a quartet of "twenty-something" Chicanos, represent an interesting and provocative spectrum of middle-class Chicana/o identities. The oldest son, José, is married, macho and homophobic. Rosario, the oldest daughter is a Beverly Hills attorney looking for a sperm donor. Her youngest daughter, Gloria, is a student at UCLA and wants to move into a commune with her Anglo boyfriend, Siddhartha. And the youngest son, Jesús, is a gay artist. But the most interesting and the most developed of the characters is really Candela. Here is a Mexican mother, liberating herself from the traditional and stereotypical role expected of her.

López is once again critical of Mexican patriarchal values, taking full advantage of her arsenal of creative and humorous devices to ridicule machismo. When Jesús reveals the fact that he is gay, an outraged Rubén returns from the dead and we discover that he is a larger-than-life parody of the Macho husband and father, interested in himself and his appetites alone. All Rubén wants to do before he "Beats the maricón" (fag) out of his son, is eat. When Candela asks him, "Didn't they feed you in hell?" he responds, "Yes, but in hell all the Mexican restaurants are full" (26).

Rubén's excessive behavior and the fact that he went to Hell tell us that he was not a good man. When the Devil arrives, disguised as an Avon Lady, "she" demonstrates a new make up called "Lucifermagic," guaranteed to "cover up black eyes, scars, scratches, cuts on the face . . . Women in East L.A. are placing large orders" (30), inferring that Rubén was abusive. Rubén is indicted by the author with the Devil's litany of physical abuses. Indeed, by telling us that "Lucifermagic" is "selling like hotcakes" in East Los Angeles (30), López implicates an entire community. When Rubén is dragged back "down" to Hell, in the fire and smoke, the moment recalls the very roots of Spanish religious folk theatre. A "miracle" has happened and once the evil man is gone, the family can go on with their lives, free of his macho excesses and redeemed from society's censure.

Figure 7. Real Women Have Curves, by Josefina López. Chingona Productions and Rasquachi Rep, Los Angeles, California, 1998. Directed by Corky Dominguez. L. to R. Julia Vera, Rosalinda Morales, Teresa-Michelle Ruiz, Tina Taylor, Miriam Peniche.

The Chicana Body: Real Women Have Curves

In 1989, López participated in the Teatro de la Esperanza's Isadora Aguirre Latino Playwrighting Lab in San Francisco, California, taught by noted Mexican playwright, Emilio Carballido. With Carballido's guidance she began to write *Real Women Have Curves* and in 1990 the Teatro de la Esperanza produced the world premiere of that play.[46] That production, directed by Hector Correa, was an instant success, particularly with female audiences. *Real Women Have Curves* became the most produced play written by a Chicana or Chicano for several years. The play has been produced by Latino and non-Latino companies – mainstream and community-based – from California to Florida, from Seattle to New York City.

[46] There are three versions of *Real Women Have Curves* in print. I will be working off the version published by The Dramatic Publishing Company, 1996. According to the playwright (telephone conversation March 20, 1999), this is the "official" version of this play.

Like López's *Simply Maria, Real Women Have Curves* is also autobiographical, centering on the character of Ana, a young Chicana who is working in her sister, Estela's, small sewing factory in East Los Angeles. The play takes place over a period of five days during which the women work to finish an order of dresses. The dramatic action is pushed forward by the women's desire to save the financially strapped business, despite various setbacks, and the situation is given comic life by the conversations between the women about life, love, husbands, boyfriends or would-be suitors, and, of course, their bodies. The women finish the order on time, Estela decides to open her own boutique and in the process the women discover and empower themselves as women and creators.

In Virginia McFerran's words, the women discover "that traditional reality and its norms for women are actually completely unrealistic."[47] This is a play about expectations – what society, especially Mechicano culture – expects of its women and how women might negate those expectations on a path towards liberation from the patriarchy. In the epilogue, Ana addresses the audience directly for the first time and concludes the play with a call for women's unity. She then relates how she did, indeed, attend NYU and when she came back her sister had opened her own boutique.

As the title suggests, *Real Women Have Curves* debates and exposes issues of the female body, especially "fat," "large," "plump" or "voluptuous" bodies, depending upon the gaze of the beholder. Based on her actual experiences, both with her body weight and working in her sister's sewing factory, López places her character at the center of the story as narrator and unhappy teenager who would rather be at NYU studying writing. In her analysis, Maria Teresa Marrero conflates the two prevalent issues in this play, body weight and immigrant status: "The fat body, like the immigrant, requires fundamental alteration in order to 'fit,' to be assimilated into the dominant, circulating norms (be they aesthetic or cultural)."[48] Marrero widens the topography of her discussion to include all Latinas struggling to survive in low paying jobs in this country. "To be a woman, undocumented and overweight places these characters as a target in the very center of a three-pronged U.S. cultural bias" (Marrero, "Real Women," p. 67). In other words, "three strikes and you're out."

---

[47] Virginia Derus McFerran, "Chicana Voices in American Drama: Silviana Wood, Estela Portillo-Trambley, Cherríe Moraga, Milcha Sanchez-Scott, Josefina López," Ph.D. dissertation, University of Minnesota, 1991 (Ann Arbor, 1991), p. 210.

[48] Maria Teresa Marrero, "Real Women Have Curves: The Articulation of Fat as a Cultural/Feminist Issue," *Ollantay*, 1 (January 1993), 63.

Reinscribing the conquest: Unconquered Spirits

In 1994–95 López's historical drama, *Unconquered Spirits*, received its world premiere, produced by the Theatre Department of California State University, Northridge, directed by Professor Ana Marie Garcia.[49] *Unconquered Spirits* is López's homage to *La Llorona*, as well as to the Mechicana pecan shellers' who went on strike in San Antonio, Texas in 1938. In her play López combines myth with history, taking her audience back and forth through time and place, from the early twentieth century to the sixteenth century and back. Always, *La Llorona* is a presence and a charac-ter. In this epic historico-mythico play the playwright attempts to draw par-allels between the present and past conditions of women in Mexico and in the United States. She is also intent on redeeming La Llorona and all women from their marginalized and demonized positions.

López serves two histories in this play. She reminds her audience of the abuses of the Colonial Church and she also brings an important event in twentieth-century *Mechicana* (read: women's) labor struggles to light. With *La Llorona* as symbol of all oppressed Mechicanas, *Unconquered Spirits* gives women a voice and a reason. While most tales of *La Llorona* simply tell of this (anonymous) "evil woman who killed her children," few of the story tellers inform their listeners of who she was and why she did what she did. In many versions, *La Llorona* is conflated with *La Malinche*, Cortés's mis-tress and alleged "traitor of the Mexican people." But in the words of Aida Hurtado, ". . . most recently Chicana feminists have reinterpreted La Malinche's role in the conquest of Mexico from traitor to that of a brilliant woman whose ability to learn different languages was unsurpassed by any of her contemporaries."[50] Just as many Chicana writers and critics are re-visiting the Malinche myth, López, too, redeems her, and thus all women, in her version of the *Malinche/Llorona* myth.[51] But the playwright does not redeem the Church.

López's writing and acting careers extend to television as well. In 1993 she was a staff writer for Fox's *Living Single* comedy series and in 1994 she was a writer, performer and segment producer for *Culture Clash*, also for Fox Television. In the fall of 1998 López entered the graduate program in

---

[49] Josefina López, *Unconquered Spirits* (Woodstock, IL: Dramatic Publishing, 1997).

[50] Aida Hurtado, *The Color of Privilege: Three Blasphemies on Race and Feminism* (Michigan, 1996), pp. 56–57.

[51] In his (unpublished) play, *La Malinche*, Carlos Morton also conflates Malinche with La Llorona. See my review of the world premiere, *"La Malinche* at the Arizona Theatre Company," *Latin American Theatre Review* 31 1 (Fall, 1997), 176–77.

screenwriting in the School of Theatre, Film and Television of the University of California at Los Angeles. López's ultimate goal is to found a theatre, film and television production company, empowering other Latinas as well as Latinos to produce their own narratives. While for some, this would be a "miracle," for López it will be the logical outcome of her ambition, talent and tenacity.

Roman Catholic nightmares: Simply Maria, or the American Dream

The last play that I will discuss in this section on Josefina López is actually her first play, *Simply Maria, or The American Dream*, a biting satire of the Roman Catholic Church.[52] This play reflects the highly theatrical early Valdezian/Campesino style in which time and place are irrelevant as the characters traverse international borders by simply crossing the stage. In López's vision the actors transform into any number of characters and allegories in this coming-of-age play centered on the young (autobiographical) Maria. López dramatizes Maria's parent's courtship and elopement in Mexico, her birth, their crossing to the United States and her dreams of becoming a writer in a comically exaggerated critique of Machismo, the Church and Mexican patriarchy.

Simply Maria is not a "simple" play and should not be dismissed as such. As she will continue to do in her later plays, López is deconstructing traditional expectations, laying the blame for attitudes of what a "good Mexican girl should be" squarely on the Roman Catholic Church. She creatively and caustically indicts the Institution through her hilarious, yet poignant portrayal of the Church and its priests. After the Priest officiates at Maria's parents' marriage, three women, who have been portraying statues of the saints in the church, come to life and transform into "three angelic girls" who chant a litany of what a Mexican girl can and cannot do. They recite that a Mexican girl must be: "Nice, forgiving, considerate, obedient, gentle, hard-working, gracious." She must like: "Dolls, kitchens, houses, caring for children, cooking, laundry and dishes." She must not: "Be independent, enjoy sex, but must endure it as your duty to your husband, and bear his children." Her goal must be to reproduce and her only purpose in life is to serve three men: "Your father, your husband and your son" (Feyder, *Shattering the Myth*, p. 119). By having the Three Marys transform into

---

[52] *Simply Maria* is published in Linda Feyder (ed.), *Shattering the Myth* (Houston: Arte Publico, 1992), pp. 113–41 and by Dramatic Publishing Company, 1996. All references are to the Feyder edition.

angelic girls, the playwright locates these ideas firmly in the name of the Church.

Later in the play Maria dreams about her "White Wedding." This time the priest lists the duties of a good Mexican wife. He asks if she will: ". . . love, cherish, serve, cook for, clean for, sacrifice for, have his children, keep his house, love him even if he beats you, commits adultery, gets drunk, rapes you lawfully, denies you your identity, money, love his family, serve his family and in return ask for nothing?" After Maria agrees to the marriage vows the priest puts a collar and leash on her and tells the groom "You may pet the bride" (132). This caricature of the priest and parody of a Catholic wedding ceremony becomes an indictment of the Church itself, for the author makes it clear that the priest does not speak in isolation. López does not release the Church from its complicity; she refuses to show any transformations in Church doctrine or in the priest's traditional interpretation of marriage. In the end, Maria is triumphant, liberating herself from her father's and the Church's literal and symbolic clenches. Like the Teatro Campesino's early *actos*, *Simply Maria* is a modern morality play. However, in this play the teachings of the Church are subverted rather than promoted and the playwright incites her female audiences to challenge the patriarchy.

Edit Villareal's baptists and voodoo: My Visits With MGM

Having been born into and raised in a Mexican Protestant home, Edit Villareal did not grow up with any love or affection for the Roman Catholic Church as her play, *My Visits With MGM*, first discussed in chapter 2, illustrates. And as might be expected, the Protestant faiths do not incite Villareal's critique. Instead, the playwright focuses her criticism on the Roman Catholic Church. The character of Father Ernie comes under scrutiny in the second act and although he is vindicated, the Church is not. Throughout the first act we have watched as Florinda converts from Baptist to Pentecostal to Roman Catholic with a vengeance. When Florinda becomes a Pentecostal, her older sister, Marta Grande, quips: "She was always looking for a macho god." To which Feliz adds: "One of those primitive types who has answers for everything and leaves nothing to choice. Especially yours . . . But Florinda was not happy as a Holy Roller either. Living in the United States convinced her that here voodoo was necessary. Magic spells and potions" (Feyder, *Shattering the Myth*, p. 151).

Villareal equates Roman Catholicism with "magic spells and potions," as well as with poverty. The playwright told me that: "My views of the church as expressed in MGM, [are] what I call the 'iconization of poverty', it makes poverty a virtuous state."[53] Feliz tells Father Ernie that her grandmother always told her that "Catholics all over the world were underdeveloped, impoverished, disease-ridden and undereducated. Second-class citizens she called them . . . in third-world conditions" (Feyder, *Shattering the Myth*, p. 190). Villareal also recognizes and satirizes the incredible power of the Church. When Feliz asks Father Ernie for help securing a job for her Aunt Florinda, he tells her: "I'll speak to the proper authorities." Feliz assumes he is referring to the police, to which Ernie replies, "The police? Of course not! I'm talking about the Church. We're much bigger than the police . . ."(189). Indeed.

Although absent from the first act, Father Ernie becomes a pivotal character in Marta Feliz's journey. Initially, it is clear that he is interested in more than Marta Feliz's soul, but he controls his lust. However, by not stopping Florinda from putting a curse on Marta Feliz, father Ernie becomes another accomplice in the realm of "voodoo." Rather than dissuade Florinda from her voodoo, he tells Marta Feliz: "You cannot resist her. Your aunt is giving you *el mal ojo* [the evil eye]" (194). The fact that Florinda is fighting for possession of the house without interference from Father Ernie makes him an accomplice to her selfish intentions.

Father Ernie wears his libido on his forehead. His immediate attraction to Marta Feliz is so obvious that he could be dismissed as laughable. His intentions are not invisible to Marta Feliz, either. As Father Ernie washes her feet, ostensibly pressing for her soul, she asks, ". . . have you ever thought of getting a real job? Where you improve people's lives, instead of maintaining the status quo?" (193). Ultimately, Villareal redeems Father Ernie. He resists his sexual attraction to Feliz and moves to Los Angeles to work with the poor and preach the theology of liberation. Ernie finally persuades Marta Feliz that she should join him in the common struggle, which she does. Father Ernie becomes the activist-priest he had always wanted to become, a model for other clerics who go against the conservative powers of the Church and fight for the rights of the poor.

Beverly Sanchez Padilla's redemptive nun

I do not know of any published Chicana/o plays that focus on contemporary nuns as visible characters. As discussed briefly earlier in this chapter,

---

[53] From the UCSD-TV series, "Necessary Theatre: Conversations With Jorge Huerta, Edit Villareal," taped February 2, 1995.

teaching nuns make cameo appearances in Milcha Sanchez-Scott's *Latina* and nuns are also mentioned (but not seen) in Cherríe Moraga's *Giving up the Ghost* and *Shadow of a Man*. In all three of these plays, the nuns are Anglo, representatives of the dominant culture. The only published play about a nun is Estela Portillo-Trambley's three-act historical drama, *Sor Juana*, about Sor Juana Inéz de la Cruz, a seventeenth-century nun and a very important historical and literary figure in Mexico.[54] However, neither Sor Juana, the person, nor *Sor Juana*, the play, should be ignored, because Sor Juana is a very important predecessor for contemporary Latinas. Like Josefina López's *Unconquered Spirits*, *Sor Juana* exposes the patriarchy of the Colonial Church, while the play also reminds Mechicanas of a brilliant seventeenth-century Mestiza who confronted the Church. Although Sor Juana was ultimately silenced by the Church for her writings, she has the last word as one of the most studied poets of the Spanish language in Mexico and other Spanish-speaking countries.

For an analysis of a play that revolves around a contemporary Mexican nun I turn to Beverly Sanchez-Padilla's *La Guadalupe que camina* (*The Guadalupe Who Walks*) directed by Ruby Nelda Perez in 1990. Although this play is unpublished, it merits attention as a singular example of a drama about a real person, a nun who challenged the Church in court. Beverly Sanchez-Padilla is a native of Albuquerque, New Mexico, where she was born in 1947. She grew up in Albuquerque and earned an undergraduate degree in Sociology/Psychology from the University of New Mexico in 1970. She also studied 16mm film and animation at the Anthropology Film Center in Santa Fe, New Mexico, from 1975 to 1976 and held a post-graduate fellowship in Urban Studies and Planning at M.I.T. from 1977 to 1978. Sanchez-Padilla moved to San Antonio, Texas, in 1984 and is currently an Artist-in-Education with the San Antonio Independent School District teaching courses in radio, film and television. In her words, "Trained in 16mm film, a veteran poet and author of five produced plays, I see myself as an interdisciplinary artist."[55] She is widely known for her plays, videos, films and performance pieces. She has written and performed one-woman pieces and other multi-disciplinary works in a variety of venues including theatres, museums, schools, churches, community centers and conferences.

---

[54] Because *Sor Juana* does not deal with contemporary Chicana/os I must leave that discussion for another study. See Estela Portillo-Trambley, *Sor Juana and Other Plays* (Tempe: Bilingual Press, 1983), pp. 143–95. This play is also published in Tey Diana Rebolledo and Eliana S. Rivero (eds.), *Infinite Divisions: An Anthology of Chicana Literature* (Tucson, University of Arizona, 1993), pp. 233–55.

[55] From Beverly Sanchez-Padilla's resume, *c.* 1997.

Figure 8. La Guadalupe Que Camina, by Beverly Sanchez-Padilla. Guadalupe Cultural Arts Center, San Antonio, Texas, 1990. Directed by Ruby Nelda Perez. L. to R. Beverly Sanchez-Padilla, Ruby Nelda Perez, Sonia Salazar, Nancy López.

Sanchez-Padilla bases all of her artistic expression on the joys and struggles of being a woman and especially a Latina in this society. In her "Artistic
Statement" Sanchez-Padilla writes: "All of my work deals with the
consciousness of a woman growing up in a transcultural world surviving,
reflecting, synthesizing and communicating past, present and future."[56] In
her conclusion to her "Artistic Statement," she clearly defines and describes
her work and her vision of the New Mechicana, the "neomestiza": "My work
is in english/spanish/movement and video and deals with researching,
retelling, rewriting, rereading, revitalizing and reconstructing stories and
lives with the purpose and vision of creating peace and the neomestiza"
(Sanchez-Padilla, 1997).

La Guadalupe Que Camina defines the neo-mestiza as an activist, a spiritual woman who loves her community and who is willing to sacrifice her
job for that community. The world premiere of this play was produced by
Mujeres Indigenas (Indigenous Women) at the Guadalupe Cultural Arts
Center in San Antonio, Texas, under the direction of Ruby Nelda Perez, in
1990. One of the most accomplished actresses performing in Latina/o
theatre, Ms. Perez also played the adult version of the central character in
this production. The event was for one night only, but the theatre was
packed and the people were both educated and entertained with this ground
breaking play. Although not quite a docu-drama, this multi-media work
dramatizes in music, video, dance, narrative and action, the life and struggles of an actual person, a Mexican nun, Rosa Martha Zarate Macias.
Zarate Macias is a native of Guadalajara who had worked for fifteen years
as a nun, teacher and community leader in San Bernardino, California,
teaching and organizing in the poorest Spanish-speaking barrios. Her
dedication to her work and her outspoken criticisms of the Church caused
the Bishop to fire her from her job in 1988, after which she was dismissed
entirely from her order. In an unprecedented action, Zarate Macias filed a
$1.5 million civil law suit in 1988 against Bishop Phillip Straling, of the San
Bernardino, California, diocese, charging employment discrimination.
Although the suit was dropped because of the laws separating church and
state, the play still makes its message clear. In a newspaper interview,
Sanchez-Padilla said: "I think the Catholic religion has been oppressive to
women and we address this in this play," while also emphasizing her belief
that her play "is not intended to condemn religious life but to point out an
'oppressive hierarchical society'."[57]

---

[56] Sanchez-Padilla's "Artistic Statement" (unpub.), dated 1997, in my files.
[57] Anon. "La Guadalupe' examines oppression in church," San Antonio Light, December 13, 1990,
      n.p.

La Guadalupe Que Camina traces the life of Zarate Macias, called Sister Lupe in the play, from her youth to her court battles with the Church.[58] The play is very bilingual since the action begins when Sister Lupe is a little girl in Mexico and all the dialogue is realistically in Spanish. We see her interactions with family members and learn of her unwavering independence and early devotion to a religious life, despite her mother's almost abusive attempts to dissuade her. She enters the convent in Mexico and is transferred to San Diego, California (fictitiously) and we watch as her life becomes more and more complicated. The period is 1970, the war in Vietnam is raging, and Sister Lupe cannot ignore the poor, especially the Mexicans. Sister Lupe finds soul mates among the religious with equal fervor for social change, but in this dramatization, they are the minority.

The Bishop, here aptly named Bishop Western, is portrayed as an offensive man who is out of touch with the Spanish-speaking community he serves. He is totally against the use of the Spanish language in the schools, a very controversial topic in the barrios. He tells Sister Lupe: "But you don't seem to understand that teaching Catechism in Spanish will not encourage others to learn the language of this country. Doing things the way you want to will cause divisions in our parish."[59] The playwright is obviously a proponent of bilingual education and this issue becomes key to the Bishop's ignorance of his flock. In this play, it is the Bishop who causes divisions, inspiring Sister Lupe to leave and join a group of "religious rebels."

The third and final act is rather brief and takes place in the courtroom where we get a taste of the arguments that were given. Sister Lupe states: "As a women [sic] and a religious we are instruments and tools of the men who run the 'official' church . . . I believe that Tonantzin the goddess of the sun [sic] in our Indian religion showed herself to Juan Diego not as a fairy tale of a passive virgin, but a symbol of truth and action"(Sanchez-Padilla, p. 29).[60] Thus the title of the play, the active Guadalupe, striving for and achieving social justice. Of course this indigenous interpretation is quite troubling to the Bishop who tells the Court: "If you look at her personal history you will see a pattern of extreme individualistic behavior"(30). As expected, the judge recites: "As a court of law we cannot operate in the arena of religious beliefs nor involve ourselve [sic] in religious matters . . . the court rules on the side of the defendant"(31).

[58] All names and places were altered in the play to avoid lawsuits.
[59] All references to this play are from Beverly Sanchez-Padilla, *La Guadalupe Que Camina*, unpub. ms. dated December 14, 1990, p. 12.
[60] Sanchez-Padilla mistakenly calls Tonantzin Goddess of the Sun. Tonantzin was Our Revered Mother and Huitzilopochtli was the God of the Sun. See Miguel Leon-Portilla, *Aztec Image of Self and Society* (Salt Lake City: University of Utah, 1992), pp. 21, 187.

La Guadalupe Que Camina is a very important piece of theatre, not because it is a "great play," but because it exposes an actual nun whose determination to help her people causes her to do battle with one of the wealthiest and most powerful patriarchal structures in the world. The very fact that the play is based on a real nun in an authentic conflict with the Church distinguishes it from all other dramatizations, since only Sor Juana is thus presented – but her case is three hundred years old. Sister Lupe's case was still pending when the play was produced, adding to the dramatic possibilities. Although she eventually lost her court battle, this nun's story is a compelling example of a religious woman who did not acquiesce to her superiors, whether male or female, certainly redeeming herself in the process.

Conclusions

All of the playwrights discussed in this chapter exhibit a strong and sincere spirituality in their plays while also often subverting what the Church teaches as redemption through Christian doctrine. The Roman Catholic faith is prominent in all of the plays and although none of the plays rejects Catholicism outright, most challenge Church authority, offering alternative forms of redemption mediated as political action. With the exception of Edit Villareal, the authors write from a Roman Catholic perspective, exposing particular prejudices and biases against that faith. As might be expected, the Protestant Villareal criticizes certain aspects of the Roman Catholic Church while redeeming Father Ernie. She also idealizes the Mexican Protestants, particularly the Baptists and Methodists.[61] In actuality, Villareal reveals more about Roman Catholicism than any real functioning of Protestantism. We do not see the Protestant churches, nor do we meet their ministers in any of the plays. And if there are Protestant miracles, we do not see them.

For miracles, we turn to Milcha Sanchez-Scott's *Roosters* and Cherríe Moraga's *Heroes and Saints*. Yet, their miracles differ markedly. When Angela ascends it is the only true miracle we witness in any of these plays. Like Cerezita, Angela has constructed a special world for herself, a safe haven from her bleak surroundings. But unlike Cerezita, Angela is "lifted"

---

[61] Besides Edit Villareal, Cherríe Moraga is the only other playwright to mention Protestants. Her characters make oblique references to the Anglo and Mechicana/o Protestants, critical of their "coldness" and the "emptiness" of their places of worship. See *Giving up the Ghost* in *Heroes and Saints*, pp. 9–10, 13–14; and *Heroes and Saints*, p. 100.

by heavenly forces, hanging suspended in space as symbol of faith and hope. Angela becomes saint-like as she had prayed for, but her transformation is not of her creation, like Cerezita's. And though Cerezita seems fated for martyrdom, Angela's future, though uncertain, does not mirror Cerezita's. Although Cerezita moves an entire community to action, and Angela's ascension affects only the immediate family, the two girls are empowered and redeemed through their miracles.

Sanchez-Scott is the only playwright discussed here that does not challenge Church authority as openly as the other playwrights. As a feminist, Sanchez-Scott is certainly aware of patriarchal abuses, but she does not focus on these issues. With the other plays, criticisms of the Church abound. In some instances, such as in the character of Padre Ladrón in Carlos Morton's *El jardín* priests clearly represent the institution as literally or metaphorically "stealing" from the people. In Cherríe Moraga's *Heroes and Saints*, Dolores tells Father Juanito that other priests don't come to the house unless you have money. Villareal's Marta Grande, in *My Visits With MGM,* categorically blames the Church for Latin America's poverty. In *Simply Maria*, López clearly condemns the Church for its disregard for women's rights and its promotion of male dominance and outright abuse. And certainly, Beverly Sanchez-Padilla's *La Guadalupe que camina* exposes a real life example of the power and abuses of the Church.

Although none of the (published) plays focuses on priests or nuns, *Heroes and Saints* and *My Visits With MGM* depict contemporary scenarios in which priests are necessary to the forward action of their plays. *La Guadalupe Que Camina* stands out as the only play about an actual contemporary Mexican nun in the United States and is also important as a play that demonstrates life in the Church. Although the main antagonist, Bishop Western, is an Anglo, Sister Lupe's Mother Superior in Mexico is an equally severe character, thus in this play villains come from both sides of the border, although the Mechicana nuns and Mechicano priests who form their own (rebel) communities are painted very favorably.

These playwrights do not attempt to negate the importance of priests or nuns in the lives of their respective communities. The playwrights understand the nature of the Mechicanos' spirituality and rather than deny that commitment, they propose models of the ideal priest and the ideal nun. These plays portray priests who are fictional; however they are not fantasies. Priests have been active before and since the Chicano Movement, working diligently for the Mechicanos' rights, and so have nuns, as evidenced in *La Guadalupe Que Camina*. In reality, Mexican and Chicano ministers have also fought alongside their brothers and sisters in social struggles, but I know of no play that dramatizes this fact.

It is interesting to note that the activist priests and nuns are usually Mexican or Chicano. The one Anglo priest, Bishop Western, in *La Guadalupe que camina*, is clearly insensitive to Mechicano needs and is portrayed as cold and vindictive. It is the Chicano priests and nuns who must come to the aid of their people, the playwrights are telling us, for they know and understand their communities. I do not believe these authors dismiss the many non-Latino religious who have joined with the people in their battles; however they have committed themselves to portraying religious who must come from La Raza. If they had scripted Anglo priests as emancipators, the playwrights would have risked the danger of being criticized for portraying "great white fathers," as though the Chicanos could not produce their own religious leaders and liberators. Father Juan Cunningham approaches the image of "Anglo savior" but he totally denies his father's heritage in favor of his mother's culture, thus regardless of his Anglo features, he is "*puro* Chicano."

Moraga, Sanchez-Padilla and Villareal each position their revolutionary priests and nuns with the people against the establishment, linking them in spirit, history and heritage. Also, the theme of Liberation Theology permeates many of the plays, from *El Jardín* to *Heroes and Saints, My Visits With MGM* and *La Guadalupe que camina*, also connecting the characters and struggles with those of the people in Latin America. Morton's two plays also link God with revolutionary theology, effectively questioning the role of the Church in the liberation of all peoples.

Each of the priests and nuns in these plays is looking for something beyond what the Church is giving them. That something is a link with their community; a sense that they are doing something more than "maintaining the status quo," as Marta Feliz puts it. Father Juan tries to offer his flock more than spiritual sustenance when even the land these people work is incapable of giving them life. The court case dramatized in *La Guadalupe Que Camina* is perhaps the most important dramatic statement about an individual religious personal commitment to her or his community, because it is based on fact. Whether in the cities or on the farms, the Mechicano is in trouble, the playwrights are telling us and if the Church will not take action, the priests and nuns must do something to change this situation.

Finally, the plays I have discussed underscore the importance of the Roman Catholic faith to the vast majority of Chicana/o playwrights. While it is the Roman Catholic Church that mainly defines the Mechicana/o experience, it is also the Institution that impels these playwrights to rebel against the patriarchy, to question its authority. Paradoxically, it is the Roman Catholic Church, with its candles and incense, its saints and, especially, its Virgin of Guadalupe that clearly defines the culture of the Chicana and Chicano in these playwrights' eyes. After reading or seeing these plays it is difficult to imagine Mechicana/os as anything but Roman Catholics; they seem inseparable, regardless of one's own beliefs. Yet we leave these plays with a sense of a love/hate relationship between the playwrights and their Church. In fact, these plays tell us that Roman Catholic Mechicana/os can deal directly with their *Virgencita Morenita*, regardless of the institutional restrictions, for She emanates from their spiritual and historical roots as brown-skinned people. The Church becomes a basis for reverence and ridicule, for a sense of community and a site of contestation. Redemption, we are told, is in the eye of the beholder, in the pen of the playwright, not in the dictates of a man-made Church.

4

Rebelling against damnation:

out of the closet, slowly

"But lesbianism, in any form, and male homosexuality which openly avows both the sexual and emotional elements of the bond challenges the very foundation of la familia."

Cherríe Moraga[1]

"I'm no queer . . . I'm a boy
From the barrio, East L.A.,
We don't do sexual ambivalence there."

Sergeant: *Deporting the Divas*[2]

"Peepo like you are dying . . .
God makes this sickness."
Dolores, *Heroes and Saints*[3]

Introduction: the discussion of homosexuality in Chicano literature and theatre

To say that homosexuality is a taboo subject in Mechicano households is to state the obvious. Not that gays and lesbians in other cultures find solace in Sunday dinners with mom and pop, but to a Mechicana/o homosexual, the cross seems even heavier. Perhaps because they take their religion(s) so seriously, as evidenced in previous chapters, Mechicana/os have always had trouble accepting homosexuality. In one of the first articles to address male homosexuality in Chicano literature, published in 1986, Juan Bruce-Novoa stated: "I do not claim that homophobia is more prevalent among Chicanos – although some would aver it – but only that as product of two societies,

---

[1] Cherríe Moraga, *Loving in the War Years* (Boston: South End Press, 1983), p. III.
[2] Guillermo Reyes, *Deporting the Divas*, Gestos 27 (1999), 133.
[3] Cherríe Moraga, *Heroes and Saints and Other Plays* (Boston: West End, 1994), p. 124.

Mexico and the United States, neither of which displays great tolerance for gays, Chicanos simply reflect the norms of the wider sociocultural context."[4]

In his important (and singular) article on Chicano male homosexuality, Tomás Almaguer posits: "Chicano men who embrace a 'gay' identity (based on the European-American sexual system) must reconcile this sexual identity with their primary socialization into a Latino culture that does not recognize such a construction: there is no cultural equivalent to the modern 'gay man' in the Mexican/Latin American sexual system."[5] Further, Almaguer argues that the Chicano gay male suffers double marginalization: first as a Chicano and then as a homosexual. He then distinguishes between those men who are gay Chicanos and those who would be Chicano gays. Which label comes first determines the effects of socialization felt from the distinct cultures affecting Mechicana/os as transcultured people in this society.

It may not be more difficult to be openly homosexual in the Mechicana/o community – this is a strictly subjective position – but the historical paucity of gay and lesbian plays indicates that the subject of homosexualit(ies) is still very charged. Certainly, the field is growing, but it has been and continues to be a slow, painful process, this "queering of the barrio." In 1981 Gloria Anzaldúa and Cherríe Moraga published their historic anthology, *This Bridge Called My Back: Writings by Radical Women of Color,* a volume which empowered many Latina writers to break the silence and proclaim a new era of dialogue regarding Mechicana sexualities.[6] The conclusion: It is not easy being a Mechicana lesbian, either. Today, there are many more Mechicana writers addressing the issues of feminism and sexualities and even challenging the pioneers.[7] But their essays and other literary works are not public events. It is one thing to read about forbidden topics without intervention, in the privacy of your home, but quite another to attend a play that exposes your community's worst fears.

If it took quite a while for the subject of human sexuality to enter into discussions of Chicano literature, early teatros and playwrights also avoided the dangerous terrain of gay or lesbian themes. In 1981 this situation

[4] Juan Bruce-Novoa, "Homosexuality and the Chicano Novel," *Confluencia,* 2 (Fall 1986), 69.
[5] Tomás Almaguer, "Chicano Men: A Cartography of Homosexual Identity and Behavior," *differences* 3.2 (1991), 6.
[6] Gloria Anzaldúa and Cherríe Moraga (eds.), *This Bridge Called My Back: Writings by Radical Women of Color* (Boston: Persephone Press, 1981).
[7] For more on the current debate over the Chicano Movement, the negation of women in that movement and a critical response to writers such as Moraga, see Deena J. González, "Speaking Secrets: Living Chicana Theory," in Carla Trujillo (ed.), *Living Chicana Theory* (Berkeley: Third Woman Press, 1998), pp. 46–77.

prompted Yvonne Yarbro-Bejarano to remark: "The exclusion of a performance of [a gay Chicano] play during the TENAZ Eleventh Festival in
the Fall of 1981 revealed the depth of resistance to considering the Chicano
theatre movement an appropriate vehicle for the exploration of questions of
sexuality."[8] Echoing this sentiment ten years later, Cherríe Moraga told an
interviewer in 1991: "Latino and Chicano theaters have been notoriously
sexist and homophobic and have not shown a great interest in doing
women's work."[9] In 1997 Guillermo Reyes affirmed the continuing fear of
lesbian and gay plays in the Latino theatre community. He writes, "If it
weren't for sympathetic gay white artistic directors or sometimes straight
white [artistic directors] none of my plays would have gotten produced."[10]
The following discussion is meant to break the barrier of silence, to challenge tropes of homosexual damnation.

Early representations of (homo)sexual characters

Estela Portillo's closeted lesbian: Day of the Swallows

Ironically, the first playwright to address the subject of lesbianism in the
Mechicano community was a heterosexual woman, Estela Portillo-
Trambley. In her play, Day of the Swallows (also discussed in chapter 1), first
published in 1972, the author explores a hidden relationship between her
protagonist, Doña Josefa, the town's "pillar of virtue," and Alysea, a young
woman she rescued from the bordello.[11] Structured like a murder mystery,
the tale unravels the secrets between the two women in the shadow of
repression and male domination. When the exposure of Josefa's sexuality is
threatened, her final act (and the end of the play) is to drown herself in the
lake.

The playwright's decision to have Josefa commit suicide has given the
critics much to discuss and to argue about. Sue-Ellen Case sees multiple
meanings in this final act: "Josefa's erotic relation to the land and her suicide,

---

[8] Yvonne Yarbro-Bejarano, "Female Subject in Chicano Theatre: Sexuality, 'Race,' and Class," in
    Sue-Ellen Case (ed.), *Performing Feminisms: Feminist Critical Theory and Theatre* (Baltimore:
    Johns Hopkins, 1990), p. 145, footnote 38. More on the play in question, *Reunion*, below.

[9] Andrea Lewis, *Mother Jones*, January–February 1991. Quoted in Lynda Hart and Peggy Phelan,
    Acting Out: Feminist Performances (Michigan, 1993), p. 88.

[10] Guillermo Reyes, "What I've discovered," *Ollantay Theater Magazine* V 2 (Summer/Autumn
     1997), 39.

[11] *Day of the Swallows* is in Roberto Garza (ed.), *Contemporary Chicano Drama* (Notre Dame, 1976),
     pp. 205–45.

a final coupling with the land, are common in homosexual writings, in which the desire which dares not write itself to another person, or within the community, but is displaced to a celebration of place becomes dispersed within the elements, as in Whitman or Lorca." [12]

Case also posits that Josefa's suicide places her in the (traditional) heterosexual perception of homosexual violence and shame, reminding the reader of Lilian Hellman's *The Children's Hour,* "or other plays in which the lesbian is sacrificed to the uses of the heterosexual community, which would use her suffering to adjust its own homophobia" (Case, "Seduced and Abandoned," p. 93). Case argues further that Josefa represents the Indian and the lesbian, both of which must be abolished: "Perhaps more accurately, Josefa the lesbian does not stand for Indian, as much as for the abolition of Indian. As lesbian, she represents that which should not be seen – that which ultimately must be eradicated" (95).

In what might be considered a stereotypical or uninformed heterosexual response to Josefa's lesbianism, Tomás Vallejos comments in passing that Josefa "is driven to lesbianism by a male-dominated society," and, further, that she becomes "unbalanced as a result of a social order that is itself inequitable and unbalanced."[13] This play is not the focus of Vallejos' study, but his brief remarks echo the beliefs of many people, both within and without the Chicana/o communities: that lesbianism is a response to male domination and that this "condition" must lead to "imbalance" and extreme acts such as suicide. His remarks are important as backdrop to any discussion of homosexualities in Chicana/o dramaturgy, for they reveal the tenor of the period (1980) before Chicana feminist and lesbian critics began to investigate and write about the literature and drama.

In his attempt to show the tragic implications in *Day of the Swallows,* another critic, Alfonso Rodríguez (also writing in 1980), believes that Josefa is "haunted by fear of disapproval from others, obsessed by her disdain for men and dominated by her lesbian passion for Alysea."[14] Referring to

---

[12] Sue-Ellen Case, "Seduced and Abandoned: Chicanas and Lesbians in Representation," in Diana Taylor and Juan Villegas (eds.), *Negotiating Performance: Gender, Sexuality and Theatricality in Latin/o America* (Durham: Duke, 1994), p. 94. The list of lesbian suicides in American drama is long. For a thorough discussion of the lesbian subject in theatre, see Jill Dolan, " 'Lesbian' Subjectivity in Realism: Dragging at the Margins of Structure and Ideology," in Sue-Ellen Case (ed.), *Performing Feminisms: Feminist Critical Theory and Theatre* (Baltimore: Johns Hopkins, 1990), pp. 40–53.

[13] Tomás Vallejos, "Estela Portillo's Fictive Search for Paradise," *Frontiers* v 2 (1980), 55.

[14] Alfonso Rodríguez, "Tragic Vision in Estella [sic] Portillo's *The Day of the Swallows,"* De Colores 5 (1980), 153.

Josefa's account of how a group of boys held her down and killed a swallow above her face when she was seven years old, Rodríguez sees this act as "a traumatic experience which conditions her whole outlook on life and leads her to regard the opposite sex as the incarnation of evil on earth" (Rodríguez, "Tragic Vision," p. 156). Again, a male critic seems to believe that lesbians must, of necessity, hate all men and therefore love women. And, again, this critic describes Josefa's suicide as a "kind of mystical insanity" (157). Further, Rodríguez equates lesbianism with an "obsession," somehow uncontrollable, which leads to disaster.

In a review of Portillo's novel, *Trini*, Cherríe Moraga argues that the "fundamental male-centered resolution" in that novel reminds her of *Day of the Swallows*: "I've always loved *Swallows*, although it is a 'classic' lesbian work in the worse [sic] sense of the 1950s view where all lesbian protagonists are punished for their disobedience to the male hegemony." She continues: "They all end up dead or howling at the moon . . . Those who follow the law of the father will be rewarded . . . those who transgress are punished."[15]

Other critics see Josefa's death as either a spiritual message or a political commentary. On the transcendental side, Juan Bruce-Novoa argues: "Portillo manages to save her protagonist by turning her suicide into a mystical union with nature, a transcendence into a more tolerant realm of existence, and a victory for life and love."[16] In her analysis, Louise Detwiler echoes Bruce-Novoa arguing that Josefa's connection with her magicians makes her death an act of liberation: "Josefa has deliberately created a more perfect union with what she considers to be divine."[17]

In contrast, Janice Dewey and María Herrera-Sobek both feel that Josefa's suicide is political and, further, in the tradition of Chicano protest theatre. Dewey asks: "How can a woman's suicide in the face of an entire towns' condemnation of her lesbian love not be considered a symbolic protest, a protest 'staged' against both the violence that leads to her own death and the farce of the lie that she lived?"[18] I agree that the issue of sexual

[15] Cherríe Moraga, "The Obedient Daughter," *Third Woman* 4 (1989), 161–62. Also in Norma Alarcón, Ana Castillo and Cherríe Moraga (eds.), *The Sexuality of Latinas* (Berkeley: Third Woman Press, 1993), pp. 157–62.

[16] Juan Bruce-Novoa, *Chicano Authors: Inquiry by Interview* (Austin: Texas, 1980), p. 163.

[17] Louise Detwiler, "The Question of Cultural Difference and Gender Oppression in Estela Portillo-Trambley's *The Day of the Swallows*," *The Bilingual Review/Revista Bilingüe* (1996), 151.

[18] Janice Dewey, "Doña Josefa: Bloodpulse of Transition and Change," in Asuncion Horno-Delgado, Eliana Ortega, Nina M. Scott, and Nancy Saporta Sternbach (eds.), *Breaking Boundaries: Latina Writings and Critical Readings* (Amherst: University of Massachusetts, 1989), p. 40.

repression and denial is very political but Josefa must die in order to make her point and all indications are that only three people will know why she committed suicide.

Passion becomes a central theme in this exploration of female sexuality and the mystery of Josefa's "magicians." Josefa's passion goes beyond the physical to the metaphysical and the spiritual as she expresses her Christian/indigenous beliefs in spirits beyond the Church's dominion. Unlike a homophobic Church, Josefa's magicians are non-judgmental, for they allow her lesbian desire, free of guilt, giving her a calming peace. She tells Alysea's Indian suitor, I had the secret of the magicians . . . the wine of love . . . the light was me; I knew that I would bear the children of light . . . the moon . . . the burning lake" (Garza, *Contemporary Chicano Drama*, p. 222). In other words, Josefa will not bear the children of man; she will not be used for procreation at all. The "wine of love" is a woman's love for another woman. Finally, the metaphor of a "burning lake" reflects Josefa's inner fire which she has had to literally subvert, presenting a cold facade to the world outside her sanctuary.

The playwright avoids telling the reader whether the village of San Lorenzo is in Mexico or the Southwest; whether these people are Mexican or Chicano. The nature of the ritual bathing connotes a Mexican setting, yet rituals still abound in certain Southwestern villages, thus the characters could be considered Chicano. Though the characters seem frozen in a previous time their attitudes are current in many Mechicano households. The village girls' dreams of "the perfect husband" permeate this play even though the author is attempting to deconstruct traditional patriarchal values.

Day of the Swallows cannot ultimately satisfy the lesbian critics who explore its faults even as they appreciate the gesture. Despite her concerns about the author's inability to avoid being "the obedient daughter" to the patriarchy, Moraga commends the play for its "daring and complex depiction of a lesbian who is actively desirous, whose desire is equal to the urges of a man, but who rightly fears for her life to face it"(Moraga, "Obedient Daughter," p. 162). Perhaps because Portillo-Trambley was heterosexual and from an earlier generation, she could not argue from a lesbian subject position as writers like Moraga or Case would years later.

Written in a form of poetry as delicate as the lace Josefa and Alysea weave, *Day of the Swallows* remained the only Chicana/o play to broach male or female homosexuality for several years. The play is studied widely in Chicano literature courses, though not produced very often, perhaps because it is technically demanding but also, I am sure, because of the sensitive subject matter. Portillo-Trambley's first play is important for the themes it explored at a time when most Chicano theatre was still in the *acto* stage, not concerned with psychological realism and certainly indifferent to sexuality aside from cheap jokes.[19] It would be several years before a full-length play about a gay Chicano would emerge.

Plays with secondary gay Chicano characters

To date, with the exception of Cherríe Moraga's *Shadow of a Man*, no full-length play in which a secondary Chicana character is lesbian has been published.[20] Notable among the early representations of secondary lesbian (and gay) characters is a 1975–76 version of the Teatro Campesino's *Fin del Mundo*. In the words of Betty Diamond, "The play is significant politically because in its analysis of personal contradictions, the Teatro [Campesino] for the first time sympathetically depicts characters usually criticized and mocked in Chicano theater and Chicano culture: lesbians, male homo-sexuals and Anglos."[21]

Diamond goes on to reveal the fact that two of the Chicanas in this play are lesbian lovers, 'Guera' and 'Prieta,' "the fair-skinned and the dark-skinned, are opposites who join together in union." Further, one of the farm workers, Olegario, also known as "Sugar," is gay and is having an affair with the Anglo sheriff, "Sam Barnes" (231). In her analysis, Diamond asserts: "Mundo [the title character] taunts Sugar for his homosexuality but we are made to realize that it is Mundo who, in his macho bravado, is 'queer' for the growers. Sugar just sleeps with the Sheriff, but he works for the strike" (231–32). Because Mundo is the central figure, Diamond discusses his rela-tionship to Sugar more than to the lesbian characters; yet another indica-tion that although Diamond believed the Teatro attempted to portray lesbian characters sympathetically, these character types (as well as the gay males) remained, in 1976, marginalized. Whether or not the usual Mechicana/o audiences were as accepting of the lesbian and gay characters as Diamond was is debatable.

---

[19] An example of cheap homosexual humor is in Ysidro Macias' *The Ultimate Pendejada* ["stupid-ity"]. Published in 1976, this play has a scene in which a Chicano student activist tells a poten-tial recruit: "I was just kidding about being militant. We just say that to scare off the putos [fags]. You're not scared are you?" In Garza, *Contemporary Chicano Theatre*, p. 144.

[20] Guillermo Reyes' comic one-act, "Bush is a Lesbian," has been produced and published. Dallas: Dialogus Play Service, 1993. The focus is actually on the husband's problems, not his wife's lesbianism.

[21] Betty Diamond, "Brown-Eyed Children of the Sun: The Cultural Politics of El Teatro Campesino" (Ph.D. Dissertation, University of Wisconsin, Madison, 1977), p. 231.

The only play of which I am aware written and produced after 1980 that features a lesbian character in a supporting role, is Cherríe Moraga's *Watsonville*, first produced in 1996. Like the version of *Fin del Mundo* mentioned above, *Watsonville* is unpublished to date and therefore this discussion will center on the plays that have featured gay Chicanos in secondary roles.[22]

Josefina López's coming out farce: Day of the Dead

A one-act play that includes a gay Chicano character is Josefina López's *Food for the Dead*, first produced in 1989, also discussed briefly in chapter 3.[23] Although this is not the central theme, there is a coming out in which the son, Jesús, brings his lover home to introduce him to his family. But when Jesús announces that he is gay, his father, Rubén, escapes from the underworld and "all Hell breaks loose," for he is determined that his son will not be a *maricón* ("fag"). Although López's play is about issues other than homosexuality, Jesús' declaration, which mirrors his mother's liberation from traditional expectations, is the crisis that catapults his father back from the dead.

In an ironic twist, Rubén admits to the family that he died of a heart attack while having sex with Candela's cousin, Ramon (López, *Food for the Dead*, p. 31). While we could infer that Rubén's death-in-coitus was his punishment for sexual transgression, ("You will go to hell for having sex with another man") it is the father's macho hypocrisy that is being exposed and ridiculed. The playwright informs the audience that in the Mechicano community "real men" can sodomize "queers" without losing their masculine identity – a common theme in several of the plays in this chapter. López was not attempting to conflate homosexual desire with death, but more importantly to reveal prevalent attitudes in the Mechicanos' so-called heterosexual normativity. Thus, she punishes the father on several fronts. First, she kills him. Secondly, she humiliates him by revealing his hypocrisy; and finally, she sends him back to Hell at the play's conclusion. Ultimately, the Devil himself comes for Rubén and once they have watched him dragged back to Hell, the family members each realize their own limitations and promise to stop judging one another.

---

[22] In Alfredo Ramos' *Last Angry Brown Hat*, a full-length play that has not been published, but which has been produced in various cities, one of the four characters is gay. In Rudolfo Anaya's (unpublished) play, *Death of a Writer*, one of the characters is gay and in his *¡Aye, Compadre!* (unpublished) there is talk of and acceptance of a gay son whom we never see.

[23] Josefina López, *Food for the Dead and La Pinta* (Woodstock, ILL: Dramatic Publishing, 1996).

This play is wonderfully farcical, but initially suffered from the playwright's lack of knowledge about homosexuality in general and male homosexuality in particular. Working on the first production at UCSD was a difficult process for López, as she states in her introductory notes to the published version: "Since I'm not gay and didn't do enough research I ended up making a lot of innocent mistakes and some of the actors from the [UCSD] production were offended" (López, *Food for the Dead*, p. 7). To her credit, López listened and re-wrote. After one of the rehearsals I asked López what she knew about the gay male experience. She answered that she had watched her "sensitive" brother suffer at the hands of her father and other men in her family. The young playwright could identify machismo in all of its manifestations, in this case as homophobia, and wanted to express her outrage and concern through the gay brother in her play.[24]

Although *Food for the Dead* is ultimately about a Mechicana's release from traditional Mexican patriarchal values and restrictions, its production in 1989 marks a new era for gay male characters in Chicano dramaturgy. And although the author was neither male nor gay, the play deserves attention for its inclusion of a gay relationship and its satirical criticism of patriarchal homophobia in Mechicano culture. When the Teatro Campesino chose to produce *Simply María, or the American Dream* in October of the same year, they added *Food for the Dead* to the bill, giving the still-emerging playwright more visibility and a strong note of validation. The plays were directed by Amy González and toured to various cities in California.

Guillermo Reyes' gay Latinos

Another playwright who is scripting gay Chicano characters and themes is Guillermo Reyes. Although not of Mexican descent, Reyes has written several plays that deal with a variety of Latina/os, some of whom are gay and Chicana or Chicano. Born in Chile in 1962, Reyes moved to the Washington, DC area with his mother when he was nine years old. When he was fifteen, the two moved to Los Angeles, where he completed high school and an undergraduate degree in Italian Literature at UCLA. He began writing plays as an undergraduate and was invited to the 1986

---

[24] Sadly, López had understood her father's attitude towards homosexuality correctly. In an interview with Ms. López in Chicago, Illinois, on October 3, 1992, the playwright told me: "When he [her father] saw the play he said that I was pretty correct in assuming that if one of his sons turns out to be gay and if he were dead, he would pray to God or the devil to come back to life to kill the son."

Hispanic Playwright's Project at the South Coast Repertory Theatre for an in-house reading of "Exile From L.A."[25]

In 1987 Reyes was accepted into the UCSD graduate playwriting program, where he studied with playwrights Allan Havis and Adele Edling Shank as well as other faculty members. As a student, Reyes developed his thesis play, *The Seductions of Johnny Diego*, which was produced by the UCSD Theatre Department in 1990 under the direction of Tony Curiel. This absurdist comedy centers on a dysfunctional, bi-cultural Irish/Chicano family that includes one gay brother and a sexually ambivalent title character, for whom everybody lusts. Although this play has not been fully produced in a professional venue, it was an important stepping-stone for the young playwright, who was virtually coming-out through his plays.

While completing his graduate studies Reyes worked as dramaturg on Chilean playwright and novelist, Antonio Skármeta's play, *Burning Patience /Ardiente paciencia*, which I co-directed with Doug Jacobs at the San Diego Repertory Theatre in 1988. This experience also introduced the playwright to the workings of a fully professional theatre. Reyes completed his M.F.A. in 1990 and moved back to Los Angeles the following year to become the Literary Manager for the Bilingual Foundation for the Arts. In this capacity Reyes could continue to write plays as well as work with the artistic director, Margarita Galbán, and producer, Carmen Zapata, and the many other professional theatre artists who work in Los Angeles's only full-time bilingual theatre company. In 1997, Reyes wrote me about his evolution as a gay, Chilean, playwright: "It took me a long time to write about being gay, Chilean and even Hispanic. I don't know why. Because sometimes intimate experiences are potentially embarrassing, discomfiting. Ultimately, writing about Chicanos, as in 'Johnny Diego,' helped me slowly creep back into my Latino-Chilean experience."[26]

Gay Latinos everywhere: Men On the Verge of a His-panic Breakdown

Reyes' most successful play to date, *Men On the Verge of a His-panic Breakdown,* was first produced at the Celebration Theatre in West Hollywood, California, in 1994, directed by Joseph Megel and featuring Felix Pire. This is a one-man tour-de-force which explores varieties of Latino characters, immigrants as well as native-born, all of whom are gay or

[25] This play is not published.
[26] E-mail to me from Guillermo Reyes, April 23, 1997.

repressed homosexuals. The play has been produced in several other venues, from Portland to San Francisco. In 1997 Megel again directed Felix Pire in the piece off-Broadway, again to great critical acclaim.

Men On the Verge of a His-panic Breakdown, which owes its title to the Pedro Almodóvar film, "Women on the Verge of a Nervous Breakdown," consists of a series of monologues in which different Latinos from diverse generations and countries tell their stories and in the process reveal what it is like to be Latino and gay. In the words of John M. Clum, "All of Reyes' characters are survivors. All have tried to assimilate to America from pasts of poverty or political exile and must survive in a capitalist system that sees them as dispensable."[27] As Clum concludes, "Reyes's monologues are simultaneously funny and sad, but they offer a catalog of fighters" (403).

Only one of the characters in this piece is Mexican American, in the monologue titled "Hispanically Correct."[28] This character, whose stage name is Edward Thornhill the Third, is an aspiring actor who has attempted to "pass" for white, for straight – for any number of performative gestures. His monologue continues the debate over Chicano identity crises, with the added caveat that Edward is also gay. The monologue begins with a phone call as we find this young man speaking in a California San Fernando Valley accent:

> Hello . . . Is this, like, the Hispanic Hotline?
> Okay, this is my first time, you know. So, like, I'm supposed to give you the dirt and you're, like, supposed to tell me if it's like Hispanically Correct. Is that right?
> Okay, so I'm, like, young and I'm glamorous, okay? And when I first came to Hollywood a couple of years ago, I, like, changed my name, I bleached my skin, and I started frequenting the trendiest straight bars in town . . .
> Never mind my real name. I can barely pronounce it, okay?
> (Clum, *Staging Gay Lives*, p. 409)

In her analysis and comparison of Reyes' monologues and the various characters in John Leguizamo's *Mambo Mouth*, Melissa Fitch Lockhart writes: "Both plays bring to the fore the exploitation that Latinos often suffer, and yet when it comes to the queer characters in these plays the indignities are not related to their sexuality as much as to their status as subalterns within

---

[27] John M. Clum (ed.), *Staging Gay Lives* (Boulder: Westview Press, 1996), p. 402. *Men On The Verge of a His-panic Breakdown* is in Clum's anthology (pp. 401–24) and is also published by Dramatic Publishing Company (New York, 1999).

[28] Clum, *Staging Gay Lives*, pp. 409–12; and Reyes, *Men on the Verge*, pp. 17–22.

United States society."[29] As Lockhart points out, Edward Thornhill the Third is also trying to pass for wealthy. Not only does he affect a British-sounding name and a lineage ("The Third"), he also instructs his (very) Mexican parents to put on "'cute little butler and maid uniforms' in order to mislead his visitors as to the true nature of his economic status" (Lockhart, "Queer Representation," 72). Thus, according to Lockhart, Edward suffers hostilities not because of his gayness but because he is not wealthy and he is not white (73). For her, the dialectic becomes a matter of class and race as we laugh at Edward's feeble attempts to be what he is not.

Although there is only one Mexican American or Chicano character in *Men on the Verge of a His-panic Breakdown*, Reyes has demonstrated through the distinct Latino "types" that we all suffer from identity crises, whether gay or straight, United States-born or recent immigrant. However, only the Chicano attempts to pass for white and wealthy, the others are proud of their Latino cultures, including the two characters in the piece that are attempting to hide their sexuality. The success of this piece inspired Reyes to continue in the monologue genre with an exploration of what it is like to be gay, Latino *and undocumented*, appropriately titled *Deporting the Divas*, to be discussed later in this chapter.

Cherríe Moraga's transgressive queers

To look at gay representation by another self-identified homosexual, we must turn to the works of Cherríe Moraga. In her first collection of essays and poems, Moraga writes about being a woman, a Chicana, a daughter, a lesbian:

> It wasn't until I acknowledged and confronted my own lesbianism in the flesh, that my heartfelt identification with and empathy for my mother's oppression – due to being poor, uneducated and Chicana – was realized. My lesbianism is the avenue through which I have learned the most about silence and oppression, and it continues to be the most tactile reminder to me that we are not free human beings.[30]

Although Moraga looks "Anglo," her sexuality kept her from ever aspiring to complete "assimilation" as a non-Chicana. In her words: "What I am saying is that the joys of looking like a white girl ain't so great since I realized I could be beaten on the street for being a dyke" (Moraga, *Loving in*

---

[29] Melissa Fitch Lockhart, "Queer Representation in Latino Theatre," *Latin American Theatre Review* 31 2 (Spring 1998), 73.

[30] Moraga, *Loving in the War Years*, p. 52.

the War, p. 52). "In this country," writes Moraga, "lesbianism is a poverty – as is being brown, as is being a woman, as is being just plain poor. The danger lies in ranking the oppressions. *The danger lies in failing to acknowledge the specificity of the oppression*"(52). She then goes on to explain that we must all come to terms with what it feels like to be a victim – any kind of victim – in order for oppressed peoples to unite.

Moraga's first play, *Giving up the Ghost*, will be discussed later in this chapter as the first play by and about lesbian Mechicanas. Her subsequent (published) plays do not revolve around gay or lesbian characters, but there are representatives of homosexuality in the two plays that followed *Giving up the Ghost*. Curiously, in her first three plays Moraga goes full-circle in exploring the theme(s) of female and male homosexualities. She begins with a play about a thwarted love affair between a Chicana lesbian and her older, heterosexual Mexicana lover. In her next play, *Shadow of a Man*, we can infer that the young girl, Lupe, will some day come out, and we can also see that her father is in love with another man, but these are not necessarily the central issues. In the following play, *Heroes and Saints*, Moraga leaves the theme of lesbianism behind and includes a gay brother and a sexually ambivalent priest, neither of whom is the central figure.[31]

Family Secrets: Shadow of a Man

Cherríe Moraga's second produced play, *Shadow of a Man*, was first developed in María Irene Fornes' playwright's Lab in 1985 and received its world premiere in 1990, directed by Fornes. The production was co-produced by Brava! For Women in the Arts and the Eureka Theater in San Francisco, California.[32] In this play Moraga explores the problems of a Chicano family torn apart by secrets: past "sins" and future possibilities of sinning. According to Yvonne Yarbro-Bejarano, the play's fundamental theme is desire. In her words, "*Shadow* traces the erotic hunger for passion and

---

[31] *The Hungry Woman: Mexican Medea*, will appear in Caridad Svitch and María Teresa Marrero (eds.), *Out of the Fringe: Contemporary Latina/Latino Theatre and Performance* (New York: TCG, 1999). In this play Moraga places a Chicana lesbian at the center of the action. María Teresa Marrero discusses a draft of this play in "Out of the Fringe: Desire and Homosexuality in the 90s Latino Theatre," *Latin American Theatre Review* 32 2 (Spring 1999), 96–98.

[32] There are two versions of this text in print. The first appears in Feyder (ed.) *Shattering the Myth*, pp. 9–48. The second, revised version is in Moraga's trilogy, *Heroes and Saints and Other Plays* (1994), pp. 37–84. Footnotes to the text will refer to the 1994 version. Yarbro-Bejarano's article refers to the San Francisco production, although she cites the ms. of the (then) forthcoming version in the Feyder anthology.

wholeness of each of the members of this family."[33] Further, Yarbro-Bejarano argues that "this is a play about heterosexuality (pace Lupe's budding lesbian sexuality) although the take on it is clearly not a traditional one" (Yarbro-Bejarano, "Moraga's 'Shadow'," p. 92).

Written in a style that combines realism and surrealism with Fornesian monologues and tableaux, this domestic drama takes place within and without the family's home as Hortensia, the wife and mother, fights in vain to hold her family together. Her son, Rigo, whom we never see, is lost to them when he marries an Anglo woman. We watch as Manuel, the father, abuses his wife and ultimately drinks himself to death. While Manuel cannot accept nor even understand his sexual attraction to his *compadre*, Conrado, the youngest daughter, Lupe, is beginning to realize her fascination with the female body. One of the biggest secrets, the Big Lie that has dissolved the marriage, is the fact that Lupe is actually Conrado's daughter. Her presence represents a sexual boundary crossing for both Hortensia and Manuel, a transgression against the morals of society and the Church. The threat of damnation dominates these characters' lives.

Unable to accept his homosexual desire, Manuel has suppressed his physical attraction to his best friend, a man who both men and women find attractive and dangerous. In what some might consider a clearly phallic reference, Hortensia tells Rosario that Conrado's very touch would make the hair on her arms "stand straight up." To this, Rosario reminds her, "Conrado was not the kina man you marry" (Moraga, *Heroes*, p. 64). Conrado is, however, every man's fantasy of masculine sexuality, certainly Manuel's. Both the wife and the husband have an irresistible attraction to someone neither can ever have. However, the night Lupe was conceived Manuel "offered" Hortensia to Conrado and, as he puts it: "I floated into the room with him. In my mind I was him. And then I was her too. In my mind I imagined their pleasure, and I turned to nothing" (71). By "turning to nothing," Manuel is allowing himself to be emasculated; he is forfeiting his heterosexual, masculine privilege for the role of objectified and subjugated woman. By imagining himself in bed with them he reveals his subconscious desire to become her, enjoying him. According to Yarbro-Bejarano, in Mechicano culture, "The male homosexual is held in contempt because he voluntarily assumes the role of woman, the penetrated *chingada* ['fucked one']." (Yarbro-Bejarano, "Female Subject in Chicano

---

[33] Yvonne Yarbro-Bejarano, "Cherríe Moraga's 'Shadow of a Man': Touching the Wound in Order to Heal," in Lynda Hart and Peggy Phelan (eds.), *Acting Out: Feminist Performances* (Michigan, 1993), p. 101.

Theatre," p. 145). Certainly, in describing his transformation into "her," Manuel does, indeed script a female, penetrated subject position; a role he cannot accept.

By turning into "nothing," Moraga tells us, the man becomes a woman, who, in the Mechicano culture is less than nothing, especially after having been violated. Tomás Almaguer notes that studies of homosexual behavior among Mexican men reveal the fact that the dominant male partner, the "inserter," does not lose his sense of masculinity. "What may be called the 'bisexual escape hatch' functions to insure that the tenuous masculinity of Mexican men is not compromised through the homosexual act; they remain men, *hombres*, even though they participate in this sexual behavior."[34] Thus by "becoming her," Manuel becomes the woman while Conrado maintains his privileged position.

Male sexuality has always been of interest to Moraga, beginning with a short story, titled "It is You, My Sister, Who Must Be Protected." The narrator, Cecelia, begins: "Maybe you'll understand this. My mother was not the queer one, but my father" (Moraga, *War Years*, p. 8). She then goes on to relate how her father has lost any feeling for her mother and seems to be much happier in the presence of men: ". . . daddy seems to love men. It's true. You know how he always gets excited with any ole new friend he makes at the plant" (11). This description of the father, published in 1983, seems a stage direction for the future character of Manuel, who also loses interest in his wife and prefers the company of men. According to Yarbro-Bejarano: "At issue in *Shadow* is not whether Manuel is gay or not; instead, the audience is invited to consider sexuality along a continuum, to explore the intersections between homosociality and homosexuality" (Yarbro-Bejarano, "Moraga's 'Shadow'," p. 92).

Hortensia tells her sister that all Manuel talks about is Conrado. In another scene, a conversation between Manuel and Rosario, Manuel tells her that Conrado is building swimming pools in Phoenix. The talk of the desert and water reminds Manuel of his youth, his innocence. He recalls when he was an adolescent living in the desert and he and his cousins were riding in the back of a truck when a desert thunder shower took them by surprise. "Then right there in the open back of the troque [truck] we tore off our clothes and took our showers in the rain. Sometimes . . . you want to be a boy like that again" (Moraga, *Heroes*, p. 55). Manuel conflates the

---

[34] Tomás Almaguer, "Chicano Men: A Cartography of Homosexual Identity and Behavior," *differences* 3.2 (1991), p. 84.

swimming pools with the clean, clear water that comes from the sky in an innocently homosocial shower scene.

A few scenes later Manuel rejects Hortensia's sexual advances, slaps her and throws her to the ground in disgust. Contrasted with the image of the pure desert shower Hortensia runs to the bathtub and attempts to douche herself with vinegar, to clear away the shame and guilt she feels for having borne Conrado's daughter. The wife becomes the bond and the division between the two men, literally, for she was the one to enjoy Conrado's passion, destroying Manuel's fantasy and his sense of male self-worth. After that night the memory of Conrado becomes a wedge between the two and the marriage is doomed. Lupe is born and Manuel sees Conrado in her eyes. When Hortensia looks at Lupe all she can see is guilt.

Hortensia begs Manuel to have sex with her but he will not even discuss the matter; he cannot tell her that she is not the object of his sexual desires and instead, beats her. The burden of their secret desires is too much for either of these people and after a visit from Conrado, Manuel finally realizes that he will never have what he truly desires and kills himself. Curiously, recall that Moraga was critical of the fact that Josefa, in *Day of the Swallows*, felt that death was her only recourse. Yet in her own portrayal of male homosexuality, Moraga, too, dooms the homosexually charged Chicano character to die. Portillo romanticized her lesbian character; Moraga paints a very negative picture of Manuel, regardless of his sexual desires.

Moraga contrasts Manuel and his sexual confusion with the twelve-year-old daughter, Lupe, coming into her own as a woman. In her portrayal of Lupe, Moraga leaves behind Corky, the blatantly masculine character she wrote about in *Giving up the Ghost*, and portrays, instead, Lupe, who *it is assumed* (and which Yarbro-Bejarano confirms, above) will eventually adopt a lesbian position. The first image we see is of Lupe's head, illuminated by a single votive candle under her chin, with "the shadow of a crucifix" looming behind her. She is in the bathroom, the only private refuge in the house, looking at her face in the mirror as she talks to herself revealing her interest in the naked female body. She has secrets which determine her character: "I can see through Sister Genevieve's habit, . . . she has a naked body under there. I try not to see [her] this way, but I can't stop . . . Sometimes I think I should tell somebody about myself . . . no matter how many times I try to tell the priest what I hold insida me, I know I'm still lying. Sinning. Keeping secrets" (Moraga, *Heroes*, p. 42).

In another scene, Lupe's lesbian desire reveals itself in a biblical allegory.

While polishing her sister's toenails, Lupe goes into an elaborate re-creation of the moment Jesus forgives Mary Magdalene, picturing Magdalene crying at Jesus' feet, wiping her hair on them. "Can you imagine what it musta felt like to have this woman with such beautiful hair *wiping* it on you? It's jus too much to think about" (70). Unfortunately for Lupe, it appears that her older sister, Leticia, is not aware of the sexual connotations in her little sister's melodramatic moment. Lupe is probably dying to tell her about her secrets but this revelation is as far as she can go. The image is both religious and sensual. As Yarbro-Bejarano states: "Paradoxically, the church also offers outlets for sexuality and subjectivity. Alongside the repression of the body and sexual desire, Catholicism provides its followers with a peculiar brand of sensuality. Moraga's writing characteristically infuses Mexican and Catholic archetypes with the 'heat' of female desire" (Yarbro-Bejarano, "Moraga's 'Shadow'," p. 100).

Framing the action of this play, the last picture literally "mirrors" the first, with Lupe, again at the bathroom mirror, revealing her final secret, to be "inside" of her girlfriend's body: "I've decided my confirmation name will be Frances cuz that's what Frankie Pacheco's name is and I wanna be in her body . . . If I could, I'd like to jus' unzip her chest and climb right in there, next to her heart, to feel everything she's feeling and I could forget about me" (Moraga, *Heroes*, 84). Lupe is already susceptible to a sense of guilt for her sexual attraction to the female body and wants to erase herself. She knows that condemnation and damnation await her.

This play is a woman's piece, originally written for four women and two "shadows;" clouded images of the men in the story. In an early draft, directed as a staged reading by José Guadalupe Saucedo for the Latino Lab in Los Angeles in 1989, Manuel and Conrado appeared only as shadows, behind a white scrim. They were never actually seen. But when María Irene Fornes directed this play in 1990, she persuaded Moraga to include the male characters as visible entities. By including the men on stage, the playwright thus objectifies them and demonstrates through their actions as well as their words, their roles in the sexual ambivalence of the whole.

Of plagues and pesticides: Heroes and Saints

As discussed in previous chapters of this book, Moraga's third play, *Heroes and Saints*, explores and exposes problems of cultural identity, assimilation and economic survival in a central California farm worker community. The main problem centers on the growers' use of pesticides; however, this play also explores the issue of homosexual desire in the character of the brother, Mario. Physically, the playwright describes him as "well built, endearingly macho in his manner" (Moraga, *Heroes and Saints*, p. 95). In other words, the actor playing Mario must "appear" masculine, giving no stereotypical (feminine) hint of his sexual preferences. Early in the play, before we know anything about his sexual orientation, Mario announces that he is going to San Francisco and his sister, Yolanda, warns him: "You better stay away from the jotos (fags). You don't wanna catch nothing." To which he replies: "I got it covered, hermana [sister]" (97). The reference can be read two ways: "Don't worry," or, more to the point, "I'll wear a condom." This foreshadowing of "jotos" and "covers" might be lost to the observer until a little later in the scene, when Father Juanito is introduced and the stage directions indicate that when Mario greets him, it is "with interest" (98).

About thirty minutes into the first act, it becomes clear that Mario is attracted to men. When Cerezita asks him to recount the "story of the Mayan god," any thoughts of indigenous folk tales are quickly dispelled. Mario relates a personal experience he had as a boy, recounting the night a handsome older cousin came into his bedroom: "The next thing I know, my young god is standing at the foot of my bed. His shirt is open to his waist . . . more Mayan rock . . . My little heart is pounding as he tells me how –" (105). We never hear what, exactly, happened between the two boys. Mario's sensual account is interrupted when a car horn breaks the fantasy and he has to leave. But it is clear that Mario loves men, for their masculine, sensuous beauty.

Once Mario has left, Yolanda refers to the man that picked him up as a "sleazy gringo," to which Cerezita responds: "He doesn't like him." "Well, for not liking him," Yolanda answers, "he sure sees him a lot." Cerezita confirms our suspicions when she replies: "He gives him things" (105). By now, it is clear that Mario is going to San Francisco to participate in the openly gay lifestyle allowed there and denied to gays and lesbians in small, unforgiving towns. It is also clear that both Cerezita and Yolanda know about Mario's sexual orientation, but they never discuss his sexuality among themselves. Mario is not closeted but there are few people in this small town with whom he can really be honest.

Towards the end of the first act Mario and Juan are sitting on a park bench, discussing life in the valley. Mario indicates that he does not think he will live forever. When Juan reminds him that he is still young, Mario responds: "I get high, Padre. I smoke and snort and suck up anything and anyone that will have me"(114). Mario then leaves when a car honks for him.

Moraga purposely paints a negative portrait of this gay Chicano, a man who abandons the family to seek a community and physical pleasures that do, indeed, make him sick. He leaves the family for the same reason so many homosexual men and women have to leave their homes. He is escaping both the bigotry of his surroundings and the living conditions the family suffers.

Still, audiences have questioned Mario's self-serving motives. In the discussion with the playwright after a reading of this play which I directed in 1993, a young Chicano protested this negative portrayal of gay Chicanos. Moraga simply responded: "If I portray this type it is because he exists. I cannot change that and I will not apologize for any of my characterizations."[35] An important part of Moraga's project is to teach playwriting workshops for gay, lesbian and bisexual Latina/o youth in San Francisco. Thus, she confronts daily the attitude among many young gay men that they might as well live recklessly, since everybody around them is dying anyway. This attitude can also be traced to the self-hatred many gays and lesbians have been taught to cultivate.

As if in response to questions about Moraga's negative portrayals, Yarbro-Bejarano concludes her article about *Shadow of Man* with the following statement: "Moraga's refusal to produce 'positive images' prohibits a complacent spectator position for non-Latino and Latino viewers alike . . . [she] examines the contradictions, the mixed messages, the positive as well as the negative. For Moraga, criticizing her culture is an act of love" (Yarbro-Bejarano, "Moraga's 'Shadow'," p. 102).

In her second book of prose and poetry, titled *The Last Generation,* Moraga expresses that critique towards her gay brothers, but with the chastising tone of a loving, older sister: "As much as I see a potential alliance with gay men in our shared experience of homophobia, the majority of gay men still cling to what privileges they can. I have often been severely disappointed and hurt by the misogyny of gay Chicanos."[36] She is critical of Chicano gay men for being "reluctant to recognize and acknowledge that their freedom is intricately connected to the freedom of women" (162). Whether consciously or subconsciously, Moraga has let this critique influence her characterization of Mario; she will not let the gay Chicano off easily in this play, as much as she loves him.

In the second act, during a farewell party for him, Dolores, acknowledges that she knows Mario is gay and cannot accept it. "I know already for a long

---

[35] I directed a staged reading of *Heroes and Saints* for the Bilingual Foundation for the Arts, in Los Angeles, California, in June of 1993. The quotes are from my personal records of the event.

[36] Cherríe Moraga, *The Last Generation* (Boston, South End Press, 1993), p. 161.

time," she tells him, continuing, "*Me choco* [It shocked or disgusted me] the first time I seen you with your hands digging into Yolie's purse like they belong there" (Moraga, *Heroes*, p. 123). A little later, Dolores tells Mario: "God made you a man and you throw it away. You lower yourself into half a man" (124). Again, Moraga reflects the Mechicano construction of gender through Dolores, telling him he is only "half a man" by "choosing" a gay lifestyle, which his mother conflates with femininity.

It is through the ultra-conservative Dolores that the playwright exposes the kinds of attitudes that abound in sectors of the community, attitudes that destroy families. In a speech that is all-too-familiar to many gay males, Dolores tells Mario that AIDS is God's punishment for his aberrant lifestyle. Death and damnation are all that Dolores sees in her son's future. Mario leaves and returns at the end of the play, obviously dying of AIDS. Although he had abandoned the family, Mario redeems himself when he shouts: "Burn the fields," inspiring the townspeople to revolt against the oppressive growers in a final cataclysmic image of the burning fields.

Heroes and Saints is not a play about homosexuality, per se, but by including the gay brother and having him contract AIDS, the playwright brings this much-needed discussion into a dialogue that demands action regarding both pesticides and AIDS. For some observers, the addition of a gay character distracts from the major issues of the play. However, in the playwright's analysis, it is important to link the deaths and disfigurations brought on by both pesticides and AIDS. Both issues continue to demand the public's attention.[37]

Plays with gay/lesbian central characters

The first gay Chicano play: Edgar Poma's Reunion

In 1981 Edgar Poma wrote what appears to have been the first produced play centered on a Chicano gay male, titled *Reunion*. The play was initially written as a ten-minute exercise for Carlos Morton's Chicano theatre workshop at the University of California at Berkeley in 1980. The play was actually written as part of the young student's own coming-out process.[38] Poma was born in 1960 in Northern California, the son of Filipino migrant workers. Having grown up in a culturally mixed California neighborhood,

[37] I have not read a critique of this play that feels Moraga is tackling too many subjects in *Heroes and Saints*. This observation comes from remarks I have heard from colleagues in the field over the years.

[38] From a letter from Mr. Poma dated February 6, 1993, in my files.

Poma understood the Chicano culture and decided to explore cultural and sexual identities in his play. What he discovered was the universality of the coming-out theme.

"I made my characters Chicano," wrote Poma, "discovering in the process that my experiences as an Asian-American paralleled certain Latino cultural values."[39] Soon after he wrote the play, two San Francisco teatros, Teatro Latino and Teatro Gusto, joined forces as Teatro Yerbabuena under the direction of the late Rodrigo Reyes to further develop and produce the play at the Mission Cultural Center in San Francisco in August of 1981.[40] The play attracted large audiences in the heart of the city's Latino community, the Mission District. According to Yvonne Yarbro-Bejarano, "Performances were followed by lengthy, lively discussions."[41]

Reunion portrays the familiar coming-out story in which the gay son brings home his lover. I say "familiar," in reference to non-Latino plays, however. In his review of the play's premiere production Francisco X. Alarcón called it "the first play dealing primarily with a gay theme *performed by a Latino theatre group* in the U.S." [italics mine] (Alarcón, "A Challenge," p. 11). I would say that *Reunion* was probably the first Chicano gay-themed play produced by *any* theatre group in the United States.

In his review of that production, Alarcón commented: "Many social demons – homophobia, sexism, 'machismo,' sexual repression, etc., – are invoked throughout the play; however, they are not dealt with in a conclusive way. The demons are never exorcised" (12). There is the danger of caricaturizing in the play, yet Alarcón concluded: "In short, *Reunion* is an excellent play, conceived and presented with great honesty"(12). As the title to Alarcón's review indicates, sexual taboos were being challenged and tested and his ultimate response to this production was to overlook the play's weaknesses and rejoice in its audacity.

Reunion did not get produced again until Teatro Chicano and Teatro Carmen, of Tucson, Arizona, mounted the play in 1986. Again, the play was greeted with mixed responses, yet the very fact that it was being produced reflected the changing attitudes that had evolved in the era of AIDS: a much bolder spirit in the gay and Lesbian Chicano communities. Although the reaction of the Tucson press was "lukewarm," the playwright felt that the

[39] From the program notes of the Teatro Chicano/Teatro Carmen production in Tucson, Arizona, June 26–28, 1986, n.p.

[40] Francisco X. Alarcón, "A Challenge to a Sexual Taboo," *El Tecolote* (San Francisco) (December 1981), 11.

[41] Yarbro-Bejarano, "The Female Subject," p. 145, footnote 38.

closing night benefit performance for the Tucson AIDS Project left the audience "enthralled."[42]

Looking back at the initial production, Poma feels that the play served a very important purpose "because it extended the power and diversity of politically charged gay Chicano students bent on improving the Chicano Studies Department and the university in general by forcing recognition, more courses, etc."[43] This play cannot be considered "great theatre" but it is nevertheless important documentation and must be recognized as the first of its kind, raising questions heretofore avoided in Chicano theatre and culture. *Reunion* remained the only play with a central gay Chicano character *written by a gay man* until 1996, when Guillermo Reyes' *Deporting the Divas* was first produced. Between 1981 and 1999, several playwrights, both gay and straight, included gay characters in their plays.[44]

Cherríe Moraga's lesbian representations

Revealing lesbian desire: Giving up the Ghost

Cherríe Moraga's first play, *Giving up the Ghost*, was originally presented as a staged reading at the Foot of the Mountain Theatre, in Minneapolis, in 1984, directed by Kim Hines. The world premiere of another, more fully developed version of this play was produced by San Francisco's gay/lesbian theatre company, Theatre Rhinoceros, in 1989, co-directed by Anita Mattos and José Guadalupe Saucedo. This version became a part of Moraga's trilogy, *Heroes and Saints and Other Plays*, published in 1994. *Giving up the Ghost* is the first play about lesbian desire, written by a lesbian, to be produced and published.[45]

In her review of the San Francisco production, Catalina Cariaga wrote that the play was initially ". . . a set of poems – women's voices emerging from Moraga's collective unconscious . . . Moraga allowed these voices to settle into three distinct characters."[46] Actually, the three women on stage represent two characters, Marisa and her younger self, known as "Corky,"

[42] Letter from Poma dated February, 6, 1993.

[43] *Ibid.*

[44] Edgar Poma continues to write plays, now focusing on Asian-Americans. He is also writing a novel. None of his plays have been published to date.

[45] The earlier version of *Giving up the Ghost* is published singly by West End Press, Los Angeles, California, 1986. The version produced by Theatre Rhinoceros is in Moraga, *Heroes and Saints and Other Plays*, pp. 1–35. All references to this play are from the 1994 edition but citations will give page references for both versions below.

[46] Catalina Cariaga, "The Poetics of *Chisme*," "Poetry Flash" [Berkeley, CA] No. 195, June 1989, np.

played by two distinct actors, and the third woman, Amalia, Marisa's lover. Focusing her analysis on the relationship between Marisa and Amalia, Cariaga writes: "Neither is quite sure how or why the love between them has come to be or if it should or will last. They either ignore or avoid these questions. Each is filled with too many inner conflicts – 'ghosts' to overcome" (Cariaga, "Poetics," np.).

Although this play has been produced in only a few venues, because of the importance of the author and because it has been published twice it has generated a great deal of interest from several literary and theatre critics. Like most writers' first plays, the initial publication of *Giving up the Ghost* has the aura of autobiography, the resonance of a soul on fire, eager to share the flames.[47] I use the term "fire" because the play suggests a burning. A burning of old ideas, an incineration of outdated attitudes; but most especially, a burning of passion. In the first version of *Giving up the Ghost* Moraga created a beautifully simple, yet considerably complex series of monologues delivered unabashedly to the audience, with very little interaction between the three women on stage. Together, these characters revealed the beauty of understanding and respecting one's self, despite society's rejections.

In Erik MacDonald's words, "through these roles, the play critiques the cultural oppression of Chicanas and analyzes individual and cultural problems of lesbian identification."[48] When Moraga published the revised version in 1994 she wrote: "This current version is based to a large degree on the Theatre Rhinoceros production"(Moraga, *Heroes*, p. 4). She had begun to explore dialogue as opposed to monologue and her directors, Kim Hines, Laura Esparza, and especially Anita Mattos and José Guadalupe Saucedo, undoubtedly informed her playwriting as they worked with her and the actors. The 1994 version is much more "complete" as a dramatic text, than the first series of poems.

In the first version there is no actual plot other than the eventual acknowledgment by Marisa of her ability to survive. Mostly, the three women talk to the audience, listed by Moraga as "The People," in the Cast of Characters; the playwright's attempt to make the collective viewers active participants in the play. The actors looked at one another, acknowledging

---

[47] Yarbro-Bejarano refers to the characters of Corky and Lupe (*Shadow of a Man*) as embodying "some autobiographical elements of Moraga's early struggles with Catholicism and sexuality." Yarbro-Bejarano, "Moraga's 'Shadow'," p. 98.

[48] Eric McDonald, *Theater at the Margins: Text and the Post-Structured Stage* (Michigan, 1993), p. 153. He is writing about the first edition of this play.

the other's presence, but there was very little "dramatic" tension or interaction between them. No debate. The debate was with the society that has given these women few options other than to conform to or rebel against patriarchal condemnation. Corky/Marisa is the central figure, the autobiographical character who narrates her journey from a young, tomboy-like Chicana who knows that she is "difernt," to the older Marisa, who has accepted her lesbian desire and wishes to express it with the older Mexican, Amalia. Amalia mourns a lost male lover, a simple man from a Mexican village. It is the man's ghost that tears Marisa and Amalia apart, leaving Marisa to mourn her other ghosts, including Corky, as she picks up the pieces of a lost relationship.

A sample of the kind of language and thought in this play may illustrate its honesty and force:

> It's odd being queer.
> It's not that you don't want a man,
> you just don't want a man in a man.
> You want a man in a woman.[49]

Yet this is not an angry outcry against men, but more of a sincere attempt to share some of the experiences a woman can go through, passing from childhood to womanhood, from innocence to wisdom. And, from naiveté to cynicism as in the rape scene described by Corky. In one of the most arresting accounts of sexual violation I have ever encountered in a play, Corky tells how, at the age of twelve, she was raped. The narrative is a mixture of comedy and pathos, told with such truth that it is an actor's dream. When a man whom she thinks is a school custodian asks her to help him fix a desk, Corky agrees and finds herself underneath the drawer, supposedly holding it for him. Eventually, he coerces his way into a sexual penetration:

> Then he hit me with it
> into what was supposed to be a hole (. . .)
> But with this one
> there was no hole
> he had to make it
> 'n' I see myself down there like a face
> with no opening
> a face with no features
> no eyes no nose no mouth

---

[49] Moraga, *Heroes*, p. 21 and *Giving up the Ghost* (Los Angeles: West End Press, 1986, 1992), p. 29.

only little lines where they shoulda been
so I dint cry.
I never cried as he shoved that thing
into what was supposed to be a mouth
with no teeth
with no hate
with no voice
only a hole. A HOLE!
(gritando[shouting])
HE MADE ME A HOLE![50]

In her analysis of this scene, María Herrera-Sobek concludes: ". . . the rape scene encodes a political metaphor for society's marginalization of women. It traces, in a few powerful lines, the socialization process visited upon the female sex which indoctrinates them into accepting a subordinate position in the socio-political landscape of a system."[51] In her study of this play, Yvonne Yarbro-Bejarano also comments upon the rape scene as startling evidence of the woman's penetrated position:

> Up to the time of the rape Corky had thought it could never happen to her because she had denied her femaleness, rejecting the role of *chingada* [the fucked one] and identifying with the *chingón* [fucker], the active, aggressive, closed person who inflicts the wound. The rape brings home Corky's sex to her as an inescapable fact, confirming her culture's definition of female as being taken.[52]

In her review of the San Francisco production Cariaga also draws attention to the rape scene. Cariaga quotes from a speech by Norma Alarcón in which she discussed "the re-occurring topic of rape in the work of women writers . . . 'Perhaps,' she [Alarcón] said, 'it expresses the forcefulness of their negation from the literature of the dominant Anglo culture' " (Cariaga, "Poetics of *Chisme*," np.). From the symbolic rape of women as writers to the actual retelling of a rape in Moraga's vision, the taboo topic is finally exposed for what it is: a political act. As Corky puts it, her "hole" had no voice. After Corky has shouted out her last line (as quoted above), Marisa wraps a rebozo around her shoulders and holds her. Marisa then takes over the scene with the following dialogue which is no longer in verse:

[50] Moraga, *Heroes*, p. 29 and Moraga, *Ghost*, pp. 42–43.
[51] María Herrera-Sobek, "The Politics of Rape: Sexual Transgression in Chicana Fiction," in María Herrera-Sobek and Helena María Viramontes (eds.), *Chicana Criticism and Creativity: New Frontiers in American Literature* (Albuquerque: New Mexico, 1996), p. 249.
[52] Yvonne Yarbro-Bejarano, "The Female Subject," p. 147.

I don't regret it. I don't regret nuthin'. He only convinced me of my own name . . . And then, years later, after I got to be with some other men, I admired how their things had no opening . . . only a tiny pinhole dot to pee from, to come from. I thought . . . how lucky they were, that they could release all that stuff, all that pent-up shit from the day, through a hole that *nobody* could get into.[53]

In her analysis of the first version of *Giving up the Ghost*, Tiffany Ann López sees the rape monologue as "the play's core scene because it synthesizes the process of seeing, touching, and naming that is necessary to her characters' process of healing."[54] López also points-out the fact that after the rape monologue Corky "disappears from the rest of the play, a narrative shift that symbolizes how such acts of violence against women serve to erase them, literally, from the social text" (173). López chooses to discuss the first version of this play because she believes that the characters are more involved with the audience, making it more "artistically confrontational" (p. 176, footnote 3). López is also better able to make her point about Corky's disappearance in the first version since there is non-verbal interaction between all three women after the rape in the second version. Yet, even in the second version, Corky soon disappears from the text and the stage, supporting López's assertion that Corky's disappearance represents the erasure of the raped woman by her community.

According to Sue-Ellen Case, *Giving up the Ghost* was exceptional beyond the Chicana/o community, making groundbreaking statements that reverberated in the feminist movement as a whole. "Within the feminist community," Case writes, "the play was exceptional for its material and multiple identity construction, in contrast to the few white lesbian plays which had appeared, without class or race specificity – taking for granted the bourgeois, white lesbian as normative" (Case, "Seduced and Abandoned," p. 99).

Yvonne Yarbro-Bejarano echoes Case in her analysis of the various subjects being de-constructed in this play. "The representation of female desiring subjects in *Giving up the Ghost* is culture-, class-, and race-specific; their subjectivity as sexual beings is shaped in dialectical relationship to a collective way of imagining sexuality. The text explores the ways in which Chicanas, both lesbian and heterosexual, have internalized their culture's concepts of sexuality" (Yarbro-Bejarano, "Female Subject," p. 145).

---

[53] Moraga, *Heroes*, p. 29 and Moraga, *Ghost*, pp. 43–44.
[54] Tiffany Ann López, "Performing Aztlán: The Female Body as Cultural Critique in the *Teatro* of Cherríe Moraga," in Jeffrey D. Mason and J. Ellen Gainor (eds.), *Performing America: Cultural Nationalism in American Theater* (Michigan, 1999), p. 169.

The "ghost" that the title refers to is multiple. Amalia cannot let go of her dead lover's ghost; Marisa cannot let go of Amalia; nor can she let go of her younger self, Corky. In the process of telling us her story, Marisa does, in fact, let go of her cultural taboos. Marisa reveals for the listener/observer, her frustrated desires and in so doing, revolts against and rejects the pro-scribed behavior expected by her community. Although it is clear from the beginning that Marisa/Corky is a lesbian, we are never quite certain what Amalia's sexual orientation is.

Unlike the naive and one-dimensional representation of lesbian desire in *Day of the Swallows*, Moraga writes from experience and can thus present us with multiple sexual identities. In doing so, Moraga paints characters that are complex in their psychology and not easily categorized nor ana-lyzed. In Norma Alarcón's words: "Moraga puts into play the concepts 'man' and 'woman' (and the parodic 'butch/femme'), with intuitive knowledge that they operate in our subjectivities, so that it is difficult to analyze them."[55]

Finally, Cherríe Moraga's *Giving up the Ghost* is a milestone in the history and evolution of a Chicana/o dramaturgy, gay or straight. Like Edgar Poma's *Reunion*, this play exposed (and exposes) its audiences to topics they might never have encountered in public spaces otherwise. Granted, the majority of audiences who witnessed Moraga's first play were women, gay and straight, and as Latinas they could only rejoice in seeing their sisters and mothers, aunts and cousins on stage as women. Desiring women. Lustful and lusty women fighting their demons. Marisa may have lost Amalia, her Mexico, but she gained a deeper understanding of herself, as did the people who allowed these characters to come into their lives, if only for an evening.

Oliver Mayer's homoerotic world of boxing in the 1950s: Blade to the Heat

Oliver Mayer was born in Hollywood, California, in 1965, the son of a Chicana mother and an Anglo father. His interest in theatre came perhaps naturally, his mother forsook an acting career to raise him, and his father was a film art director in Hollywood. When Mayer was a teenager his father

[55] Norma Alarcón, "Making 'Familia' From Scratch: Split Subjectivities in the Work of Helena María Viramontes and Cherríe Moraga," in María Herrera-Sobek and Helena María Viramontes (eds.), *Chicana Criticism and Creativity: New Frontiers in American Literature* (Albuquerque: New Mexico, 1996), p. 229.

died, leaving him and his mother to form a very special bond of love and mutual support. He was raised in Studio City, California, where he attended high school. While in junior high school he saw Luis Valdez's play, *Zoot Suit*, an event that changed his life. In an interview in 1997 he told William Nericcio:

> Probably my best experience in the theater was when I saw *Zoot Suit* . . . I was a teenager with pimples and attitude and a lot of rage inside me and nowhere to put it. I was in a dangerous place. In a way that show changed my life. It was so sexy and fun and alive, and it had such joy that all these years I can still feel the thrill of watching Eddie Olmos as El Pachuco, of those lives created on stage by Luis Valdez. He gave me a kind of high water mark in my life.[56]

When Mayer enrolled as a freshman in Cornell University in 1986 he discovered that he was one of only twenty-seven Chicana and Chicano students out of a total population of sixteen thousand undergraduates. Like other Chicana/os who find themselves isolated in an Ivy League college, Mayer and his peers founded a Chicano student organization called M A S A (Mexican American Students' Association) to create a sense of community.[57] Because he is fair-skinned, over six-feet tall and has a non-Hispanic last name Mayer could easily have "passed" for Anglo, but he chose, instead, to celebrate his bi-cultural heritage. After Cornell, Mayer attended Oxford University for one year and then enrolled in the M.F.A. Program in Playwriting at Columbia University in New York City. While at Columbia Mayer studied with Howard Stein, head of the Playwriting Program and whom Mayer credits with his success as a playwright.

In 1989, immediately after completing his M.F.A., Mayer became an Associate Literary Manager at the Center Theatre Group (Mark Taper Forum) in Los Angeles. He remained in that position until 1997, writing plays and reading the many manuscripts a literary associate is required to review for potential production. This experience gave Mayer a very valuable introduction to the world of regional theatre, offering the playwright an intimate knowledge of the inner workings of the distinct world of non-profit theatre. As a member of the staff of Los Angeles' most prestigious professional theatre company, Mayer could interact with a virtual "Who's Who" of the theatrical and cinematic world of Los Angeles.

[56] William Nericcio, "Interview With Oliver Mayer," *Performing Arts* [Music Center of Los Angeles County] (March–May, 1996), p. P–5–P7. This is the program for the Mark Taper Forum production of *Blade to the Heat*.

[57] From a discussion by Meyer in my seminar, May 4, 1999.

One of Mayer's first plays, titled *Young Valiant,* was given a professional reading at the South Coast Repertory Theatre's Hispanic Playwright's Project in 1989, directed by José Guadalupe Saucedo.[58] *Young Valiant* is an autobiographical two-act play that centers on a twelve-year-old boy, his Chicana mother and his Anglo father. The boy, called simply, "Boy," has a good relationship with his father but wants to know what it is like to make love to his mother. Thus this play is Mayer's re-interpretation of the Oedipal myth in which the boy's incestuous urges are not acted out. The love of the father for both his wife and his son is clear as is the age-old rivalry between both males for the wife/mother/nurturer. The play is a loving homage to his father, a strong, "man's man" who fears his impending old age just as the boy begins to feel his sexual awakening.

Other plays include *Joe Louis Blues* directed by Abdul Salaam El Razzac at the Los Angeles Theatre Center in 1992 and *The Chess Machine,* which had a staged reading in the Mark Taper's "Mentor Playwrights Reading Series" the same year, directed by Oskar Eustis. In the program to that reading, Mayer thanks Cuban-American playwright, Eduardo Machado, for "All the right exercises." In 1994 *Ragged Time* was produced at the Royal Court Theatre, London, directed by Hattie MacDonald. In 1997 *The Road to Los Angeles* was produced at SPARC (Public Art Center), in Venice, California, as a work-in-progress directed by Natsuko Ohama and also had another workshop production at the San José Repertory Theatre, San José, California. In 1999, Mayer was working on a screenplay of *Blade to the Heat* produced by Madonna for national television.

The play that interests us here is Mayer's best-known work to date, *Blade to the Heat,* a heterosexual man's exploration of homoeroticism in the world of professional boxing.[59] Following his father's influence and example, Mayer was fascinated by the sport of boxing from early childhood on. Mayer had boxed as a young man; had worn his black eyes as badges of honor, making his father proud of the fact that his son was a "real man." Years later, in 1991, Mayer began to wonder how people in and out of the boxing world would respond if they discovered that a boxer were gay. Although he is not gay, Mayer acknowledges the sexuality/sensuality of the boxing ring. He knew a great deal about the history of boxing and recalled that in 1959 an African-American boxer, Emile Griffiths, had killed another

---

[58] *Young Valiant* is published by the South Coast Repertory Theatre's Hispanic Playwright's Project, Vol. 11, No. 1 (1989).

[59] Oliver Mayer, *Blade to the Heat* (New York: Dramatists Play Service, revised 1996). All references to this play are from this revised version, which is the version the playwright prefers.

Figure 9. Blade to the Heat, by Oliver Mayer. New York Shakespeare Festival, 1994. Directed by George C. Wolfe. L. to R. Maricela Ochoa, Paul Calderon.

boxer in the ring after the boxer had accused him of being homosexual. Mayer decided to write a fictional play based on this event, leading to the world premiere production of *Blade to the Heat* at the Joseph Papp Public Theatre in 1994, directed by Artistic Director, George C. Wolfe. It was a very spectacular production and although the play received mixed reviews Mayer was now among the elite of the theatrical world, joining the ranks of many playwrights whose professional careers had (and have) been launched in that venue. Mayer was the third Chicano playwright in history to have his play fully produced by a major company in New York City and *Blade to the Heat* was the fourth play about Chicana/os to be produced in New York City as well.[60]

Explaining the origins of the title Mayer told William Nericcio:

> In metallurgy when you put a blade or some kind of metal to the heat or the fire you test the m-e-t-t-l-e of the m-e-t-a-l and judging from its amalgam, from how many parts iron to whatever, it will either break or it will get stronger. I'm writing about a world of cultural fusion where mixed-blooded, Latin and black people are undergoing trial by fire. And they either break or they get stronger.
>
> (Nericcio, "Interview," p. 6)

After the New York production, the late Ron Link directed the play for the Center Theatre Group and he and Mayer made changes to the text, re-focussing the play on the characters and their actions, rather than on the spectacle. *Blade to the Heat* is about a fictitious young Irish-Mexican boxer, Pedro Quinn, struggling with his sexual, cultural and athletic identity. At the beginning of the play Pedro is asexual; he has not had the time to get involved with women and is very much a loner. Quinn has always dreamed of being a champion boxer and the opening scene of the play is the match in which he wins the World Championship from an Afro-Cuban boxer, Mantequilla Decima, in a split decision. The play is cinematic in structure, moving seamlessly between the boxing ring, the locker room and other settings as we follow the rising tension between Quinn, Mantequilla and a Puerto Rican boxer named Wilfred Vinal.

The world of boxing is contrasted with the world of entertainment in the form of Quinn's best friend, Garnet, an African-American performer

---

[60] The reader is reminded that the first (and only) Chicano play produced on Broadway to date is *Zoot Suit*, produced in 1979. Other plays by or about Chicana/os produced off or off-off-Broadway are Milcha Sanchez-Scott's *Roosters*, Carlos Morton's *Pancho Diablo* and *El jardin*. All of these plays are discussed in other chapters of this book.

who has made a career impersonating James Brown and Jackie Wilson. Impersonation is an overriding theme in this play, set in a time when appearances were so important. Early on, Vinal accuses both Mantequilla and Quinn of being "*maricónes*," queers, an accusation that sets the major conflict into motion. The world of athletics is a fascinating site of male–male relationships, homoeroticism incarnate to some observers. The suggestion that a boxer (or any athlete) could be gay challenges the myth of heteronormativity on the playing field.[61] The remainder of the play is a series of encounters between the boxers, their trainers, friends and Mantequilla's girlfriend, Sarita. Each encounter establishes a character's heteronormativity, homosexuality or variation on the theme of sexuality.

Sarita is necessary for Mantequilla's image; he publicly flaunts her to prove his heterosexuality. When Mantequilla begins to have nightmares that he is, indeed, homosexual, his insecurities mount, affecting his ability to make love to Sarita, adding to his fear and frustration. According to the playwright, Mantequilla is heterosexual but his doubts arise because everybody believes that Quinn is "soft," and to lose the title to a "*maricón*" is tantamount to being one – no worse fate could be imagined in the world of boxing.[62] Mantequilla has a very homoerotic dream/nightmare in which two fighters, "their faces obscured, are grabbing and clutching each other." As the dream continues, the stage directions tell us their fighting becomes "more like they're fucking than fighting" and Mantequilla awakens from his nightmare screaming: "N O L O S O Y!!!!" [No I'm not!] (Mayer, *Blade*, p. 26).

While Sarita performs Mantequilla's heterosexual identity, Garnet's character initially hints at Quinn's homosexuality – he performs impersonations, after all. But any hints of Quinn's homosexuality give way to an outright signal when he and Garnet begin to kiss late in the play. Quinn cannot sustain the moment, however, and bites Garnet, drawing blood. As he wipes the blood from his lips, Garnet tells Quinn: "That's all you know" (38) and, indeed, Quinn does not know how to love any human being; he can only punch.

The character of Sarita, the only (speaking) woman in the play, is crucial to the constructions of masculinity in this play, especially in its time. In the 1950s it was very easy to "cover" one's sexuality by performing heteronormativity with a pretty woman on one's arm. And, unlike today's more enlightened observers, gay or straight, in the 1950s nobody questioned a

---

[61] For an informal introduction to homosexuality in professional sports see Dan Woog, *Jocks: True Stories of America's Gay Athletes* (Los Angeles: Alyson Books, 1998).

[62] Mayer told us he believes Mantequilla is heterosexual in a discussion in my seminar, May 4, 1999.

man's heterosexuality if he had a girlfriend and especially if he was married. Thus, Sarita becomes the "key" to Quinn's sexual identity crisis when she tells Mantequilla that she knew Quinn in high school, but that "We did nothing," meaning they did not have sex (27). Sarita inadvertently, adds to Mantequilla's fear that he has been defeated by a "maricón"; if Quinn was not interested in her sexually, he must be queer. When Sarita goes to the gym to speak with Quinn, his trainer, Jack, shouts joyfully: "I knew that boy flew straight!" (40), thankful for a woman's presence to dispel the gossip that plagues the man and the world he loves. Appearances.

It is the character of Wilfred Vinal that is the most transgressive in this play. He is the first publicly to accuse Mantequilla and Quinn of being *maricónes*. Immediately following his defeat by Mantequilla Vinal gets up and shouts into the microphone: "Let that little fag kick your ass. Fucking Pedro Queen! Ain't no fag ever gonna beat me"(21). Vinal is the character most in touch with his sexuality and with a clear assessment of what goes on in the minds of some boxers. Further, he is not afraid to speak about it. He tells Quinn's trainer, Jack, "Then there's the other kind. They're here because they like the smell of men. They like to share sweat . . . only a pair of wet trunks between his johnson [penis] and yours. They like it. And they like to take a whupping for liking it. That's just the way it is." Vinal tells Jack: "I'd fuck him! I'd fuck you." When Jack tells him "You're sick," Vinal glibly answers: "I tell it like it is. If some dude wants to go down on me, bring him on! I'll fuck anything! But nobody fucking me, I draw the line. Baby!" (31–32).

The action leads to the inevitable match between Mantequilla and Quinn, the final moments of the play. The match is close but when Mantequilla kisses Quinn on the mouth, as if to prove to him that he *is* queer, Quinn's anger, frustration and confusion take over. It is not a sensual kiss we observe, but a deadly one – a threat of violence rather than an expression of sexual passion. Because the audience has heard Mantequilla declare his heterosexuality all along, they know that this kiss is not transgressive; they do not panic. In the last action of the play, as Mantequilla lay dying on the mat, Pedro kisses him as he pleads, helplessly, uselessly: "Come back" (Mayer, *Blade*, p. 48). It is the epilogue to the previous Kiss of Death as Pedro speaks the final lines of the play and the scene goes into its final blackout. A kiss is not just a kiss in the boxing ring.

Guillermo Reyes' sexual border crossers: Deporting the Divas

I feel a certain amount of pride and responsibility for the evolution of *Deporting the Divas* by Guillermo Reyes. As director of the various stages in the evolution of this play, from the first reading to two subsequent fully staged versions, I am intimate with this play. The original version of *Deporting the Divas* was a loosely connected collage of scenes, playlets and monologues which had its world premiere at the Celebration Theatre, Los Angeles, California, under my direction in March of 1996. Unfortunately, the piece never came together because the through-line remained unclear. The playwright completely re-structured and re-wrote the play for a second production at the Borderlands Theatre of Tucson, Arizona, in the summer of 1996 under the direction of Chris Wilken. This production met with great success and I then directed a further revised version co-produced by the Teatro de la Esperanza and Theatre Rhinoceros in San Francisco, California, the following fall (1996). The San Francisco production, too, was very well received and is the version I will discuss here.[63]

Deporting the Divas is ultimately a love story, but Reyes positions that story within a framework that allows him to investigate and subvert inter-sections of gender, sexuality, sexual object choice, and immigrant status. The play takes place in San Diego and Tijuana, geographically symbolizing the other borders that are traversed in this play. The play combines various the-atrical styles: monologues and story theatre, in which the characters break the fourth wall to narrate and even to comment on the play itself; psycho-logical realism, and film noire fantasy. Because the location of the action shifts from place-to-place with cinematic frequency the setting must be a backdrop to the action, with furniture or set props that take on multiple functions. Sometimes the characters literally tell the audience where they are, other times, the dialogue reveals the new setting. All of the scenes revolve around Michael González, his work and his private life.

González is a Chicano Border Patrol officer in his late twenties, who is a married father of two children and who has never thought of himself as gay. When Michael's wife leaves him because "my arms are cold," he meets Sedicio, an openly gay Mexican student in his Spanish class and the two fall in love and have an affair. After a series of scenes that show the develop-ment of the affair and other aspects of Michael's work, he breaks up with Sedicio and re-unites with his (unseen) family. In the epilogue, Michael returns to the barn on the border where it all started at the beginning of the

---

[63] *Deporting the Divas* is in *Gestos* 27 (1999), pp. 109–58. All references are to this edition.

Figure 10. Deporting the Divas, by Guillermo Reyes. Miracle Theatre Company, Portland, Oregon, 1998. Directed by Michael Menger. L. to R. Andrés Alcalá, Jason Maniccia, Dan Palma, Rob Harrison, Jack Lozano.

play: the site of a Mexican gay wedding in the desert that ignited a socio/sexual confusion and curiosity in him. In this, his final monologue, Michael ends with the hope that his "divas" will return to him and "transport me to that grand, fabulous world where I will arise, one day, ready and eager to face the music and sing along!" (Reyes, *Divas*, 72).

Although we have watched Michael explore a new side of his sexuality, we have also witnessed his embarrassment at the thought; he can only enjoy Sedicio's seductiveness in private settings. Sedicio is an activist for gay and immigrant rights and, ironically, an undocumented Mexican himself – a fact which he reveals to Michael before they begin their affair. In a clever reversal of sexual borders, it is the undocumented Mexican who can be openly comfortable with his sexuality, while the citizen must hide his. Further, as an undocumented gay immigrant, Sedicio represents everything Michael has been taught and trained to fear and to reject, both figuratively and literally.

Michael enters the relationship fully aware of Sedicio's undocumented status, ignoring this "complication" as he tries to negotiate his desire. Ultimately, it is all too much for Michael and he breaks-up the relationship. In the penultimate scene Sedicio comes to Michael's home and offers him what he has wanted all along, anal intercourse. Sedicio shows him a condom and says: "This is what you needed, isn't it?" (155). But although Michael has fallen in love with Sedicio, his wife is pregnant and they are going to get back together. When Michael suggests "a discreet affair on the side" (156), this will not satisfy Sedicio so he leaves Michael alone on stage to narrate the close of the story.

This play is an ensemble piece in the tradition of collective theatre, with each of the four actors playing other characters in Michael and Sedicio's lives and imaginations. Within these multiple representations and multiple characters, it is the love affair between the Chicano and the Mexican that interests us here. It should be clear from their first encounter that there is a connection between Michael and Sedicio, a sexual/sensual energy. When Michael and Sedicio get together for coffee, Michael reveals his true intentions, to go to bed with another man, when he asks Sedicio: "When do we cut to the chase and do it?" Sedicio, who was the first to blurt-out his sexuality, retreats and tells him: "But . . . I'm into dating" (123). Contrary to popular perception of sex among most gay men, Sedicio will not jump into anybody's bed without a relationship.

The relationship that develops between the two men is almost platonic. Sedicio has "rules" about sex. After several weeks of romantic interludes,

Michael tells Sedicio he wants more than what they have been experiencing and Sedicio tells him, "I'm not ready for that type of sex." After some
bantering back and forth, Sedicio refers to his "soft-core approach to eroticism," but Michael wants more intimate sex. Sedicio responds: "You either
believe in a relationship or you believe in a series of quick insertions. I've
already made that mistake before without lubricants and without emotional
attachments and I don't know which one is more painful" (127).

Although his relationship with Sedicio is paramount, other forces con-
spire against Michael to add to his confusion. Early in the play, in his duties
as a Border Patrolman, Michael encounters Miss Fresno, who begs him to
deport her. She is a Guatemalan of German descent, an ex-cheerleader who
has "passed" for female *and* Anglo all her/his life – a true border crosser. She
tells the mesmerized Michael: "Mommy's the one who discovered my
unusual talents. On her death bed, she held my hand and whispered in my
ear: 'You look like a white woman mija. Use it!'" (116). Michael is convinced
that Miss Fresno is what she appears to be, a beautiful, white, Anglo woman
– certainly not an undocumented immigrant – and refuses to deport her.
This flashback happens early in the play, preparing the audience for
Michael's fascination with men dressed as women.

Reyes traverses multiple sexualities in this play. Michael has had an on-
going fantasy of being a Santa Monica police Sergeant who falls in love with
a tango transvestite, Sirena Angustias. The fantasy comes to life and we
watch Michael as the Sergeant, relate his story, in a film noire parody that
is the comic highlight of the play. Sirena is played by a man, but according
to the stage directions, "she is not just a camp impersonation of womanhood, she is womanhood, at least in its 1940s incarnation of masochistic
suffering heroine with a hidden past and tremendous destructive passion"
(129). The Sergeant/Michael tells Sirena he can dance the tango with her
"As long as you're dressed as a woman of course, I'm no queer." Sirena, held
dramatically in his arms, looks out at the audience with a knowing smile
and says: "Of course not." The detective continues: "I'm from the barrio,
East L.A., we don't do sexual ambivalence there . . ." (133).

Suddenly, Sedicio interrupts the tango fantasy to confront Michael and
question his sexual object choices. Sedicio tells Michael: "I know quite well
I'm attracted to men, and I don't see myself falling for transvestites. Face it.
This tango fantasy is a perfect example of political repression that you, as a
man, have absorbed into your psyche." "I don't think so," Michael responds,
but Sedicio has more to say, "Yes, you're really attracted to men, but
somehow it's more acceptable that he'd be dressed up as a woman. It's a
mask, it's a closet, get over it" (134).

This moment, both the interruption of the fantasy and the questions regarding Michael's sexual object choices, come from the more experienced Sedicio. Sedicio has been around long enough to accuse Michael of fooling himself – that he somehow believes that he is maintaining a masculine role by fantasizing an affair with a man dressed as a woman. And although he is not critical of drag artists, Sedicio has no interest in cross-dressing. The result of this confrontation is not really conclusive; we do not learn why Michael fantasizes about Sirena while also having an affair with a masculine gay man *dressed as a man*. But the question has been raised by the playwright, a question no other Chicana/o play attempts to pose.

Mirroring his encounter with Miss Fresno in the first act, Michael has another crucial experience in the second act, another moment in which he must re-evaluate his own choices as a man and as a Border patrolman. In perhaps the most moving scene in the play, Michael has to deport an ailing AIDS patient, Silvano, to his native El Salvador. Silvano is a haughty, over-confidant diva who will not go peacefully. He claims that his wealthy father "owns" El Salvador but it is clear that his family abandoned him long ago because of his sexuality. Now that he is going home to die, Silvano retains his elegance, pride and dignity, teaching Michael a lesson in courage in the face of imminent death. It is an incredible moment of pathos and humor, for Silvano will not be pitied. "I'm not demented," Silvano tells Michael, "I'm just fabulous!" (146).

The major divas of the title, Sedicio, Miss Fresno, Sirena, and Silvano, all serve to reinforce Michael's confusion as we watch him tentatively embrace a homosexual relationship and then reject any commitment. Each of these characters, whether real or in his imagination, teaches him something about himself. Silvano teaches Michael to appreciate the divas in his life, especially Sirena. When Michael tells him that Sirena "lives in the imagination," Silvano responds: "Why live anywhere else?" (147). In the words of noted Latin American theatre scholar, George Woodyard, "*Estos personages funcionan como tentación para Michael y como proyección de sus inquietudes sexuales, especialmente Sirena*" ("These characters function as temptations for Michael and as projections of his sexual anxieties, especially Sirena").[64]

However, because this play exists on different levels of reality, there are

[64] Woodyard was analyzing a draft of the text, not a performance. George Woodyard, "Rompiendo las fronteras: El teatro de Guillermo Reyes," Théatre et Territoires Espagne et Amérique Hispanique (1950–1996). Teatro y Territorios España e Hispanoamérica. Actes du Colloque International de Bordeaux 30 janvier–1 février 1997 (Bordeaux: Maison des Pays Ibériques, 1998), p. 338. Coordination: Sara Bonnardel, Genvieve Champeau.

points of contrast between the realistic and complex characters of Michael
and Sedicio and most of the other exaggerated characters they encounter
(and perform). By taking his audience from reality to fantasy and back
again, Reyes mirrors the fractured nature of the gay Latino or Latina experience. Anything can happen in the world of these "Divas," just as anything
can happen in the daily lives of the people who function in a queer identity.
Multiple realities, settings and contradictions abound as Reyes explores and
explodes heteronormativity and homonormativity. Michael returns to his
traditional marriage because that is what he was taught to do. By his
parents, by his culture and by his Church. But will he avoid damnation?

Conclusions

Who is writing gay and lesbian plays?

The theme of homosexuali(ties), like women's issues, came late in the
development of contemporary Chicano theatre. With the exception of
Estela Portillo-Trambley's *Day of the Swallows,* plays about gay, lesbian or
bisexual central characters did not appear until the 1980s, led by lesbian
playwright, Cherríe Moraga, whose plays have dealt with varieties of male
and female sexualities. Prior to *Reunion*, by Edgar Poma, and *Giving up the
Ghost,* by Moraga, lesbian and gay characters were mostly marginalized
(onstage or usually off), exploited for derogatory or comic purposes only.
While Moraga remains the only openly gay Chicana to write plays
about (homo)sexualities, no published play about a gay Chicano has been
written *by a gay Chicano* to date. Of the published works discussed in this
chapter, only one of the plays about gay men is by a gay man, Chilean-born
Guillermo Reyes.

The most prolific playwrights to date are Moraga and Reyes, who write
about gay and lesbian desire from experience, calling upon their personal
trials, triumphs and understanding to create characters that are more than
stereotypes. Gay-themed plays written by heterosexuals sometimes create a
tension between the text and reality, as in Portillo-Trambley's *Day of the
Swallows* or Josefina López's *Food for the Dead.* López's play is too brief to
fully explore the gay issues it touches upon, but *Day of the Swallows* has
clearly interested critics from every corner of academia. *Blade to the Heat* is
Oliver Mayer's heterosexual attempt to explore homophobia in the world
of boxing and I believe he succeeds. It is important to recall, however, that
both directors of Mayer's play were gay men and their gay sensibility gave

the production a "homosensuality" that Mayer probably could not have staged or imagined so effectively.

After reviewing the list of heterosexual playwrights scripting gay characters, the obvious question is: Where are the gay and lesbian Chicano playwrights? Certainly, every community of artists has its share of homosexuals, and the Chicano theatre community is no different. And yet, I cannot name one gay Chicano playwright who has published a play that deals with homosexuality. In reality, lesbian and gay Chicana/o performance artists are the most prominent and public performers of homosexual identities, scripting one-person pieces which they have performed all over the country and abroad. The growing list of gay and lesbian performance artists includes Los Angeles-based Luis Alfáro,[65] and Monica Palacios,[66] and Minneapolis-based Ric Oquita. In San Antonio, Texas, visual artist, David Zamora Casas and dancer/actor Paul Bonin-Rodríguez perform one-man pieces addressing issues of homosexuality as well.[67] Each of these artists has told me they are working on plays but none have been published to date.

Still, the concerns expressed by Chicana/o critics in the early 1980s about the paucity of gay and lesbian plays are being addressed, however slowly and cautiously. The road has been challenging and daunting. As María Teresa Marrero aptly states: "These authors seek the ambiguity of the gaps, of the poetic, of the theatrical. It is a space hard won by fifteen years of their individual productions."[68] All but one of the plays discussed here are published and all have been produced in a variety of venues. And although it is difficult to get a gay-themed play produced in the Mechicana/o community, the list of teatros and community cultural centers that have produced the plays I've discussed is impressive. These teatros include the Miracle Theatre Company, in Portland, Oregon, Su Teatro, in Denver, Colorado, Teatro de la Esperanza, in San Francisco, California, Teatro Visión, in San José, California, and the Chicago Latino Theatre Company in Illinois. The cultural centers that have produced some of these plays include the Guadalupe Cultural Arts Center, in San Antonio, Texas, the Mission Cultural Center in San Francisco, California, and El Centro Cultural de la Raza in San

---

[65] Luis Alfáro's one-man piece, *Downtown* is in Holly Hughes and David Román (eds.), *O Solo Homo* (New York: Grove, 1998), pp. 313–48.

[66] For an excellent introduction to the works of Monica Palacios, see Alicia Arrizón, *Latina Performance: Traversing the Stage* (Bloomington: Indiana, 1999), pp. 139–48. Chapter 5 of Arrizón's book addresses queer Latina performers and subjectivity.

[67] See Bradley Boney, "The Lavender Brick Road: Paul Bonin-Rodríguez and the Sissy Bo(d)y," *Theatre Journal* 48 1 (1996), 35–57.

[68] Marrero, María Teresa, "Out of the Fringe," 88.

Diego. Little by little, teatros and cultural centers are developing audiences willing to support these plays and playwrights.

Where's the (male) nudity?

Mechicana/o audiences are still afraid of transgressions such as nudity on stage. Noting that many (Anglo) gay male plays of the 1990s include male nudity, John M. Clum states, "the nakedness, the forcing of the gaze and narcissistic enjoyment of that gaze, the forbidden freedom of the uncovered penis, and the assumption that viewing the penis is a pleasurable act all represent, not male sexuality, but gay sexuality . . . *The danger in the willfully nude male body is homosexuality*" [italics mine].[69] I emphasize the last sentence because it signifies, for me, a recurring realization regarding the plays I have discussed. With the exception of *Blade to the Heat*, there is no nudity in these plays, male or female. Indeed, there is very little *sexuality* present, because many producers, regardless of their sexual orientation, are afraid of the danger to which Clum alludes. And the playwrights have to write what they think will get produced.

Along with the dream/nightmare of two (barely visible) nude boxers in *Blade to the Heat* there is a scene in which Mantequilla takes a shower. The audience is confronted with full, frontal male nudity, but the threat Clum infers is averted by Sarita's presence, towel in hand, confirming Mantequilla's heterosexuality. The naked body is something Latinas and Latinos do not display easily; the naked queer body would be even more transgressive and dangerous. Despite the gay male nudity in Anglo dramas, there are no nude queer Chicana/o bodies in any of these plays, nor in any Chicana/o dramas I have seen or read to date.

Curiously, the two openly gay writers, Reyes and Moraga, are somewhat restrained in their depiction of homosexual desire. The stage directions in the second version of *Giving up the Ghost* call for Amalia and Marisa to share a very tender, sensuous kiss, but the degree of sensuality they bring to this scene is mediated by a variety of considerations. Moraga is very comfortable with expressing and exposing lesbian sensuality, but are the actors? And what of the audience? I have seen two versions of this play and they differed markedly in their expressions of lesbian desire. The discomfort of the actors in one version was palpable, in the other version their desire was totally believable. In both instances, the actors were hetero-

[69] John M. Clum, *Acting Gay* (New York: Columbia, 1992), p. 21.

sexual; the good actor makes a kiss real, no matter what her sexual orientation may be.

The gay male kiss has been known to send some people into "heterosexual panic," regardless of their culture. While *Blade to the Heat* is one example of a play that confronts its audiences with two men kissing, the kisses are restrained. Quinn begins to kiss Garnet but he cannot sustain it. And, as mentioned, Mantequilla's kiss is not sensual but violent. Reyes seems even more reticent in his portrayal of gay sexuality in *Deporting the Divas*, calling for one long kiss between Michael and Sedicio and a truncated kiss at the end of the play when Michael refuses Sedicio's sexual advances. Nothing more to demonstrate one man's desire for the other. We do see the kiss between the Sergeant and Sirena, but that the kiss is not transgressive. If performed well, we come to perceive of Sirena as a "real woman," and there is no shock in the kiss.

The last word

I believe the playwrights discussed in this chapter are telling us as much about the Mechicano communities' attitudes towards homosexuality in their silence as they are demonstrating through their plays. What the playwrights do not say, or show, is sometimes more revealing than what they do. Their reticence is understandable in the context of everything I have discussed in the previous chapters. The Mechicana/o mythos does not include homosexualities. Yet, when I wrote my first book on Chicano theatre in 1980, there was only one play in print that addressed these issues, however clumsily. I could not have written this chapter in 1980. And although Mechicanas and Mechicanos do not seem to have changed much in their attitudes towards homosexuality, we do have a new generation of playwrights willing to risk censure and, yes, damnation, by writing about a topic most people wish would go away. Certainly, the advent of AIDS, which has had and continues to have a major impact on the Latina/o communities, has opened dialogue where there was none.[70] But it is still a very slow process and there are times I feel that the Mechicano community is many years behind the dominant society.

Thankfully, there are now playwrights, performance artists, actors,

---

[70] See: David Román, "Teatro Viva!: Latino Performance and the Politics of AIDS in Los Angeles," in Emilie L. Bergmann and Paul Julian Smith (eds.), *¿Entiendes? Queer Readings, Hispanic Writings* (Duke, 1995), pp. 346–69; Alberto Sandoval, "Staging AIDS: What's Latinos Got to Do With It?," in Taylor and Villegas, *Negotiating Performance*, pp. 49–66.

directors and producers willing to risk producing plays that openly discuss and confront homosexualities. Brave, bold, and even audacious individuals and organizations willing to attack all forms of internalized and externalized homophobia in the Mechicano communities. To date, the performance artists are the most audacious. But with these pioneers to inspire, motivate and propel them, the next generation of Chicana/o theatre artists will hopefully be even bolder, braver and much more audacious rebels as they deal with their myths, mysteries, redemption and damnation.

Afterword

On finding a Chicana/o *mythos*

I have often wondered about a Chicano aesthetic in teatro, a peculiarly
Chicana/o form of dramatic expression, unique to the Chicana/o alone. But
as I looked at the history and evolution of Chicano theatre since 1965 I could
not find one, particular aesthetic. Initially, I could define Chicano theatre
by describing the Teatro Campesino's *actos* or the *mitos* as aesthetic forms
that were peculiar to the Valdezian collective and individual imaginations.
Some observers have termed the early period a "rasquachi aesthetic," referring to the unsophisticated, unpretentious nature of the *acto* and other theatrical statements being created in the 1960s and seventies. But even the
actos have their roots in a centuries-old tradition of Italian street theatre as
well as in other forms of political sketches, performed in various world cultures. What made any of these early performances "Chicana/o" was simply
the fact that they were created by, for and about Chicana/os.

Today, there is not a particular artistic style in Chicana/o theatre, as I
hope this book has demonstrated. Most of the plays I have discussed are
rooted in Western European traditions, the children of realism and its
various permutations: absurdism, expressionism, surrealism, etc. But as I re-
read the plays, reviewed my records of productions I have directed or seen,
as I wrote and re-wrote, I found myself confronting, not an aesthetic, but a
Chicana/o mythos. What I discovered in this project was a common source,
a thread linking these plays and playwrights to one another: Mexico. Not a
Mexico of corrupt politics, drug lords and police extortion, but a Mexico of
indigenous symbols, of pyramids and poetry: *flor y canto*, flower and song.
A living Mexico, evident in the faces of Mechicana/os living and working
in any city in the United States that they call home.

Unlike all of the other Latina/o immigrants living in the United States, the Chicana/os have no desire to "go home" because the United States is home. But their plays tell us that they do not want to forget Mexico, her colors, her joy, her pain and her history. The Mexico expressed in the plays I've discussed (and any other Chicana/o plays, really) is designated, generally, through signs as opposed to geographical locale, for few of these plays take place in Mexico. But it is the image of Mexico that makes the plays Chicana/o. But, "What," one could ask, "makes, or identifies *anything* as Chicana/o?"

What makes this vase "Chicano?" I will ask my students, having drawn a rudimentary flower vase on the board. It is only a chalk outline of a basic vase, curvilinear, but with no true signifiers of its cultural origins. It could be a classic Greek vase, but there are no Greek figures dancing on this vase, nothing but an outline. The students cannot identify the vase's "ethnicity," until I ask them to imagine a Virgin of Guadalupe painted on it. Suddenly, what else could it be but a Mexican or Chicano vase? If not sculpted by a Mechicana/o, the vase was at least decorated by someone who was attempting to appeal to a Mexican Roman Catholic mythos. Is this stereotypical? Perhaps, but stereotypes are based on reality or they would not be stereotypes. In that simple image of a Mexican icon, the vase and whoever holds it becomes an extension of the reality painted on the ceramic. Depending upon what s/he does with that vase, the holder is either a believer or a non-believer, a Roman Catholic or not. But the connection to Mexico is inescapable.

Chicana/o playwrights invoke Mexican icons in order to position themselves as Americans of Mexican descent. Anglo icons or heroes generally do not appear in Chicana/o plays and, when they do, they are not the central figures. Rather, Chicana/o playwrights often create the Anglo characters as deconstructions of dominant histories in order to demystify traditional images of "the great White Hero." Anglo characters in a play may be good or they may be bad but the stories do not belong to them. Rather, the stories, the struggles, the demons and myths belong to the Mechicana/os on stage and in the audience. Traditional myths are exploded in order to define new myths and old, untold histories of the Chicana and Chicano as the children of the Children of the Sun.

A re-occurring symbol of the Aztec people is the so-called Aztec Calendar Stone, actually a representation of the Fifth Sun, popularized in plaster castings and found on the walls of rooms in some of these plays. Little, if anything, is said about this stone in the plays but its presence is an enigmatic reminder of a culture nobody knows much about. A more recognizable image which also has its roots in indigenous cultures is an altar to a deceased relative on stage. The altar is a living symbol of the dead, adorned with a picture or pictures of the deceased, burning candles, foods and objects that gave that person a place in her/his cosmos. In other instances, Mexico is invoked through indigenous flute music, drums or Spanish guitars defined by Mexican strums. The musical sounds of Mexico permeate every one of these plays.

Chicana/o playwrights recall Mexico in their ancestors, the parents or grandparents who made the sacrifice to leave their homeland to return to the homeland, "Aztlán." In all immigrant cultures, the homeland is seen through the nostalgic lens of the border crossers, a place that no longer belongs to them, as they attempt to make this new land their own. But in the case of the Chicana/o characters, the border is a construction, literally and metaphorically, a river or a fence that they can cross legally, although they have to prove their citizenship at each crossing if they "look Mexican." Mexico is on their brown faces, their Spanish, Indian and African features, and in their humility.

Mexico becomes a mythical place as does the barrio in which the native-born were raised. When the Chicana/o characters speak of their youth, growing up in a barrio, it is usually a place that is free of today's violence and drugs. The people may have been poor, but they were good people, hard working and eager to hold their families together despite the obstacles. Their tenacity is represented in a plant growing in a rusty coffee can, an image that might transport many a barrio-raised Chicana/o back to their own barrio, images of a mother, an aunt or another elder faithfully watering that plant as symbol of everyone's determination to survive. Mexico is in that coffee can, a miniaturized "*ranchito*," just as Mexico is in the brown, wrinkled hands that tend it.

Mexico is in the kitchens in each of these plays. Some scenes literally take place in the kitchen and, if not, a bowl of beans is usually boiling away offstage, literally or metaphorically. The women no longer go to the river to wash the clothes, but they talk about that time, remember the hardship and the camaraderie. If characters are making hand-made tortillas these are probably the most visible image of a Mexico long abandoned, for few contemporary Chicanas (much less Chicanos) will make their own tortillas today. But the smells of the kitchen immediately establish a Mexican home and the chilies and corn growing in the garden affirm this image. These playwrights know that much of today's Mexican cuisine dates to pre-Conquest times. Corn, beans, chilies, tomatoes, turkey – even cotton, we owe to the Mesoamericans and the playwrights are careful to include these symbols in their plays, declaring the world's debt to their ancestors' wisdom.

The playwrights recall and conjure Mexico through the strongest symbol of all, language. Not one of the plays I have discussed is written totally in English or all in Spanish. As many examples throughout this book have shown, more often than not, the language spoken in the plays is a combination of Spanish and English and the hybrid mixture, "Spanglish," which only the Chicana/os can truly articulate. It is the language of the characters that defines them as either Mexican, Anglo or Chicana/o and it is their religious iconography that links them to both the Spanish Roman Catholic Church and their indigenous forefathers and mothers. The images of the Virgin of Guadalupe, Malinche and *La Llorona* permeate many of these plays, sometimes literally and usually subliminally because every Mechicana is a daughter of all three. And every Mechicano is a son of Cortez and Malinche.

All people in all cultures are the consequences of myth and mystery and most cultures have their own forms of redemption and damnation but these concepts seem particularly meaningful to the Mechicana/o. Indeed, I believe they define a Chicana/o mythos, progressing naturally from myth, to mystery, to redemption and damnation in the Mechicana/o communities. Chicana/o playwrights demonstrate a strong fascination with the power and influence of the Church, its representatives and those within and without that Institution who would rebel against damnation. The curious conflation of Christianity and indigenous philosophy that permeates Mechicana/o cultures defines a Chicana/o mythos, a duality that is represented in every indigenous deity and which translates for the Chicana/o as Jesucristo/Quetzalcóatl, Guadalupe/Tonantzin, or the Father/Mother, Ometeotl/Omecihuatl. By embracing all of these concepts and more, contemporary Chicanas and Chicanos are rebelling against the systematic obliteration of their histories, re-creating their own mythos.

A note on mainstreaming and professionalism

Each of the plays I have discussed has been influenced by either a mainstream "project," a teatro, or both. Most of the plays have been produced in mainstream theatres as well as in teatros, and although the productions have differed in all respects, from budgets to facilities, the plays have generally been well received by Mechicana/o and non-Latina/o audiences. While I initially feared that the plays might suffer a kind of "white washing" in the mainstream play development projects, the fact that each of the plays has also been produced by teatros affirms the integrity and validity of the texts. In other words, Chicana/o artistic directors would not have produced these plays if they thought they were not representative of their communities, regardless of the often dysfunctional families they portrayed. Many have taken risks with transgressive queer plays, slowly educating their audiences, opening dialogue where there was none.

An inevitable outcome of all that has happened in the Chicana/o theatre community since *Zoot Suit* was first produced is the fact that Mechicana/o audiences have become more educated, more middle class, as the players have become more professional. This is not to say that working-class people do not attend professional Chicana/o productions. From what I have observed in teatros and mainstream theatres across the country, Mechicana/os from all walks of life will find their way to a play that addresses their community. Certainly, it was clear that Mechicana/os attending *Zoot Suit* in Los Angeles in 1978–79 were not all middle class, but no other play by a Chicana or Chicano has generated the enthusiasm and interest of that groundbreaking production. The success of most of the plays discussed in this volume, despite rising ticket prices, is proof that Mechicana/os continue to want to see themselves on stage. This does not mean, however, that the working-class communities are being left behind, because there are still community-based teatros seemingly in every center of Mechicana/o population.

As mentioned in the Introduction, Chicano/Latino theatre companies continue to produce plays from various Latina/o communities in cities and towns across the country. The list of teatros is long and varied. The leading California theatres are El Teatro Campesino (San Juan Bautista), Kinán Valdéz, Director; El Teatro de la Esperanza (San Francisco), Rodrigo Duarte-Clark, Artistic Director; the Bilingual Foundation for the Arts (Los Angeles), Margarita Galbán, Artistic Director and Carmen Zapata, Producing Director; Latino Theatre Company (Los Angeles), José Luís Valenzuela, Artistic Director; Teatro Visión (San José), Elisa Marina González, Artistic Director; Teatro Familia (San José), Adrian Vargas, Artistic Director; and Teatro Máscara Mágica (San Diego), Bill Virchis, Artistic Director. In New Mexico Ramon Flores is the Artistic Director of *La Compañía de Teatro de Alburquerque*; in Denver, Colorado, Tony Garcia is the Artistic Director of El Centro, Su Teatro and Antoñio Sonera heads the Teatro Milagro in Portland, Oregon. Juan Ramirez is the Artistic Director of the Chicago Latino Theatre Company in Illinois, Barclay

Goldsmith is the Artistic Director of Borderlands Theatre, in Tucson, Arizona, and Cora Cardona is the Artistic Director of Teatro Dallas in Texas. Teatro Latino de Minnesota, in Minneapolis/St. Paul is headed by Virginia McFerran. Every one of these teatros has contributed in some way to one or more of the plays discussed in this volume.

Major cultural centers have also been important to the development of Chicana/o drama and include the Guadalupe Cultural Arts Center in San Antonio, Texas, and the South Broadway Cultural Center, in Albuquerque, New Mexico. The California centers include the Mission Cultural Center, in San Francisco, the Centro Cultural de la Raza in San Diego, and La Plaza de la Raza, in Los Angeles. These are the cultural centers with the longest trajectories and with a history of commitment to producing Chicana/o plays. Sometimes these venues will present travelling plays while others, such as the Guadalupe Cultural Arts Center, has a producing arm with a full-time producer, Jorge Piña, and various educational and performing teatro programs. Often, the centers will co-produce productions with a teatro or even a non-Latina/o theater company, bringing together audiences from more than one constituency.

Alongside the more established groups, there are newer, younger teatros everywhere, groups which I seem to "discover" wherever I travel. These troupes are not necessarily known outside of their immediate surroundings but they are actively producing *actos*, plays and other performances for their own communities. In other words, the tradition begun by the Chicano Theatre Movement and TENAZ has not died, as some might aver, but it has transformed. Today's teatros are not necessarily aligned with universities and colleges, and I find that often the participants are young and older community members who hold "real" jobs while expressing their theatrical objectives through a teatro of some kind. Most of the members of these troupes have no interest in becoming professional theatre artists, especially if they live outside of the major centers of professional Latina/o theatre such as Southern California, the Bay Area (Northern California), Chicago or New York. Instead, these teatristas are fulfilling a need to participate in their communities in an active, socio-political and artistic way by producing plays such as those discussed in this book. But, unlike their predecessors, these teatristas know what a professional play should look like and they have much higher performance standards than the earliest student teatros.

Where do we go from here?

At a meeting in San Juan Bautista in the early 1980s Luís Valdez reminded the participants that there were not enough Chicana/o plays to fill a season yet. He was right, but as this book has hopefully demonstrated, that is no longer the case. While the plays I have addressed here would fill three or even four seasons, I have not discussed all of the plays by and about Chicana/os that have been published to date. Further, such is the productivity of Chicana/o playwrights writing today that I could not have discussed all of the plays that have been produced but which remain unpublished. Not only are there more than enough Chicana/o plays to fill a few seasons, most of the teatros of which I am aware produce plays from other communities as well. Teatros across the country are producing plays by other Latina/os living in the United States as well as producing plays by Latin American and other communities. Some theatre companies produce Latin American plays in English only, while others might produce the plays only in Spanish. In a few rare instances, the theatre companies will produce these plays in both languages, alternating performances from night-to-night.

While there are still teatros that call themselves "Chicano theatre companies," the growing numbers of theatre artists from other United States Latina/o communities has affected both the participants in the teatros and the audiences they serve. In cities like Chicago, Los Angeles and San Francisco, the teatros are composed of artists from all parts of the Americas. Yet, on the East Coast, from New York to Miami, the mixture of communities reflected in the theatre companies does not include many Chicanas and Chicanos because there are few theatre artists of Mexican descent living in those parts of the United States. There are Mexican theatre artists living in New York, as there have always been, but they are mainly non-English speaking and thus could not participate in a bilingual Chicana/o production. I discovered this first-hand, the two times I directed bilingual plays for the Puerto Rican Traveling Theatre in New York City.

This is not to say that Chicana/o plays have not been produced east of Chicago. As noted throughout this book, the three major Latina/o companies in New York City, INTAR, Repertorio Español and the Puerto Rican Traveling Theatre, have each produced and/or presented Chicana/o plays. However, when these and other East Coast companies produce a Chicana/o play they usually cannot find Chicana/o actors and thus one encounters a curious mixture of accents on stage, from Argentina to Colombia,

Nuyorican to Iberian Spanish. But producers on the East Coast continue to look for plays that reflect the Mechicana/o experience just as Chicana/o teatros in other parts of the country broaden their repertoires with plays that emanate from other United States Latino communities.

The publication of United States Latina/o plays has made those texts available to other communities, as have the workshops discussed in this book. One of the very positive results of both the mainstream projects as well as the play development programs in the teatros, has been the interaction between the various playwrights, directors and actors. For example, each year, when people from across the country gathered in Costa Mesa or San Francisco to listen to their plays and to one another and to hear audience responses to their works, life-long friendships and collaborations were forged. Directors met and worked with actors from the Los Angeles or Bay Area Latina/o actors' community and playwrights were introduced to actors and directors whom they had never met. Thus, when the play was produced by a professional company somewhere else, the playwright could recommend an actor s/he had seen in one of the readings in such projects as the Hispanic Playwright's Project, or Teatro de la Esperanza's playwriting workshop. Certainly, this is how I "discovered" talent across the country – actors, playwrights, directors and designers that I could then recommend to my producers or to other companies looking for professional talent.

It is important to note that all of the playwrights and directors I have discussed (and many that I have not been able to include here), have undergraduate degrees, usually in theatre or drama, and most hold a Master of Fine Arts degree in acting, directing or playwriting. This was not the case in 1980, when few teatristas were training in or studying theatre. Further, many of these playwrights are, themselves, now college and university professors teaching in theatre and drama departments. The full-time professors are Cherríe Moraga, Carlos Morton, Guillermo Reyes, Luís Valdez and Edit Villareal. Other playwrights, such as Josefina López, Oliver Mayer, Beverly Sanchez-Padilla and Milcha Sanchez-Scott have taught playwriting classes and/or workshops. Of the directors I have mentioned, Tony Curiel, José Cruz González, Marcos Martinez, José Luís Valenzuela and Bill Virchis are each full-time college professors who manage to teach and direct in a variety of venues throughout the country. The Mechicana directors, such as Cora Cardona, Laura Esparza and Norma Saldívar are actively engaged with either their own companies or other theatres and teatros. Although there are more professional Chicana directors than there were in

1980, this brief listing demonstrates an obvious gender gap in the artistic director ranks, a situation that will hopefully improve with the next generation.

The greatest challenge to Chicana/o theatre artists as we enter the twenty-first century is no different than the challenges to all theatre artists now and throughout history: to get their dramatic statements on stage and in print. To be seen by as many people as possible, from as many cultures as possible. The challenge to any artist is to keep re-inventing her/himself, revising the art form without fear of criticism. As any writer knows, the art of writing is re-writing and in the collaborative process that is theatre, the re-writing becomes more than an individual endeavor. Theatre is perhaps the most collaborative of the arts and as Chicana/o theatre artists explore new ways of saying and seeing, it is incumbent upon them to be honest in their statements, unafraid to challenge tradition even as they promote traditions that reach back thousands of years.

It has been said that art is essential in a civilized society and Chicana/o dramatic art is certainly fundamental to a better understanding of who the Mechicana/os are and who they were. The playwrights cannot rely on Hollywood to tell their stories, so they must continue to write for the theatre because it is much easier to get a play produced than it is to see your screenplay turned into a film. Just ask Luís Valdez. Many of the people I have written about in this book – playwrights, directors and actors – are also involved in film and television but their real love is live theatre. Hollywood pays the bills but the stage feeds the soul, especially when the magic we all look for in a theatrical event happens: that intangible but palpable connection between the actor and the audience, between the intentions of the production team and the eager reception of those ideas.

I believe that every one of the playwrights and other theatre artists I have written about in this book sees the theatrical space as a temple, a very special place where magic can happen. Those of us who work in the theatre know about that feeling of ritual every time an audience gathers, eager to share in the approaching event. Initially the early Mechicana/o audiences were satisfied to get their teatro on the run, on flatbed trucks or in other untraditional theatre spaces. When the plays moved indoors another energy was aroused, no less anticipatory, as the audience began to fill the house. The anticipation that runs through the auditorium as the lights dim and the performance begins to unfold. To a theatre artist there is no greater thrill than seeing your work, "work." Seeing the audience laugh where you wanted them to, cry when you knew they would and applaud because their lives have been touched. That is, quite simply, magical and mythical, mysterious and redemptive.

I believe that all artists must fight against discrimination because they are artists, must battle daily damnation of anything or anyone that challenges the status quo. Although I titled the chapter on homosexuality "Damnation," in effect, the entire community of Mechicana/os has been and continues to be damned by virtue of its invisibility. As 1980 approached, *Time Magazine* declared that the decade of the 1980s would be "The Decade of the Hispanic," but few, if any changes seemed to occur in the Reagan years. But with the phenomenal growth of the Latina/o populations in the United States, with all that has happened in electoral politics in the 1990s, the new millennium does, indeed, look promising for these communities. Despite the growth of a Mechicana/o middle and upper income population, however, there remains much to be done to improve the conditions of the Mechicana/os. Problems still plague the community, just as they did in 1980: access to education and health care, injustice in the courts, police brutality, women's rights, internal and external racism, homophobia in the barrios – these are continuing issues, as demonstrated in the plays I have discussed.

The theatre artists I have written about in this volume (and the many others I could not discuss), write, act, direct, design or produce because they have to. They teach because they must, whether through their work on stage or in a classroom. These theatre artists are reaching an ever-widening audience with their tales of myth, mystery, redemption and damnation as they continue to express a mythos that gives their audiences an identity in a country that tries to erase that identity. If we are doing our job right, the younger generation of *teatristas*, our students, will learn to challenge us and take teatro into new and different directions. But always, I predict, there will be a sense of identity, however fractured, of a history and of place that will be called "Chicana/o." To be a Chicana or a Chicano is to recognize the oppression, to try to understand it and to attempt to change it. That is how Chicana/o theatre began and that is how it will continue.

Bibliography

Plays

Alfaro, Luis. *Downtown*. In *O Solo Homo*, edited by Holly Hughes and David Román. New York: Grove, 1998, pp. 313–48.

Alurista. *Dawn*. *El Grito* 7, 1974, pp. 55–84.

    Dawn. In *Contemporary Chicano Drama*, edited by Roberto J. Garza. University of Notre Dame Press, 1976, pp. 103–34.

Anaya, Rudolfo. *Who Killed Don José?* In *New Mexico Plays*, edited by David Richard Jones. Albuquerque: University of New Mexico Press, 1989, pp. 197–231.

Chávez, Denise. *Plaza*. In *New Mexico Plays*, edited by David Richard Jones. Albuquerque: University of New Mexico Press, 1989, pp. 79–106.

Fernández, Evelina. *How Else Am I Supposed to Know I'm Still Alive?* In *Contemporary Plays by Women of Color*, edited by Kathy A. Perkins and Roberta Uno. New York: Routledge, 1996, pp. 158–67.

Franco, Cris, Luisa Leschin, Armando Molina and Diane Rodríguez. The LA LA Awards. In Franco, *et al. Latins Anonymous: Two Plays*. Houston: Arte Público, 1996, pp. 12–52.

García, Anthony J. *The Day Ricardo Falcon Died*. In Anthony J. Garcia, *Su Teatro: 20 Year Anthology*. Denver: El Centro Su Teatro, 1990.

    Little Hands Hold the Wind. In Anthony J., Garcia, *Su Teatro: 20 Year Anthology*. Denver: El Centro Su Teatro, 1990.

    Ludlow: El Grito de las Minas. In Anthony J., Garcia, *Su Teatro: 20 Year Anthology*. Denver: El Centro Su Teatro, 1990.

Girón, Arthur. *Money*. In *Necessary Theater: Six Plays About the Chicano Experience*, edited by Jorge Huerta. Houston: Arte Público, 1989, pp. 258–315.

Huerta, Jorge A. *El Renacimiento de (Rebirth of) Huitzilopochtli*. In *El Teatro de la Esperanza: An Anthology of Chicano Drama*, edited by Jorge A. Huerta. Goleta: El Teatro de la Esperanza, 1973, pp. 98–123.

Leschin, Luisa, Armando Molina, Rick Nájera, and Diane Rodríguez, *Latins Anonymous*. In Franco, *et al., Latins Anonymous: Two Plays*. Houston: Arte Público, 1996, pp. 55–101.

López, Josefina. *Confessions of Women from East L.A.* Woodstock, IL: Dramatic Publishing Co., 1997.

Food for the Dead (and) La Pinta. Woodstock, IL: Dramatic Publishing Co., 1996.

Real Women Have Curves. West Hollywood: Mercedes Management, 1988.

Real Women Have Curves. Woodstock, IL: Dramatic Publishing Group, 1996.

Simply María. In *Shattering the Myth: Plays by Hispanic Women*, edited by Linda Feyder. Houston: Arte Público, 1992, 113–41.

Simply María. Woodstock, IL: Dramatic Publishing Company, 1996.

Unconquered Spirits. Woodstock, IL: Dramatic Publishing, 1997.

Macías, Ysidro. *The Ultimate Pendejada*. In *Contemporary Chicano Theatre*, edited by Roberto J. Garza. University of Notre Dame Press, 1976, pp. 135–64.

Mares, E. A. *I Returned and Saw Under the Sun: Padre Martínez of Taos*. Albuquerque: University of New Mexico Press, 1989.

Lola's Last Dance. In *New Mexico Plays*, edited by David Richard Jones. Albuquerque: University of New Mexico Press, 1989, pp. 63–78.

Meyer, Oliver. *Blade to the Heat*. New York: Dramatists Play Service, 1996.

Young Valiant. South Coast Repertory Theatre's Hispanic Playwright's Project 2, no. 1, 1989.

Montoya, Richard, Rick Salinas and Herbert Siguenza. *A Bowl of Beings*. In Montoya, *et al.*, *Culture Clash: Life, Death and Revolutionary Comedy*. New York: TCG Publications, 1999, pp. 57–106.

The Mission. In Montoya, *et al.*, *Culture Clash: Life, Death and Revolutionary Comedy*. New York: TCG Publications, 1999, pp. 1–56.

Radio Mambo. In Montoya, *et al.*, *Culture Clash: Life, Death and Revolutionary Comedy*. New York: TCG Publications, 1999, pp. 107–64.

Moraga, Cherríe. *Giving up the Ghost*. Los Angeles: West End Press, 1986.

Giving up the Ghost. In Cherríe Moraga, *Heroes and Saints & Other Plays*. Albuquerque: West End Press, 1994, pp. 1–35.

Heroes and Saints. In Cherríe Moraga, *Heroes and Saints & Other Plays*. Albuquerque: West End Press, 1994, pp. 85–149.

Heroes and Saints. In *Contemporary Plays by Women of Color*, edited by Kathy A. Perkins and Roberta Uno. New York: Routledge, 1996, pp. 230–61.

Shadow of a Man. In *Shattering the Myth: Plays by Hispanic Women*, edited by Linda Feyder. Houston: Arte Público, 1992, pp. 9–48.

Shadow of a Man. In Cherríe Moraga, *Heroes and Saints & Other Plays*. Albuquerque: West End Press, 1994, pp. 37–84.

Morton, Carlos. *El cuento de Pancho Diablo*. *El Grito Del Sol* 1, July–September, 1976, pp. 39–85.

El cuento de Pancho Diablo. In Carlos Morton, *Johnny Tenorio and Other Plays*. Houston: Arte Público, 1992, pp. 153–92.

El jardín. *El Grito* 7, 1974, pp. 7–37.

El jardín. In Carlos Morton, *The Many Deaths of Danny Rosales and Other Plays*. Houston: Arte Público, 1983, pp. 105–28.

Johnny Tenorio. In Carlos Morton, *Johnny Tenorio and Other Plays*. Houston: Arte Público, 1992, pp. 25–52.

Las Muchas Muertes de Richard Morales. *Tejidos* 1, no. 3, Spring, 1977, pp. 28–50.

Las muchas muertes de Danny Rosales. In *Teatro Norteamericano Contemporaneo*, edited by David Olguin. Mexico City: Ediciones el Milagro, 1995, pp. 324–95.

Las muchas muertes de Richard Morales (*The Many Deaths of Richard Morales*). Conjunto, Casa De Las Américas, La Habana, Cuba 44, abril–junio, 1980, pp. 74–109.

The Many Deaths of Danny Rosales. In Carlos Morton, *The Many Deaths of Danny Rosales and Other Plays.* Houston: Arte Público, 1983, pp. 7–49.

The Many Deaths of Danny Rosales. In *Types of Drama*, edited by Sylvan Burnet, Morton Berman, William Burto and Ben Draya. New York: R.R. Donnelley & Sons, 1997, pp. 809–32.

Rancho Hollywood. In Carlos Morton, *The Many Deaths of Danny Rosales and Other Plays.* Houston: Arte Público, 1983, pp. 50–86.

Rancho Hollywood. In *The McGraw Hill Book of Drama*, edited by James Howe and William Stephany. New York: McGraw Hill, 1995, pp. 978–98.

Nájera, Rick. *The Pain of the Macho.* In Rick Nájera, *The Pain of the Macho and Other Plays.* Houston: Arte Público, 1997, pp. 7–52.

Latinologues. In Rick Nájera, *The Pain of the Macho and Other Plays.* Houston: Arte Público, 1997, pp. 53–92.

A Quiet Love. In Rick Nájera, *The Pain of the Macho and Other Plays.* Houston: Arte Público, 1997, pp. 93–151.

Pérez, Judith and Severo Perez. *Soldierboy.* In *Necessary Theater: Six Plays About the Chicano Experience*, edited by Jorge Huerta. Houston: Arte Público, 1989, pp. 18–75.

Portillo-Trambley, Estela. *Autumn Gold.* In Estela Portillo-Trambley, *Sor Juana and Other Plays.* Tempe: Bilingual Press, 1983, pp. 37–99.

Blacklight. In Estela Portillo-Trambley, *Sor Juana and Other Plays.* Tempe: Bilingual Press, 1983, pp. 100–42.

Day of the Swallows. In *El Espejo*, edited by Herminio Ríos and Octavio Romano V. Berkeley: Quinto Sol, 1972, pp. 149–93.

Day of the Swallows. In *We Are Chicanos*, edited by Philip D. Ortego. New York: Washington Square, 1973, pp. 224–71.

Day of the Swallows. In *Contemporary Chicano Theatre*, edited by Roberto J. Garza. University of Notre Dame, 1976, pp. 206–45.

Puente Negro. In Estela Portillo-Trambley, *Sor Juana and Other Plays.* Tempe: Bilingual Press, 1983, pp. 1–35.

Sor Juana. In Estela Portillo-Trambley, *Sor Juana and Other Plays.* Tempe: Bilingual Press, 1983, pp. 143–95.

Sor Juana. In *Infinite Divisions: An Anthology of Chicana Literature*, edited by Tey Diana Rebolledo and Eliana S. Rivero. Tucson: University of Arizona Press, 1993, pp. 233–55.

Sun Images. In *Nuevos Pasos: Chicano and Puerto Rican Drama*, edited by Jorge A. Huerta and Nicolás Kanellos. *Revista Chicano-Riqueña 7*, invierno, 1979, pp. 18–42.

Reyes, Guillermo. *Bush is a Lesbian.* Dallas: Dialogus Play Service, 1993.

Deporting the Divas. Gestos 27, 1999, pp. 109–58.

Men on the Verge of a His-panic Breakdown. In *Staging Gay Lives*, edited by John M. Clum. Boulder: Westview Press, 1996, pp. 401–24.

Men on the Verge of a His-panic Breakdown. New York: Dramatic Publishing Company, 1999.

Romero, Elaine. *Walking Home.* Ollantay 4, no. 1, 1996, pp. 127–74.

Sánchez-Scott, Milcha. *The Cuban Swimmer.* Theatre Communications Group, *Plays in Process* v, no. 12, 1984.

Dog Lady. In *Best Short Plays of 1986,* edited by Ramón Delgado. New York: Applause Books, 1986.

Dog Lady. Theatre Communications Group, *Plays in Process* v, no. 12. 1984.

Evening Star. New York: Dramatists Play Service, 1989.

Latina. In *Necessary Theater: Six Plays About the Chicano Experience,* edited by Jorge Huerta. Houston: Arte Público, 1989, pp. 75–141.

Roosters. In *On New Ground,* edited by Elizabeth Osborn. New York: Theatre Communications Group, 1987, pp. 243–80.

Roosters. American Theatre Magazine, September, 1987, pp. 1–11.

Roosters. New York: Dramatists Play Service, 1988.

Solís, Octavio. *Man of the Flesh. Plays from South Coast Repertory,* Vol. iii. New York: Broadway Play Publishing, 1998.

La Posada Mágica. Plays from South Coast Repertory, Vol. ii. New York: Broadway Play Publishing, 1998.

Prospect. TheatreForum 5, 1994, pp. 79–99.

Santos & Santos. American Theatre Magazine, November, 1995, pp. 35–57.

Teatro de la Esperanza. *Guadalupe.* In *Necessary Theater: Six Plays About the Chicano Experience,* edited by Jorge Huerta. Houston: Arte Público, 1989, pp. 208–57.

La víctima. In *Necessary Theater: Six Plays About the Chicano Experience,* edited by Jorge Huerta. Houston: Arte Público, 1989, pp. 316–65.

Valdez, Luis. *Bandido!* In Luis Valdez, *Zoot Suit and Other Plays.* Houston: Arte Público, 1992, pp. 95–153.

Bernabé. In *Contemporary Chicano Theatre,* edited by Roberto J. Garza. University of Notre Dame Press, 1976, pp. 30–58.

Bernabé. In *West Coast Plays 19/20,* edited by Robert Hurwitt. Berkeley: California Theatre Council, 1982, pp. 21–51.

Bernabé. In Luis Valdez, *Luis Valdez – Early Works: Actos, Bernabé and Pensamiento Serpentino.* Houston: Arte Público, 1990, pp. 134–67.

Dark Root of a Scream. In *From the Barrio,* edited by Lilian Faderman and Omar Salinas. San Francisco: Canfield Press, 1973, pp. 79–98.

I Don't Have to Show You No Stinking Badges. In Luis Valdez, *Zoot Suit and Other Plays.* Houston: Arte Público, 1992, pp. 156–214.

The Shrunken Head of Pancho Villa. In *Necessary Theater: Six Plays About the Chicano Experience,* edited by Jorge Huerta. Houston: Arte Público, 1989, pp. 142–207.

The Shrunken Head of Pancho Villa. In *West Coast Plays 11/12,* edited by Robert Hurwitt. Berkeley: California Theatre Council, 1982, pp. 1–61.

Zoot Suit. In Luis Valdez, *Zoot Suit and Other Plays.* Houston: Arte Público, 1992, pp. 23–94.

Villareal, Edit. *My Visits With MGM (My Grandmother Marta).* In *Shattering the Myth: Plays by Hispanic Women,* edited by Linda Feyder. Houston: Arte Público, 1992, pp. 143–208.

Articles and books

Anon. "Edit Villareal: Already in Her 30s, She Turned to Writing." *Los Angeles Times,* February 14, 1993, Calendar, pp. 72, 74.

Abrams, Richard A. "Chicana playwright struggles with 2 cultures." *Austin-American Statesman,* December 6, 1981, sec. A, p. 24.

Acuña, Rudolfo. *Occupied America: A History of Chicanos,* 3rd edn., Harper and Row, 1988.

Alarcón, Francisco X. "A Challenge to a Sexual Taboo." *Revista Literaria De El Tecolote* (San Francisco, California) 2, December, 1981, pp. 11–12.

Alarcón, Norma. "Making 'Familia' from Scratch: Split Subjectivities in the Work of Helena María Viramontes and Cherríe Moraga." In *Chicana Creativity and Criticism: New Frontiers in American Literature,* edited by María Herrera-Sobek and Helena María Viramontes. Albuquerque: University of New Mexico Press, 1996, pp. 220–32.

Allen, Howard. "Matadors and Mysteries." *American Theatre Magazine,* January, 1995, p. 12.

Almaguer, Tomás. "Chicano Men: A Cartography of Homosexual Identity and Behavior." *Differences* 3, no. 2, 1991, pp. 75–100.

Anzaldúa, Gloria, and Cherríe Moraga (eds.). *This Bridge Called My Back: Writings by Radical Women of Color.* New York: Kitchen Table Press, 1981.

Arkatov, Janice. "Playwright Enters World of Cockfighting in 'Roosters'." *Los Angeles Times,* June 15 1988, sec. 5, p. 3.

Arrizón, Alicia. "Chicanas en la escena: teatralidad y performance." *Ollantay* 4, no. 1, 1996, pp. 21–32.

   Latina Performance: Traversing the Stage. Bloomington: Indiana University Press, 1999.

Avila, Kat. "The Genesis of Edit Villareal's M G M ." *Ollantay* 4, no. 1, 1996, pp. 52–57.

Boney, Bradley. "The Lavender Brick Road: Paul Bonin-Rodríguez and the Sissy Bo(d)y." *Theatre Journal* 49, no. 1, pp. 35–57.

Breslauer, Jan. "Southwest Passage." *Los Angeles Times,* May 23, 1993, Calendar, pp. 3, 26–30.

Broyles-González, Yolanda. *El Teatro Campesino: Theater in the Chicano Movement.* Austin: University of Texas Press, 1994.

   "What Price 'Mainstream?' Luis Valdez's *Corridos* on Stage and Film." *Cultural Studies* 4, October, 1990, pp. 281–93.

Bruce-Novoa, Juan. "Estela Portillo." In *Chicano Authors: Inquiry by Interview,* edited by Juan Bruce-Novoa. Austin: University of Texas Press, 1980, pp. 164–81.

   "Homosexuality and the Chicano Novel." *Confluencia* 2, Fall, 1986, pp. 69–77.

Burciaga, José Antonio. "Didn't Know I Was Funny Until People Started Laughing." *Ollantay* 4, no. 1, 1996, pp. 111–19.

Campa, Arthur L. "Spanish Religious Folk Theatre in the Spanish Southwest." *The University of New Mexico Bulletin, Language Series* 5, June, 1934, pp. 5–157.

Cariaga, Catalina. "The Poetics of *Chisme.*" *Poetry Flash (Berkeley)* 195, June, 1989.

Case, Sue-Ellen. "Seduced and Abandoned: Chicanas and Lesbians in Representation." In *Negotiating Performance: Gender, Sexuality and Theatricality in Latin/o America,* edited by Diana Taylor and Juan Villegas. Durham: Duke University Press, 1994, pp. 88–101.

Chipman Waite, Rachel. "Milcha Sánchez-Scott: An Emerging Latina Voice." MA thesis, University of Oregon, 1993.

Corrales, José. "A Walk Over New Terrain." *Ollantay* IV, no. 1, 1996, pp. 124–26.

Daniel, Lee A. "The "Other" in *Teatro Chicano.*" *Ollantay* 4, no. 1, 1996, pp. 103–8.

"A Texas Tenorio: Carlos Morton's 'Johnny Tenorio'." *Ollantay* 4, no. 1, 1996, pp. 66–73.

de la Roche, Elisa. *Teatro Hispano!: Three Major New York Companies.* New York: Garland Press, 1995.

Derus McFerran, Virginia. "Chicana Voices in American Drama: Silviana Wood, Estela Portillo-Trambley, Cherríe Moraga, Milcha Sánchez-Scott, Josefina López," Ph.D. dissertation, University of Minnesota, 1991.

Detwiler, Louise. "The Question of Cultural Difference and Gender Oppression in Estela Portillo-Trambley's *The Day of the Swallows.*" *The Bilingual Review,* 1996, pp. 146–52.

Dewey, Janice. "Doña Josefa: Bloodpulse of Transition and Change." In *Breaking Boundaries: Latina Writings and Critical Readings,* edited by Asunción Horno-Delgado, Eliana Ortega, Nina M. Scott, and Nancy Saporta Sternbach. Amherst: University of Massachusetts Press, 1989, pp. 39–47.

Diamond, Betty. "Brown-eyed Children of the Sun: The Cultural Politics of El Teatro Campesino." Ph.D. thesis, University of Wisconsin, Madison, 1977.

Dolan, Jill. "Lesbian Subjectivity in Realism: Dragging at the Margins of Structure and Ideology." In *Performing Feminisms: Feminist Critical Theory and Theatre,* edited by Sue-Ellen Case. Baltimore: Johns Hopkins, 1990, pp. 40–53.

Elam Jr., Harry. "Of Angels and Transcendence: An Analysis of *Fences* by August Wilson and *Roosters* by Milcha Sánchez-Scott." In *Staging Difference: Cultural Pluralism in American Theatre and Drama,* edited by Marc Maufort. New York: Peter Lang, 1995, pp. 287–300.

Taking It to the Streets: The Social Protest Theater of Luis Valdez and Amiri Baraka. University of Michigan Press, 1997.

Foster, David William. "Guillermo Reyes's 'Deporting the Divas'." *Gestos* 27, 1999, pp. 103–08.

Frischmann, Donald H. "El Teatro Campesino y su mito Bernabé: un regreso a la madre tierra." *Aztlán,* Autumn, 1981, pp. 259–70.

Gómez-Quiñones, Juan. *Chicano Politics: Reality and Promise, 1940–1990.* New Mexico: 1990.

González, Deena J. "Speaking Secrets: Living Chicana Theory." In *Living Chicana Theory,* edited by Carla Trujillo. Berkeley: Third Woman Press, 1998, pp. 46–77.

González, José Cruz. "From Director to Playwright: El otro lado." *Ollantay* 4, no. 1, 1996, pp. 109–10.

Green, Judith. "She's at that stage." *San Jose Mercury News,* 12 November 1989, Arts and Books, p. 5.

Guzmán, Ralph. "Mexican-American Casualties in Vietnam." *La Raza* 1, no. 1, 1970, pp. 12–15.

Habell-Pallán, Michelle. "Family and Sexuality in Recent Chicano Performance: Luis Alfaro's Memory Plays." *Ollantay* 4, no. 1, 1996, pp. 33–42.

Heffley, Lynne. "Shakespeare in Baggy Pants." *Los Angeles Times,* July 10, 1997, Calendar, p. 42.

Hernández, Ellie. "The Gaze of the Other: Interview with Cherríe Moraga." *Ollantay* 4, no. 1, 1996, pp. 58–65.

Herrera-Sobek, María. "The Politics of Rape: Sexual Transgression in Chicana Fiction." In *Chicana Creativity and Criticism: New Frontiers in American Literature,* edited by María Herrera-Sobek and Helena María Viramontes. Albuquerque: University of New Mexico Press, 1996, pp. 245–56.

Hornby, Richard. "A Review: "Bandido!" *Ollantay* 4, no. 1, 1996, pp. 175–78.

Huerta, Jorge A. *Chicano Theater: Themes and Forms.* Tempe: Bilingual Press, 1982.

"Moraga's *Heroes and Saints:* Chicano Theatre for the 90s." *TheatreForum* 1 1992, pp. 49–52.

"Looking for the Magic: Chicanos in the Mainstream." In *Negotiating Performance: Gender, Sexuality and Theatricality in Latin/o America,* edited by Diana Taylor and Juan Villegas. Durham: Duke University Press, 1994, pp. 36–48.

"*La Malinche* at the Arizona Theatre Company." *Latin American Theatre Review* 31, no. 1, Fall, 1997, pp. 176–77.

"Negotiating Borders in Three US Latino Plays." In *Of Borders and Thresholds: Theatre History, Practice and Theory,* edited by Michal Kobialka. Minneapolis: University of Minnesota Press, 1999, pp. 154–83.

"An Overview of Chicano Dramaturgy Since *Zoot Suit.*" *Ollantay* 4, no. 1, 1996, pp. 91–102.

"Some Thoughts on Casting 'Deporting the Divas'." *Gestos* 27, 1999, pp. 159–61.

"Taking 'La Catrina' to the Streets: A Mexican Play About Death in New York City's *Barrios.*" In *Cultures de la Rue: Les barrios d'Amérique du Nord,* edited by Geneviève Fabre and Catherine Lejeune. Paris: Cahiers Charles v, Université Paris 7 Denis Diderot, 1996, pp. 77–89.

Hurtado, Aida. *The Color of Privilege: Three Blasphemies on Race and Feminism,* University of Michigan Press, 1996.

Kanellos, Nicolás. *A History of Hispanic Theatre in the United States: Origins to 1940.* Austin: University of Texas Press, 1990.

Kelley, Ken. "The Interview: Luis Valdez." *San Francisco Focus,* (September, 1987), pp. 51–53, 93–102.

Langworthy, Douglas. "Customizing Culture: An Interview with the Playwright [Octavio Solís] by Douglas Langworthy." *American Theatre Magazine,* November, 1995, p. 34.

Lea, Aurora Lucero-White. *Literary Folklore of the Hispanic Southwest.* San Antonio: Naylor Company, 1953.

León-Portilla, Miguel. *The Aztec Image of Self and Society.* Utah: University of Utah Press, 1992.

Pre-Columbian Literatures of Mexico. Norman: University of Oklahoma Press, 1966.

Limón, José. *Dancing with the Devil: Society and Cultural Poetics in Mexican-American South Texas.* Madison: University of Wisconsin Press, 1994.

Lockhart, Melissa Fitch. "Queer Representation in Latino Theatre." *Latin American Theatre Review* 31, no. 2, Spring, 1998, pp. 67–78.

López, Tiffany Ann. "Performing Aztlán: The Female Body as Cultural Critique in the

Teatro of Cherríe Moraga." In *Performing America: Cultural Nationalism in American Theater,* edited by Jeffrey D. Mason and J. Ellen Gainor. Michigan, 1999, pp. 160–77.

Loynd, Ray. "TV Reviews: 'La Carpa': Bittersweet Love and Chicano Social History." *Los Angeles Times,* June 16, 1993, sec. F, p 7.

Macau, Michelle. "Talking with Vira and Hortensia Colorado." *Ollantay* 4, no. 1, 1996, pp. 43–51.

Mariscal, Jorge (ed.). *Aztlán and Vietnam: Chicano and Chicana Experiences of the War.* Berkeley: University of California Press, 1999.

Marrero, María Teresa. "Out of the Fringe: Desire and Homosexuality in the 90s Latino Theatre." *Latin American Theatre Review* 32, no. 2, Spring, 1999, pp. 87–103.

"Real Women Have Curves: The Articulation of Fat as a Cultural/Feminist Issue." *Ollantay,* 1, no. 1 1993, pp. 61–70.

Martínez Paredes, Domingo. *El Popol Vuh Tiene Razón.* México: Editorial Orión, 1968.

Mason, Susan. "Romeo and Juliet in East LA." (Yale) *Theater,* Spring, 1992, p. 88.

McDonald, Eric. *Theater at the Margins: Text and the Post-Structured Stage.* Ann Arbor: University of Michigan Press, 1993.

Monge Rafuls, Pedro R. "Teatro Chicano." *Ollantay* 4, no. 1, 1996, p. 5.

Moraga, Cherríe. "Art in América con Accento." In *Negotiating Performance: Gender, Sexuality and Theatricality in Latin/o America,* edited by Diana Taylor and Juan Villegas. Durham: Duke University Press, 1994, pp. 30–36.

The Last Generation: Prose and Poetry. Boston: South End Press, 1993.

Loving in the War Years: lo que nunca pasó por sus labios. Boston: South End Press, 1983.

"The Obedient Daughter." *Third Woman* 4, 1989, pp. 161–62.

"The Obedient Daughter." In *The Sexuality of Latinas,* edited by Norma Alarcón, Ana Castillo and Cherríe Moraga. Berkeley: Third Woman Press, 1993, pp. 157–62.

Waiting in the Wings. Ithaca: Firebrand Books, 1997.

Morton, Carlos. "Critical Response to 'Zoot Suit' and 'Corridos'." *University of Texas, El Paso – Occasional Paper Series* 2, 1984.

"La Serpiente Sheds Its Skin – The Teatro Campesino." *Drama Review* 18, December, 1974, pp. 71–75.

"Soy Fronterizo." *Ollantay* 3 no. 1 1995, pp. 76–78.

Morton, Carlos, and Lee A. Daniel "Chicano Theater." *Ollantay* 4, no. 1, 1996, pp. 2–4.

Paz, Octavio. *The Labyrinth of Solitude: Life and Thought in Mexico.* New York: Grove, 1961.

Prieto Stambaugh, Antonio. "La actuación de la identidad a través del performance chicano gay." *Debate Feminista* 7, abril, 1996, 285–315.

"Artes Visuales Transfronterizas y La Descontrucción de la Identidad." Ph.D. thesis, Universidad Nacional Autónoma de Mexico, 1998.

Pross, Edith E. "A Chicano Play and Its Audience." *The Americas Review* 19, no. 1, 1986, pp. 71–79.

Ramírez, Elizabeth C. *Footlights Across the Border: A History of Spanish-Language Professional Theatre on the Texas Stage.* New York: Peter Lang, 1990.

Ravicz, Ekdahl Marilyn. *Early Colonial Religious Drama in Mexico: From Tzompantli to Golgotha.* Washington: Catholic University Press, 1970.

Reyes, Guillermo. "What I've Discovered." *Ollantay* 5 no.2, 1997, pp. 38–40.

Ríos-C, Herminio "Introduction." *El Grito* 7, 1974, pp. 4–6.

Rodríguez, Alfonso. "Tragic Vision in Estella [sic] Portillo's *The Day of the Swallows.*" *De Colores* 5, 1980, pp. 152–58.

Román, David. "Teatro Viva!: Latino Performance and the Politics of AIDS in Los Angeles." In *¿Entiendes? Queer Readings, Hispanic Writings*, edited by Emilie L. Bergmann and Paul Julian Smith. Duke, 1995, pp. 346–69.

Romero, Elaine. "Finding My Voice." *Ollantay* 4, no. 1, 1996, pp. 120–23.

Roys, Ralph L. *The Book of Chilam Balam of Chumayel*. Norman: Oklahoma, 1967.

Schmidhuber, Guillermo. "El teatro chicano o la sabiduría de heredar el patrimonio hispano." *Ollantay* 4, no. 1, 1996, pp. 9–20.

Schwartz Seller, Maxine (ed.). *Ethnic Theatre in the United States.* Westport: Greenwood, 1983.

Shank, Theodore. *American Alternative Theater.* New York: Grove, 1982.

"A Return to Mayan and Aztec Roots." *Drama Review* 18, December, 1974, pp. 56–70.

Steiner, Stan and Luis Valdez (eds.). *Aztlán: An Anthology of Mexican-American Literature.* New York: Random House, 1972.

Sternbach, Nancy Saporta. " 'A Deep Racial Memory of Love': The Chicana Feminism of Cherríe Moraga." In *Breaking Boundaries: Latina Writings and Critical Readings*, edited by Asunción Horno-Delgado, Eliana Ortega, Nina M. Scott and Nancy Saporta Sternbach. Amherst: University of Massachusetts Press, 1989, pp. 48–61.

Sullivan, Dan. "El Teatro Campesino in a Halloween Program." *Los Angeles Times*, November 3, 1970, sec. IV, p. 9.

"Homecoming of a Dead GI." *Los Angeles Times*, September 25, 1971, sec. II, p 8.

Valdez, Luís. *"Pensamiento Serpentino."* Cucaracha Press: 1973.

"Pensamiento Serpentino." In Luís Valdez, *Luis Valdez – Early Works: Actos, Bernabé and Pensamiento Serpentino*. Houston: Arte Público, 1990, pp. 168–99.

Valle, Victor. " 'Corridos' moves from stage to KCET." *Los Angeles Times*, October 5, 1987.

Vallejos, Tomás. "Estela Portillo's Fictive Search for Paradise." *Frontiers* 2, 1980, pp. 54–58.

Vega, Manuel de Jesús. "El Teatro Campesino Chicano y la Vanguardia Teatral: 1965–1975." Ph.D. dissertation, Middlebury College, 1983.

Villareal, Edit. "El Teatro Ensemble de UCSD: First International Tour." *The Américas Review* 17, no. 2, Summer 1989, pp. 73–83.

"Los Vendidos . . . Johnny Tenorio . . . El Teatro Ensemble de UCSD International Tour." *Theatre Journal* 41, 1989, pp. 231–33.

Weinberg, Mark S. *Challenging the Hierarchy: Collective Theatre in the United States.* Westport, Connecticut: Greenwood Press, 1992.

Woodyard, George. "Rompiendo las fronteras: El teatro de Guillermo Reyes." In *Théâtre et Territoires Espagne et Amerique Hispanique (1950–1996) (Teatro y Territorios España e Hispanoamérica): Actes du Colloque International de Bordeaux 30 janvier – 1 février 1997*, edited by Sara Bonnardel and Genviève Champeau. Bordeaux: Maison des Pays Iberíques, 1998, pp. 333–43.

Worthen, W. B. "Staging América: The Subject of History in Chicano/a Theatre." *Theatre Journal* 49, May 1997, pp. 101–20.

Yarbro-Bejarano, Yvonne. "Cherríe Moraga's 'Shadow of a Man': Touching the Wound in Order to Heal." In *Acting Out: Feminist Performances*, edited by Lynda Hart and Peggy Phelan. University of Michigan Press, 1993, pp. 85–101.

"The Female Subject in Chicano Theatre: Sexuality, 'Race,' and Class." In *Performing Feminisms: Feminist Critical Theory and Theatre*, edited by Sue-Ellen Case. Baltimore: Johns Hopkins University Press, 1990, pp. 131–49.

Yarbro-Bejarano, Yvonne and Tomás Ybarra-Frausto. "Zoot Suit y el movimiento Chicano." *Plural*, April, 1980, pp. 49–56.

Ybarra-Frausto, Tomás. "Alurista's Poetics: The Oral, the Bilingual, the Pre-Columbian." In *Modern Chicano Writers: A Collection of Critical Essays*, edited by Joseph Sommers and Tomás Ybarra-Frausto. Englewood Cliffs, NJ: Prentice Hall, 1979, pp. 117–32.

"I Can Still Hear the Applause. *La Farándula Chicana: Carpas y Tandas de Variedad.*" In *Hispanic Theatre in the United States*, edited by Nicolás Kanellos. Houston: Arte Público, 1984, pp. 45–61.

CD-ROM, film, video

Avila, Carlos, and Edit Villareal. "La Carpa." *American Playhouse*, PBS, video, 1993.

Huerta, Jorge. "Interview with Luis Alfaro." *Necessary Theatre*, UCSD-TV, January 31, 1995. NOTE: The "Necessary Theatre" interview series is available from the University of California, San Diego Bookstore web site.

"Interview with Yareli Arizmendi." *Necessary Theatre*, UCSD-TV, February 17, 1995.

"Interview with Tony Curiel." *Necessary Theatre*, UCSD-TV, March 3, 1995.

"Interview with Evelina Fernández." *Necessary Theatre*, UCSD-TV, January 20, 1995.

"Interview with Josefina López." *Necessary Theatre*, UCSD-TV, February 16, 1995.

"Interview with Alma Martinez." *Necessary Theatre*, UCSD-TV, October 2, 1997.

"Interview with Carlos Morton." *Necessary Theatre*, UCSD-TV, March 3, 1995.

"Interview with Diane Rodríguez," *Necessary Theatre*, UCSD-TV, February 10, 1995.

"Interview with José Guadalupe Saucedo." *Necessary Theatre*, UCSD-TV, January 20, 1995.

"Interview with Luis Valdez." *Necessary Theatre*, UCSD-TV, November 20, 1997.

"Interview with José Luis Valenzuela." *Necessary Theatre*, UCSD-TV, February 24, 1995.

"Interview with Edit Villareal." *Necessary Theatre*, UCSD-TV, February 2, 1995.

Sanchez-Scott, Milcha. *Roosters*, American Playhouse Theatrical Films, WMG and Olmos Productions, co-producers. Rental copies available from various video rental stores.

"El Teatro Campesino: From the Fields to Hollywood." CD-ROM produced by El teatro Campesino, 1999. Available from El Teatro Campesino's web site.

Index

Note: Italic pages refer to illustrations.